A HISTORY OF MARXIST-LENINIST ATHEISM AND SOVIET ANTIRELIGIOUS POLICIES

A History of Marxist-Leninist Atheism and Soviet Antireligious Policies

Volume 1 of A History of Soviet Atheism in Theory and Practice, and the Believer

Dimitry V. Pospielovsky

Professor in Modern European and Russian History
University of Western Ontario, Canada

St. Martin's Press   New York

© Dimitry V. Pospielovsky, 1987

All rights reserved. For information, write:
Scholarly & Reference Division,
St. Martin's Press, Inc., 175 Fifth Avenue, New York, NY 10010

First published in the United States of America in 1987

Printed in Hong Kong

ISBN 0–312–38132–8 (cloth)
  0–312–38133–6 (pbk)

Library of Congress Cataloging-in-Publication Data
Pospielovsky, Dimitry, 1935–
A history of Marxist-Leninist atheism and Soviet
antireligious policies.
(A History of Soviet atheism in theory and
practice, and the believer; v. 1)
Bibliography: p.
Includes index.
1. Persecution—Soviet Union—History—20th century.
2. Soviet Union—Religion—1917–   . 3. Atheism—
Soviet Union—History—20th century.   I. Title.
II. Series: Pospielovsky, Dimitry, 1935–   .   History
of Soviet atheism in theory and practice, and the
believer; v. 1.
BL2765.S65P67   vol. 1 [BR1608.S65]
BL2765.S65P67   vol. 1   210'.8' 0947 s   86–14623
[BR1608.S65]   vol. 1   [272'.9' 0947]
ISBN 0–312–38132–8
ISBN 0–312–38133–6 (pbk.)

To my mother, Mariamna née Ushinskaia

Contents

General Introduction to the Three-Volume Work

Religious belief and the Churches have survived in the Soviet Union in the face of some sixty-five years of continuous persecution, unprecedented in history in intensity, although varying in degree and thrust, depending on the external and internal circumstances. According to approximate calculations, given in our book on the history of the Russian Orthodox Church under the Soviets, the toll of Orthodox clergy has been in the region of 40 000 priests, probably as many monks and nuns, and incalculable millions of lay believers. The number of functioning Orthodox churches has been reduced from over 60 000 (this includes parish and monastic churches and institutional chapels) before the revolution to less that 7000 in the late 1970s. Other religions, except perhaps the Baptists, have seen the numbers of their churches and temples reduced by at least the same proportion. And yet in the last decade and a half or so, more and more voices in the Soviet Union have been heard claiming not only religious survival but even revival, primarily of Christianity. According to all oral evidence, both of Soviet-Russian clergy remaining in the Soviet Union and of recent émigrés, this neophytic phenomenon is almost entirely limited to those under 40 years of age, while their parents mostly remain outside any religion. Hence, whatever the numbers and proportions, the current 'churchification' of the intelligentsia is largely not a carry-over from one generation to the next, nor is it a simple revival of a tradition, because the tradition of the Russian intelligentsia, at least since the 1860s, has been predominantly one of a rather passionate atheism and positivism.[1]

The main purpose of this study is a step-by-step presentation and analysis of the changing styles, strategies and tactics of the

---

1. See *Vekhi*, a collection of essays on the Russian intelligentsia by N. A. Berdiaev, S. N. Bulgakov, M. O. Gershenzon, A. S. Izgoev, B. A. Kistiakovsky, P. B. Struve, S. L. Frank (Moscow, 1909; repr.: Frankfurt/M.: Possev, 1967). Also: Jeffrey Brooks, '*Vekhi* and the *Vekhi* Dispute', *Survey*, vol. 19, no. 1 (86) London, Winter 1973.

never-ending Soviet attack on religion and on believers. This will include as detailed and documented an account as possible of the direct persecutions, of which the most massive occurred in the following periods and under the following pretexts:

February 1918 to late 1920. A bloody attack on the clergy and active laity was conducted under the pretext of their opposition to communism, their real or alleged sympathy for the Whites, and the resistance of lay believers to the nationalization of all church property in accordance with the Soviet decree of 23 January 1918.

1921 to 1923. This wave of arrests of clergy and laity, with executions of some of the most influential and popular church leaders, was officially motivated by their resistance to the confiscation of all church plate of any value, including liturgical vessels.

1922 to 1926. Persecution of the traditional Orthodox Church and her faithful clergy and laity for their refusal to join the state-supported Renovationist schism.

1926 to 1927. Arrests, exile and imprisonment of masses of bishops, as well as some regular parish clergy faithful to them, for an attempt to elect a patriarch secretly.

1928 to 1934. Arrest and liquidation of clergy and lay activists for refusing to accept Metropolitan Sergii's wording of the Declaration of Loyalty to the Soviet State and for breaking administrative connections with him.

1929 to 1930. The beginning of mass liquidation of rural parishes and their clergy and lay supporters under the guise of the collectivization and 'dekulakization' campaign.

1933 to 1934. Destruction of the remaining monastic communities and the liquidation of monks and nuns, along with many members of the urban and rural clergy, particularly renowned preachers and spiritual fathers.

1936 to 1939. Almost total liquidation of religious temples, clergy and active lay believers of all faiths.

1959 to 1964. Khrushchev's physical attack on the Church and all other religious faiths, closure and destruction of the majority of the temples reopened during the religiously 'tolerant' era of 1941 to 1957, arrests and deportations of large numbers of clergy and laity – all under the pretext of imminent construction of communism, incompatible with faith in the Supernatural.

These are just highlights of the most massive attacks, which will be accounted for and discussed in greater detail in their proper context in this volume.

The other aim of this study is to trace the continuing religious life in the country: how the believers preserve their faith and even multiply their numbers in these conditions; how, if at all, they are affected by this aggressive state atheism and anti-religious propaganda; finally, how and why there is a growing movement of adult baptisms and return to the Church after all these years of concerted attack, and this despite the absence of any organized religious education.

Finding sources for this study was a complex and uneven process. There was no problem in locating masses of the officially printed Soviet antireligious propaganda of all categories: from the allegedly scholarly studies of the Soviet 'religiologists' to the primitive attacks on religion in the mass press and, in particular, in the Soviet specialized general circulation antireligious journals, newspapers, brochures and books. The available data in the direct Soviet persecutions of the Church are more difficult to assemble. Only a very small percentage can be obtained from official Soviet publications. Official admissions of persecutions have been made only where they could be blamed on the Church's hostility 'to the young Soviet republic' (the Civil War Years), or on the believers' resistance to the implementation of Soviet laws on the nationalization of church property or confiscation of church valuables (1918 to 1922), or, finally, on Stalin's excesses. But even here gross understatement is the rule. Therefore, most of the material on persecutions comes from testimonies of witnesses, unofficial letters and secret diocesan reports smuggled abroad, the multiple *samizdat* publications of the last two decades (which even include, on occasion, internal secret party documents not meant for print, with open admissions of persecutions) and statements (written and oral) by the émigrés from the Soviet Union of all periods.

Most of the existing Western studies of Soviet atheism limit themselves to the official Soviet sources. Only a small minorty of Western scholars, such as Professor Bohdan Bociurkiw, the Rev. Michael Bourdeaux and his co-workers at Keston College, make wide use of *samizdat* in reporting persecutions of religion in the Soviet Union; however, in most cases these relate to the post-Stalin era. This study uncovers a considerable volume of direct witness and documentation on the persecutions of the 1920s and 1930s, dispersed mostly in masses of Russian émigré publications and archival collections pertaining to the time, and largely forgotten and ignored until now. This author firmly believes that only a combination of the material from the official Soviet literature with the information collected in the above fashion, followed by a systematic study of the persecutions during each separate period of Soviet history in question, will enable the reader to gain a realistic picture of the true horrors and magnitude of the permanent Soviet war against the Church.

As for the life of the Church and the believer under these conditions, their attitudes, and the religious revival of the last decades, here again most of the information comes from *samizdat*[1] from all decades of the Soviet era, as well as from interviews with Russian churchmen and religious intelligent-sia, both those who remain in the USSR and recent émigrés. The wartime émigrés and documents of the German occupy-ing forces during the Second World War are also very important sources for the religiosity and the life of the Church from the 1920s to 1940s.

Soviet-Russian fine literature (the *belles-lettres*), particularly of the last decade-and-a-half, has ever more frequently reflected the growing interest in matters spiritual, the Church, and Christian ethics of times past and present. This source has also been tapped for the current study.

The objective Western reader may be bewildered occasional-ly by the obvious 'disproportion' of credibility rendered by this author on the one hand to the official Soviet data, and on the other, to the unofficial data of *samizdat* and the testimonies of Soviet believers. The 'bias' of this book is to give more credence to the latter and to doubt the former, even to present evidence showing its mendacity whenever possible. There are several reasons for this 'inequity'. First of all, there is the old Russian saying: the one who has not been caught by the hand is not a

---

1. Although the term *samizdat* appeared only in the early 1960s, the Church, the theologians and other church authors have used similar methods for the writing and dissemination of their literature from the early 1920s, after the regime had deprived the Orthodox Church of printing presses, to the present day.

thief. The reader will soon see that the official Soviet claims, declarations, the writings of the Soviet 'scientists' of atheism or, as the Soviets call them, 'religiologists', will constantly be 'caught by the hand', mostly by comparing contradictory and mutually exclusive statements and claims made by such authors and institutions in different years, under different circumstances although relating to the same events or periods. Second, the believers, and the dissidents with their *samizdat*, are the parties under attack; they have to weigh carefully every statement they make. They are taking tremendous responsibility for every one of them. One is not likely to make frivolous irresponsible statements when the price for any 'disseminated information' that contradicts the general line of the communist party of the given moment is loss of a job, of the right to receive education, of liberty, and even of life on occasion. Although errors of transmission of information and even errors of judgement may still occur, deliberate misinformation emanating from the religious[1] and *samizdat* circles in general is very unlikely.

The study will be far from exhaustive in its coverage, for the following reasons. First, there is no way to achieve a quantitative analysis or to assess the degree of religious or atheistic penetration in the whole country, categories of believers, etc., our sample of interviewees being too limited in numbers and categories. Second, we have extremely little information on the parallel processes (if there are any on any comparable scale) among the common workers and peasants. Further, as our interviewees as well as *samizdat* writings are limited almost exclusively to the intelligentsia, and predominantly to that of Moscow, Leningrad and half a dozen other major cities, we are forced to concentrate our study and analysis predominantly on the Russian Orthodox Church, for this is the Church which most of the neophytic intelligentsia join; and it is her theology, traditions and legacy which are discussed and deliberated in almost all *samizdat* religious and religio-philosophic documents, as well as in the Christian-orientated works of some officially tolerated literary and artistic figures. In addition, although there are plenty of *sàmizdat* documents of the

---

1. This, of course, excludes official public statements by the official spokesmen of the Churches, especially when they are made for the Western media.

unofficial branch of the Baptist Church and of the Pentacostalists coming from the Soviet Union, they are limited to petitions against persecutions, reports on persecutions and imprisonments, collections of prayers and hymnals. Being neither an intellectual nor a theological phenomenon, the sects simply have not provided us with material which could be analyzed, generalized and conceptualized.

Although in the chapters on religious persecutions and antireligious propaganda the study will give brief accounts of attacks on religions other than the Orthodox Church, the concentration is on the Orthodox Church in all parts of the book, whether it is the study of Soviet atheism and its attitudes to the Orthodox Church or of the life of the Church and the believers. The reason is that Orthodoxy is the national and historical Church of the three core peoples of the Soviet Union: the Great Russians (or Muscovites), the Ukrainians (or the Little Russians),[1] and the Belorussians. In contrast to the multireligious scene in North America and to the supra-natural character of the Roman Church in the traditionally Roman Catholic nations of western Europe, Orthodoxy (using the vernacular and possessing no extra-territorial centralized Church administration) is not only a religion but a way of life, the very cultural matrix of the daily life in the countries where it has become the national Church. Russian literature, art, folk traditions, habits (where they survive), and attitudes have been formed or at least saturated by Orthodoxy from within. Therefore, the atheistic revolt of Marxist Bolshevism had to match Orthodoxy in its totality in order to crush it as the national way of life. Being only institutionally and ideologically antireligious as is Marxism in most other East European states, to allow a broader scope of religious toleration than in the USSR (in all cases except Albania) would not be effective. The attack had to be so total as to shatter the entire national culture in all its aspects. Hence the attempts of contemporary Russian nationalists to reconstruct Russian culture, Russian art and literature, inevitably brings a revival of Orthodoxy, of elements of Orthodox culture. That is why Orthodoxy is so central to any

---

1. The terms 'Great' and 'Little' Russians are of Byzantine origin, wherein the core area of a nation was called 'Little' while the zones of its later imperial expansion received the appellation 'Great'.

study of Russian nationalism. In fact this work, along with its predecessor, *The Russian Church Under the Soviet Regime* (St Vladimir's Seminary Press, 1984), is a rather bulky 'introduction' to a study of Russian nationalism and its relationship to the Orthodox religious revival, which is yet to be written.

This study is historical, hence the philosophy and the philosophical legacy and ideology of Marxist-Leninist atheism are only briefly discussed in a single chapter in the first volume. A philosophically inclined reader interested in a more profound study of the philosophical and ideational roots and concepts of Marxist-Leninist atheism is strongly advised to read James Thrower's *Marxist-Leninist 'Scientific Atheism' and the Study of Religion and Atheism in the USSR*. Dr Thrower's use of inverted commas in the title of his book has the same connotation as this author's preference for the term 'High Brow' Atheism instead of 'Scholarly' or 'Scientific' (see Volume 3 of this study).

Acknowledgements

Although all the errors and shortcomings in this work are solely my own responsibility, a number of individuals and institutions have greatly contributed to its 'delivery' if not to its 'birth'. Without their help the 'child' would have had many more defects and the birth would have been much more painful.

First, I owe my thanks to Dr Edward Manukian. Chapter 1 of this book is largely his work. As a professional Marxologist with the equivalent of a doctoral degree in philosophy from Leningrad University, he was the right person to write the theoretical chapter. My son, Andrew Pospielovsky, a fourth-year Russian history honours student at the University of Western Ontario at the time of this writing, compiled the bibliography and the Appendix on Soviet antireligious legislation, wherefore I owe him many thanks. I should also express my deep gratitude to the Social Sciences and Humanities Research Council of Canada and The University of Western Ontario Academic Development Fund, without whose grants the research that went into writing this study would have been impossible. I owe my thanks to the administration and staff of the Hoover Institution Library and Archives, the Bakhmeteff Russian Émigré Archives at Columbia University, the Dr Lieb Archiv at the Basel University Library, the Widener Library and the Russian Research Center at Harvard University, the Library of Congress and the Kennan Institute for Advanced Russian Studies. Much of the first-hand information in this study would simply not have been there had it not been for the willing co-operation of scores of recent Russian émigrés and other persons directly involved in the life of the contemporary Church in the USSR, who had granted interviews or wrote letters about their experiences to this author.

Last but not least, I owe my thanks to Mrs Pamela Hutchins-Orr for her excellent style-editing and proof-reading of the manuscript, to Miss Joanne Lemon for having speedily and efficiently typed it, and to my wife, Mirjana, for helping me very importantly with bibliographical research at the partial cost of her summer holidays and for compiling the index.

SOME TECHNICAL POINTS

Italics. Unless otherwise noted, all italics within quotations are in the original. The exceptions are the normal use of italics to indicate a title or a foreign term.

Transliterations. Generally, the Library of Congress system is used, with the following exceptions:

In personal names 'sky' ending is used instead of 'skii'; 'ya' and 'yu' are used in personal names to depict 'ю' and 'я', instead of 'ia' and 'iu', e.g. Yaroslavsky, not Iaroslavskii.

'X' is used to transliterate the Russian 'ks' throughout.

A single apostrophe (') is used for both the soft (ь) and the hard (ъ) signs.

The Calendar. Prior to February 1918 the Julian Calendar was used in Russia, which was thirteen days behind the Western Gregorian one in the twentieth century. Wherever the Old Calendar is used, it is indicated as o.s., i.e. old style.

Abbreviations. These are noted in the appropriate places in the main text and in the notes and references whenever a certain title is used more than two or three times. For example, *Bezbozhnik u stanka* becomes *Bezbust*. Similarly, such oft-repeated publication cities in bibliographical references as Moscow, Leningrad, St. Petersburg, Petrograd, New York become respectively: M., L., Pbg., P., N.Y.

DIMITRY V. POSPIELOVSKY

Introduction

'Communism begins at the outset . . . with atheism.'

(Karl Marx)

This volume sets the scene, as it were, for a study and systematic presentation of the antireligious propaganda and persecution of believers in the Soviet Union. It presents the Marxist-Leninist rationale for such policies, by outlining the relationship between the Marxist philosophical tradition and atheism, and then follows this up with a chronological and thematic account of the official antireligious policies of the Soviet State.

Many Western scholars have underestimated the role that aggressive and intolerant atheism plays in the political behaviour of the Soviet government. Others have uncritically accepted the formal but inaccurate allegations often mady by church leaders from the Soviet Union in official declarations abroad, according to which it is only the Communist Party which is militantly atheistic and is in conflict with the Church, whereas the government takes a neutral stand towards religion. Yet such outstanding specialists on the subject as Bohdan Bociurkiw and James Thrower strongly warn against such a fallacy and show that militant atheism, suppression and persecutions for faith have had a high priority in the policies of all Soviet leaders, being an organic legacy of the whole Marxist philosophical tradition, intensified in Lenin by the militantly atheistic legacy of the nineteenth-century Russian radical intelligentsia, such as Belinsky, Chernyshevsky and others.[1] This thesis is substantiated amply by Dr Edward Manukian, a professional philosopher and Marxologist.

As for the attempt to separate the policies and powers of the Communist Party from those of the Soviet government, any informed student of Soviet affairs knows that the government is only a subordinate executor of the will and policies of the Communist Party of the Soviet Union (CPSU) Central Committee Politburo and its Secretariat. Moreover, the current Constitution (1977), Article 6, plainly states:

> The leading and guiding force of Soviet society and the nucleus of its political system, of all state organizations and

public organizations, is the Communist Party of the Soviet Union.

And Article 51 adds, 'citizens of the USSR have the right to associate in public organizations' only inasmuch as this is 'in accordance with the aims of building communism'. Thus, although the very next (52nd) Article declares, 'Citizens of the USSR are guaranteed freedom of conscience ... [and] the right to profess or not to profess any religion', the preceding articles make it plain that the choices, priorities and policies of the Communist Party are inseparable from those of the government, and, second, as the Church is not aiming at building communism (at least not the Marxian one) she is *not* a public organization, hence cannot logically be a legal person in the context of the Soviet Constitution.[2] Therefore, although Soviet citizens may have the theoretical right to profess any religion, they have not a constitutionally guaranteed right to *belong* to a religous organization or church. This is fully in accord with the 1929 legislation 'On Religious Associations' and its amendments of 1975, which forbid the establishment of genuine parishes (not to mention any other religious groups or associations, which are all banned) with lists of members and regular dues. Since this legislation, as well as the Constitutions of 1936 and 1977, explicitly forbid all forms of 'religious propaganda', but allow 'atheistic propaganda' (the latter according to two constitutions), the legal and constitutional right to profess any religion, if strictly interpreted, becomes the right to a *secret* personal religion without any external and visible manifestations. Whereas prior to 1929 – when both believers and atheists enjoyed the right to the propagation of their views, and the Communist Party had not been mentioned in the earlier Constitutions of 1918 and 1924 – there was still some meaning in distinguishing between the Communist Party and its subordinate organizations (the *Komsomol*, the Young Pioneers, and their press) on the one hand, and the Soviet government on the other, and in blaming the antireligious struggle on the Party alone, such claims lost all meaning after 1929, and definitely since 1936.[3] The above constitutional clauses have only made final on paper the aims of the Communist theory going back to the very origins of Marxism-Leninism, particularly in the writings of Friedrich Engels.[4]

A textbook of the methodology of teaching 'scientific atheism' within the context of the study of the CPSU and its history, published by the Moscow amalgamated universities' press in 1975 in order to convince the party lecturer how important it is to attack religion in his lectures on communism, constantly stresses the actively antireligious accent in the whole history of Marxism, from Marx's famous statement that 'religion is a sign of an oppressed creature ... a soul of the soulless order of things. Religion is the *opiate* of the people', to L. I. Brezhnev's statement at the 24th Party Congress about the necessity of a 'permanent and uncompromising struggle with the survivals of the past' which the textbook immediately interprets as struggle against religion.[5] It stresses that because the shortage of funds and the difficulty of illegal transportation into Russia of the first Lenin newspaper *Iskra*, published in Switzerland, dictated the necessity of using as little paper for each issue as possible, only the most urgently important subjects were printed, and among these, 'already in the first few issues of *Iskra*, sixteen articles were dedicated to atheism'. The Russian Social Democratic Workers Party Programme adopted at the Second Party Congress under Lenin's leadership, in 1903, already promised the 'confiscation of all land belonging to monasteries and churches'. The same congress had adopted a resolution on the necessity of work among religious sectarians, and a paper was published by the Bolsheviks in Geneva in 1904 especially for the sectarians under the editorship of V. D. Bonch-Bruevich.[6] The purpose of this work was to turn the sectarians and the Old Believers against the Orthodox (State) Church to weaken and if possible split her – a policy that was carried out by the Soviets during the first decade of their reign.[7]

This temporary differentiation of antireligious policies was reflected in Lenin's writings of 1909: 'A Marxist,' he wrote, 'must be a materialist, i.e. an enemy of religion; but he must be a dialectical materialist, i.e. his struggle against religion ought not to be an abstract one . . . purely theoretically based . . . but a concrete one, based on class struggle.'[8] This 'dialecticism' was interpreted later, both by Lenin and his heirs, as making the character, intensity and style (methodolgy) of antireligious policies dependent on the practical possibilities and needs of the party and its policies of the given moment. In the later attacks of the so-called 'mechanicists' by the dialectical materialists and by the official party line on militant materialism and militant atheism, the subordination of both to the concrete needs and policies of the party at the given moment was termed *partiinost'* in their philosophy and in the antireligious struggle.[9]

Lenin never really ceased his war against religion. The Leninist legal Petersburg monthly *Prosveshchenie* (The Enlightenment), from its first issue in 1912 and throughout, paid considerable attention to attacks on religion. Studies appeared with detailed calculations of the proportion of taxpayer's money going to the Church, protesting that this was money wasted, implying that the Church and the clergy were parasites, although actually most of the state funds transferred to the Church went to its huge network of primary schols. There were vaguely veiled blasphemous poems by the Bolshevik poet Demian Bedny in every issue. One issue contained a story by Gorky with an open attack on the monastic clergy, presenting it as greedy, gluttonous, drunk, and dishonest.[10] Another attacked the 'god-building' theories of Lunacharsky, a Bolshevik ideologist and a future Commissar of Education (Enlightenment), because Lunacharsky dared to see Marxism as a religion or counter-religion, a religion deifying man and man's ability to build a perfect society of communism. The attacking article concluded: 'Lunacharsky's ideas are a force hostile to the enlightenment of the working masses in the spirit of Marxism.' This was in accord with Lenin's later reprimand to Lunacharsky's ideological *confrère*, Gorky: 'any religious idea, any idea of any god at all, any flirtation even with a god, is the most inexpressive foulness . . . it is the most dangerous foulness, the most shameful "infection"'.[11]

The high priority that Lenin attached to combating religion is demonstrated not only by the early antireligious legislation which will be discussed later, but also by the fact that he found it appropriate to organize political education courses in the middle of the Civil War (October 1918) when the very survival of the communist regime was very much in question and when antireligious education and the training of atheistic propagandists were of utmost importance.[12]

Thus there is a continuity in these policies from the time when the party had been only a tiny group of revolutionary conspirators to the era of its seizure of power and control of the state. The fact that, from the very first days in power to the present, government agencies in charge of overseeing the Church have been formally or informally a part of the secret or political police organization, further illustrates how much importance the Communist leadership has always attached to the struggle against religion. Indeed, the very first top Soviet supervisors over Church affairs included, among other communist leaders, Leon Trotsky, and Tuchkov the real operator and planner of church policies, who was one of the leading figures in the GPU.[13] In view of all these factors this study will not be occupied with the hair-splitting differentiation between the Soviet State and the Communist Party, but will treat all the attacks and campaigns against religion in the Soviet Union as official policy, and such organizations as *The League of the Militant Godless* or the *Znanie Society* (Knowledge) as expressions of the official policies of the Soviet State in regard to the Church. The very fact that these have been executed by such societies rather than directly by the State always gives the Soviet government or its governing Communist Party the option of changing its position on the religious front by accusing individual authors or societies of abusing power or using wrong methods. This duality also gives the Church and believers the possibility of occasionally gaining some respite by appealing to the central authorities against the local ones. Needless to say, it is obvious to scholars that any distinction between the Soviet government and the Communist Party is purely artificial.

1 The Philosophical Foundations of Soviet Atheism

'Only one secular doctrine in the modern world retains the scope of traditional religion in offering an interpretation of human existence . . . and direct[ing] their actions which transcend those offered by their immediate situation: Marxism.'

(Macintyre, cited by Thrower)

To many people interested in understanding present realities in the Soviet Union a theoretical analysis of Marxist philosophy may seem at first to be an abstract scholarly enterprise, irrelevant to everyday life in the Soviet Union today. We will try to prove, however, that such an analysis is actually the only efficient way to gain an insight into the processes that have been taking place in Soviet society for the last seven decades. Soviet leadership sees itself as a political force normatively guided by the principles of Marxist-Leninist ideology. Hence an understanding of this ideology provides us with an understanding of the actual processes of policy formation in the USSR.

Simple observations of daily events within the Soviet system are far short of helping us make sense of what is going on, or what is still to happen in that country. Outside observations do not and cannot reveal the intricacies of the political motivations that drive Soviet authorites towards ideological goals alien to Western views. A very important point is missed by empiricist-minded foreign observers. This is the fact that in the world of Communism every social event is placed in a broader context of concerns and premeditated manipulation of the whole system of existing social structures and institutions, a manipulation justified in the name of the great goals of Marxism-Leninism. It is only by studying the world-view of Communist leaders that one can reconstruct the rationale of their actions which along with their means are invariably chosen with a view to ideological ends.

For us in the West it is important to realize the basic fact that in the USSR all state policies, with no exception whatsoever, are designed and carried out as an implementation of the world-view commitments of the Communist Party. The Party has an unlimited and unquestionable authority over every aspect of social life. This state of affairs is explicitly stated and hence legitimized in the content of the Soviet Constitution. The Party openly defines itself as the political force determined to implement the social and cultural models developed initially by Marxism-Leninism; hence all Soviet policies emerge from a complicated, controversial process of rationalization and readjustment of the Communist world-view to the realities of the twentieth century.

The general point we want to make in this chapter is that a genuine insight into any particular aspect of policy formation in the USSR can be properly achieved only when we understand the specific Marxist-Leninist ideological frame of mind that is characteristic of the Soviet decision-makers.

*   *   *

This exercise is devoted to the analysis of the nature of Soviet atheism. In the larger scheme of things state-enforced atheism in the USSR turns out to be merely one of the many ways in which the Soviet leadership ensures continuous reorganization of the existing social structures. This is, generally speaking, the functional result of atheistic policies that an entire succession of governments in the Soviet Union pursued after the October Revolution of 1917. However, the issue of why these policies were designed in the first place and how exactly they were carried out in real life deserves a detailed historical analysis. It should not be brushed away by stating simplistic generalizations.

The actual history of Soviet atheism is an enormously interesting story of the grand ambition of Marxist-Leninist ideology to reshape existing forms of social consciousness, to reorganize and redirect people's beliefs. In addition, it is the story of the actual failure of the Communist Party to eradicate the faith in God and organized religions in the USSR. In spite of the efforts of several generations of militant and fully state-supported communist propagandists, religion is still practised in that country.

Indeed, the history of Soviet atheism is the story of intellectual, political and physical struggle, the implications of which have a profound world importance.

It is a fundamental fact that in every single detail Marxism is incompatible with views emanating from a faith in the Supernatural. Furthermore, Communism is persistently and openly hostile to them. This hostility is not a matter of secondary importance, it is not a contingently developed interaction between competing intellectual systems. This hostility towards religion is the core of the teaching of historical and dialectical materialism – the philosophical doctrine of the Communist Party of the USSR.

Marxist philosophy takes pride in proclaiming itself the most fundamental, thoroughly scientific critique of religion. Marxism-Leninism aims at the so-called 'demystification' and 'destruction' of religious beliefs and sentiments. In addition, it openly elaborates an educational–administrative offensive intended to methodically dismantle the instructional base of religious life, namely the Church.

Some observers of the Soviet system have pointed out that temporary historical compromises can exist between Marxist atheism and Church administrations in the USSR, and others state that religion still exists in that country after more than six decades of persecution. Sometimes there is co-operation between the Soviet state and the Orthodox Church on issues concerning world peace and the prevention of nuclear war.

It is our intention to prove that whatever these concrete compromises might be, Marxism-Leninism is determined to destroy religious consciousness and to eradicate the existing forms of religious practices in the long run. The tactical manoeuvres introduced by Soviet authorities under the pressure of political circumstances should not be perceived as a possibility for peaceful co-existence between atheism and religion. A closer analysis of basic Soviet strategies will reveal conclusively that any attempts at mutual tolerance are unconvincing and short-lived. Co-existence between atheistic materialism and the religious interpretation of reality is theoretically and practically impossible. Hostility towards religion is not a matter of contingency, but a profound,

fundamental world-view commitment of the official ideology
of Communism.

* * *

As we stated earlier, it is theoretically important to trace the
formation and trends of the development of Marxist atheism.
Understanding where Marx comes from helps us see where he
ends intellectually. From the very outset of his philosophical
career, Karl Marx was deeply involved in the debates surrounding the philosophy of religion in early-nineteenth-
century Germany. The maturing of Marx's thought took place
among bitter controversies concerning the proper interpretation of the Hegelian philosophical legacy. For the Hegelians,
philosophy as a reflective analytical enterprise was bound to
serve the superior insights of a religious comprehension of the
world. Hegel's rationalizations of the fundamentals of Christian faith, as expressed in his elaborate philosophy of Spirit,
were substantially reinterpreted after his death in 1831.
Hegel's philosophical heritage was heavily debated by the so-
called Young Hegelians (B. Bauer, M. Stirner, D. Strauss) on
the one hand, and Ludwig Feuerbach on the other. In this
crossfire between materialism and idealism, young Marx lined
up with materialism. Thus, from the very start, he initiated an
atheistic teaching which could never compromise even with the
most unorthodox, most liberal forms of religious philosophy.
Feuerbach became the intellectual mentor of Marx's profound
hatred for all Christian principles. It is enlightening to examine
some further detail on the intellectual affiliation of Marx with
Feuerbach. Although he was not a blind follower of Feuerbach,
Marx was profoundly inspired by his ideas at the onset of his
career.

This story once again starts with Hegel. Hegel often
criticized the dogmatic theology of his day, meanwhile retain-
ing a deep intellectual interest in the ontological and epistemological assumptions of Christianity. His philosophical theory of
reality as well as his theory of knowledge were in principle
compatible with the system of theological views held at the time.
Religious explanations of the deepest questions of Being were
viewed as unquestionably valuable, but needing some additional clarification, systematization and argumentative justi-

fication. Their validity was taken for granted. In short, the enterprise of philosophy was viewed by the great German dialectician only as an exercise in the conceptual justification of unquestionable truths of faith.

Feuerbach, on the contrary, tried hard to dissociate philosophy from religion. He wished to give philosophers intellectual autonomy in the high matters of ontology (that is, in the interpretation of reality). This independence was to be sought by way of an outright rebellion against the conceptual foundations of theology. The decisive intellectual blow against the intellectual strongholds of the traditional Christian Church, so ancient in time, was to be delivered, in Feuerbach's opinion, by substituting for traditional religion the new and much more sublime religion of humanity.

Feuerbach argued that this move would undermine Christianity's intellectual monopoly on such fundamentals as human dignity, the meaning of life, morality and purposefulness of existence. He believed that the new religion would manage to redirect man's need for worthwhile goals in life into the mainstream of materialism. This would provide a freedom of human action, which faith and professional theology, in his view, had suppressed for ages.

Feuerbach took a critical stand regarding Hegel's rationalistic explanation of human behaviour. Hegel's view that rationality of human action emerges from the hidden determinations of the Spirit of History (*Zeitgeist*) was in Feuerbach's opinion nothing more than a subservience by means of a theory to the *Weltanschauung* of rational theology, which he saw as wrong in principle. In his view it was an empty speculative expression of the religious conception of the divine Providence which Feuerbach considered to be simply nonsensical.

The materialist philosopher believed that human nature can be truly dignified only if it is appreciated in its own right, independent of any relation to the notion of the Almighty. Human nature, conceived of being itself divine or of supreme perfection, was to be elevated to the rank of a new subject of worship. Feuerbach thought that this new worship would be much more sincere and worthy of its idol. Temples should be built for Man's consciousness of himself, while old churches as Houses of the Lord should be demolished without any regret or mercy. As a materialist he believed that religious 'deceptions' were not worthy of any compromise or tolerance. They had to be destroyed.

Feuerbach himself understood that individual men were indeed undeserving of the effort and the enthusiasm needed for a new religion. He thought, however, that mankind was worthy at least as a collective entity. Humanity transcends individual idiosyncrasies, and human nature, as such, compromises the worthy subject of a new admiration.

Feuerbach wrote that 'the antithesis of divine and human is altogether illusory, that it is nothing more that the antithesis between human nature in general and the human individual'.[1]

Christianity, in Feuerbach's view, emerged as an early, primitive, unsophisticated, rather distorted self-knowledge of man. He stated that in Christian religion man simply extrapolated and projected onto the Heavens the attributes of the human race as such. This act, however, gradually made man a subservient slave of his own illusory creation. The philosopher states:

> All divine attributes, all the attributes which make God God, are attributes of the (human) species — attributes which in the individual are limited, but the limits of which are abolished in the essence of the species.[2]

Feuerbach insisted that the liberation of intrinsic human dignity from the reign of illusory images by the human mind in the form of religious beliefs could be achieved only if traditional faith was mercilessly attacked by a more decent and humanizing intellectual system. Religious commitments should be intellectually and emotionally destroyed by the catharsis of an intensive hatred towards the old God. All previous religious institutions should be ruthlessly eradicated from the face of the earth and from the memory of coming generations, so that they could never regain power over people's minds through deception and the promotion of fear from the mystical forces of the Heavens. At this point young Marx was completely fascinated by Feuerbach's 'humanistic zest', and he adopted Feuerbach's open rebellion against the powerful tradition of Christianity unconditionally as an intellectual revelation. Very early in his career, Marx bought the seductive idea that the higher goals of humanity would justify any radicalism, not only the intellectual kind but the

social and political as well. The extremes of political action
could be forgiven if the cause were right. The fact that most of
the higher goals of Feuerbach were totally Utopian in nature
did not bother Marx in the least. At this point in his intellectual
development, the materialistic alternative to Hegel's legacy in
Germany was all that mattered to him. He wrote with full
admiration for Feuerbach's intellectually destructive enterprise:

> I advise you, you theologians and speculative philosophers,
> to rid yourselves of the concepts and prejudices of the old
> speculative philosophy . . . and there is no other road toward
> truth and freedom than this 'stream of fire' (Feuerbach).
> Feuerbach is the purgatory of our time.[3]

Obviously Marx began his own theory of reality with a
complete intellectual disdain for everything that religious
thought, represented, theoretically, practically or emotionally.
The cultural contributions of religion over the centuries were
dismissed as unimportant and irrelevant to the well-being of
the human mind. It is important to make a specific point about
the relationship between Feuerbachian and Marxian thought.
Although influenced by Feuerbach, Marx was in no way his
orthodox follower. He related to Feuerbach more as a fellow
member of the intellectual brotherhood of atheistic-
materialists. They had a common enemy, in all forms of
idealistic interpretation.

The necessity for the autonomy of Man and his world from
the realm of supernatural forces was perceived by Marx not as a
Utopian dream conjured up by Feuerbach in isolation, but as
the axiomatic ontological truth formulated by the materialist
school of thought since ancient times. This tradition of
philosophy dated back to ancient Greek atomism, and hence it
had in Marx's eyes not only and equal but an even more
respectable history than Christianity. The great intellectual
value of even the most naïve forms of early materialism
emerged in Marx's view from the fact that materialist philosophers had in principle liberated human beings from the
necessity to suppress their natural potential for action and
domination over reality. Materialism does not constrain
human expansion, it does not preach modesty or obedience to

any idols of omnipotent and omniscient gods. And that appealed to Marx enormously.

In his doctoral thesis entitled *On the Differences Between the Natural Philosophy of Democritus and the Natural Philosophy of Epicurus* Marx embarked on atheism not as an intellectual accident, but as a conscious choice to affiliate professionally with the method and the world-view of materialism as such. It was obvious at this point that reading Feuerbach was not the only source of inspiration for Marx's atheism. The fascination with Feuerbach's war against Christianity was for young Marx nothing more than an expression of his own readiness to pursue in an antireligious struggle all the social and political extremes that materialistic determination required in principle.

Yet, as David Aikman, in his most profound and erudite study of Marx and Marxism, notes, the clue to Marx's passionate and violent atheism, or rather *anti*-theism, cannot be found in an intellectual tradition alone. He traces Marx's anti-theism to the young Marx's preoccupation with the Promethean cult of 'Satan as a destroyer ... emphasis on destruction for its own sake [is present] in so much of the Marxist tradition.'[4]

Aikman traces Marx's passionate hatred for Christianity in particular to his fascination with Satan as a liberator by means of destruction of everything created by God or by a Christ-oriented historical tradition. The inspiration for this cult of the Satan, Aikman sees in the cult of Prometheus characteristic of such eighteenth- and early nineteenth-century figures as Goethe, Shelley and Byron, as well as in the various strains of radical socialism, particularly in the communistic-Utopian religious sects. Aikman follows the Igor' Shafarevich thesis that all socialistic-communistic doctrines, from the extreme sects to Marxism, share three fundamental aims: (i) abolition of private property; (ii) destruction of religion (an established Church in particular); (iii) destruction of the family.[5]

Marx was primarily a revolutionary, ready from the outset of his philosophical career to demolish the established cultural and political order of things without compromise. Intellectually Marx rationalized his hatred for religion as a symptomatic expression of the alienation of humans from their own real world. Religious consciousness had to be wiped out along with the conditions that brought about that alienation. For Feuerbach and the Neo-Hegelians of the left, religious consciousness remained the main target of passionate intellectual attacks in nineteenth-century Germany. For Marx, religion, like all other forms of consciousness, was a superstructure determined by the economic base, which would be destroyed after the economic liberation of man from exploitation had been achieved. Yet in the high priority given to the aim of destroying religion can be seen from the fact that even before he devised a political programme the destruction of religion by that as-yet-undesigned state had already been proclaimed by Marx in the following violently revolutionary terms:

> When the political state as political state comes violently into being . . . the state can and must proceed to the *abolition of religion*, to the *destruction* of religion.[6]

Marx's understanding of religion as a distorted representation of the real world suggested that the struggle against the 'opium of Christian faith' had to be reinforced by a more fundamental struggle against the conditions that produced religious consciousness in the first place. He was convinced that:

> to abolish religion as the illusory happiness of the people is to demand their real happiness; the demand to give up illusions about the existing state of affairs is the demand to give up a state of affairs that needs illusions.[7]

Marx proclaimed the necessity to turn the 'critique of heavens' carried out by young Hegelians and Feuerbach into the grandiose enterprise of the 'critique of the earth': that meant, to abolish the complex conditions that had required the illusory consolations, which in Marx's opinion religion had tried to offer for thousands of years.

Marx writes in his thesis on Feuerbach that to criticize religion without criticizing the secular base of religion is only a futile exercise. In this document of the mature Marxist view, a departure from Feuerbach's thinking is offered and a new vision of militant materialism is openly stated. Marx writes explicitly:

Feuerbach starts out from the fact of religious self-estrangement, of the duplication of the world into a religious, imaginary world and a real one. His work consists in resolving the religious world into its secular basis. He overlooks the fact that after completing his work, the chief thing remains to be done. For the fact that the secular basis lifts off from itself and establishes itself in the clouds as an independent realm, can only be explained by the inner strife and intrinsic contradictoriness of this secular basis. The latter must, therefore, first be understood in its contradictoriness and then, by the removal of the contradiction, revolutionized in practice.[8]

Thus Marx further elaborates Feuerbach's idea that religion is an illusory form of human fulfilment. He turns the naïve atheism of his times into a more complicated world-view to be remembered as Marxism. Friedrich Engels is another prominent contributor to the ideas of Communism. Over a period of over five decades he collaborated with Marx in every major aspect of the formation of the dialectical-materialistic outlook on reality. Actually it is Engels who popularized 'dialectical materialism' and tried to systematize the principles of the new teaching. At the time when Marx gradually became preoccupied with the problems of political economy Engels emerged as the thinker who was much more open to the burning political and cultural controversies of the day, who was willing and able to take up practical issues and analyze them in relation to the fundamentals of Communist ideology. Since debates about the history and the nature of Christianity were widespread in the nineteenth century in almost all the West European countries, Engels became more and more interested in religion and in religious controversies. He published a number of books independently of Marx. In these works he tried to deal with the issues he treated in a somewhat popular but much more explicit manner than the analysis provided earlier in co-authorship with Marx in *The German Ideology*.

In his works *Anti-Düring* and *Ludwig Feuerbach and the End of Classical German Ideology* (1886), Engels elaborated on criticism of the idealistic world-view in general, including religious outlooks on reality. He insisted that idealism stems from the inability of men to cope with the forces of nature and the chaos of social life, that religion constitutes nothing more than a fantastic reflection in the human mind of those powers which determine the miserable conditions of human existence in the earlier stages of history. Engels underlines the materialistic position which holds that with the increase of man's control over natural and social processes, religion will vanish from the society of the future, since the very causes of human desperation that bring about religious views in the first place, will gradually disappear. He wrote:

> When . . . man no longer merely proposes, but also disposes — only then will the last alien force which is still reflected in religion vanish; and with it will vanish the religious reflection itself, for the simple reason that there will be nothing left to reflect.[9]

Since a religious outlook on life and reality was rationalized by Engels only as a false consciousness, bound to disappear as mankind's understanding of the world and of society deepens, he considered religious sentiments and beliefs totally incompatible with the moral and intellectual standards of communism.

All his life Engels kept in close contact with the leaders of Social Democratic and Communist parties in Europe and with the founders of the First International (the political union of communist movements in the nineteenth century), urging them to spread and cultivate atheism as the only admissable alternative to the 'old idealistic nonsense'. He insisted that the truly successful antidote to the deceptions of theology can be found in science.

Engels suggested that the scientific education of the masses on a large scale is an effective way to overcome all the fears, illusions, and desperations associated with a religious outlook on nature and life. In his view, sciences are intrinsically materialistic; they explain away all the mysteries on which religion thrives. They therefore restore the confidence of man in himself, and his own powers encourage him to control his life and dominate in his interaction with nature, instead of being left to the whim of its blind and cold mercy.

Engels became a relentless proponent of the wider spread of scientific knowledge. He wrote about the great scientific discoveries of the nineteenth century and their support for the principles of dialectical materialism in all his popular works intended for the ordinary ranks of the Communist movement. In biology, physics, chemistry, anthropology and psychology in the second half of nineteenth-century culture Engels looked for arguments in favour of materialism and against any theological explanations of the world.

In his *Anti-Düring* he proposed to the ordinary German Social Democrats a 'scientifically substantiated' exposition of the dialectical method and the Communist world outlook in general. The book was considered by several generations of Marxists to be a concise encyclopedia of dialectical and historical materialism. In Engels's view, modern science provided sufficient confirmation of the profound philosophical insights of the materialistic tradition; they exemplified the ontological and epistemological principles stated by Marxism as a monistic system. Engels wrote:

> The real unity of the world consists in its materiality and this is proved not by a few juggled phrases, but by a long and wearisome development of philosophy and natural sciences.[10]

For him, speculative philosophy so prominent in the tradition of idealism and rational theology had become totally obsolete in view of the magnificent success of positive scientific knowledge. Even materialism, much more open to the facts of the world of practice and experience, had to change its form, although it should preserve its sound content. Engels proclaims that:

> Modern materialism ... is not a philosophy but a simple conception of the world which has to establish its validity and be applied not in a science of sciences standing apart, but within the actual sciences. Philosophy is, therefore, 'sublated' here, that is, both overcome and preserved; overcome as regards its form, and preserved as regards its real content.[11]

Engels's deep conviction that materialistic atheism gains profoundly by relying on the achievements of the sciences spread quickly among Communist followers. Later it became the basic idea guiding the strategy and providing the content of the Soviet educational offensive against all manifestations of religious consciousness in the USSR. The fact that scientific views are often accepted by religious thinkers never bothered Marxist atheists.

The third major person who contributed profoundly to the shaping of modern Communist ideology in the USSR was Vladimir Ilyich Lenin. Lenin's chief source of philosophical education was the writings of Marx and Engels. His views, however, evolved in the unique cultural context of Russia and hence they were substantially influenced by the intellectual traditions of that country. As far as atheism is concerned Lenin made it the immediate political task of the party. Since he considered that in Russia religion was the basic ideological tool used by the ruling classes to keep the exploited masses in subordination, Lenin believed atheistic propaganda to be an urgent necessity. It had to be used as effectively as possible to weaken the influence of the Orthodox religion among the workers and peasants in the Russian empire. The intention was to prepare the transition of the exploited classes to new forms of materialistic consciousness, which were believed to be more appropriate for the builders of the new social order of Communism.

Lenin considered theoretical ideas important not in and for themselves, but as guidelines and weapons in the relentless class struggle raging in society. He took upon himself the responsibility of organizing an intellectually enlightened Party as the vanguard of the oppressed and hence 'to apply practically the materialist analysis and the materialist estimate of all aspects of life and activity of all classes, strata and groups of the population'.[12]

For Lenin, theoretical debates, even abstract philosophical systems, could never be comprehended in isolation from the totality of social life. He could not admit in principle the idea of objective, neutral academic research, since he was rationalizing within the tradition of historical materialism all intellectual activity as being perpetrated by and subjected to class interest. He was so deeply convinced of the partisan nature of philosophical debates that, amidst the acute daily political battles he had to fight constantly, he found time and energy to produce his book *Materialism and Empirio-criticism* and to keep extensive notes from his readings of the works of Aristotle, Descartes, Kant and Hegel. He believed that in those works he could find an answer to the deepest questions concerning the ideological class struggle of the day and therefore be much more forceful and efficient in the political arena of his own historical period.

For Lenin, even the smallest traces of idealism in the views of his political opponents or collaborators were equivalent to concessions to the mystical religious view of reality, and therefore, directly or indirectly, supported ideological dominance over the exploited classes. Since he believed that religion preaches preservation of the existing status quo and subordination and humility on the part of the faithful, he ascribed political significance to every idealistic or religious claim and thus made them the primary target of ideological attacks. Convinced of the fundamental argument of militant materialism, Lenin went far beyond the Russian tradition of political atheism of Belinsky, Herzen and Pisarev and became the proponent of a systematic, aggressive and uncompromising movement of atheistic agitation, organized and fully supported by the party. He became the founder of a whole institution of professional atheistic propagandists, who spread all over the country after the revolution and played a very important role in the attack on the churches and the conversion of the faithful to the beliefs of the 'science-based materialistic world-view' of the communists.

Lenin's unequivocally hostile attitude toward religion grew into a distinctive feature of the Bolshevik version of atheism. Compared with much milder views popular within the Social Democratic Party for example, Bolshevik atheism allowed for no compromise whatsoever with widely held religious views and sentiments even if this meant alienating some of the sympathetic, leftist-minded yet religiously believing intellectuals, workers or peasants. In this respect Lenin directed some severe criticism at Anatoli Lunacharsky. The latter was a Marxist Bolshevik, who, however, tried, unlike the hard-line followers of Lenin, to accommodate religious sentiments to the world-view of Communism.

Lunacharsky's views on the relationship between atheism and religion carried a substantial resemblance to the Utopian ideas of Feuerbach of 'a new religion of humanity' – a religion compatible with the sciences and different from the Christian tradition. Lunacharsky articulated the so-called programme of

bogostroitel'stvo – god-building. In it he proclaimed that
although traditional religion was conceptually wrong and
ideologically biased towards the interests of the exploiting
classes, it still cultivated in the masses emotion, moral values,
desires which revolutionaries should take over and manipu-
late. Those should be gradually transformed into the positive
humanistic values of a communist morality instead of opposing them and trying to destroy the basis of the psychological
and moral integrity of millions of religious people. Lunacharsky believed that by gradually replacing the traditional idea of
God with a new vision of humanity – in his view, a worthy object
for love and admiration – socialism would achieve the greatest
possible success. This would come with the least possible
confrontation, without abuse of the cultural status quo and the
whole historical tradition of European civilization. Lenin was
infuriated by these ideas, by what he perceived as giving in to
religious obscurantism. He considered Lunacharsky's position
harmful in the extreme, since, according to Lenin, it dissolved
Marxism into a mild liberal reformism. He thought that this
position obscured the fact that the Church is a servant to the
state, that religion all along has been a tool of ideological
suppression of the masses. Lenin tried to expose the god-
building programme as a dangerous and totally unnecessary
compromise with the most reactionary forces in the Russian
empire. Under the circumstances, he appealed to militant
atheism as a criterion for the sincerity of Marxist commitments,
as a testing principle. It was his view that ideological and
political conformism would weaken the theoretical principles
of the party and the revolution, if left unpunished.

In his response to Lunacharsky, Lenin writes:

> Those who toil and live in want all their lives are taught by
> religion to be submissive and patient while here on earth, and
> to take comfort in the hope of a heavenly reward. But those
> who live by the labour of others are taught by religion to
> practice charity whilst on earth, thus offering them a very
> cheap way of justifying their existence as exploiters and
> selling them at a very modest price tickets to well-being in
> Heaven. Religion is opium for the people. Religion is a sort of
> spiritual booze, in which the slaves of capital drown their
> human image, their demand for a life more or less worthy of
> man.[13]

So Lenin refused to allow for any compromise in the theoretical heritage of Marxism. He had the example of Marx's earlier rejection of Feuerbach's proposals for a religion of humanity, but in addition he had the conviction that under the confrontation of intense political pressures even the slightest deviation from the principles of materialism and atheism could degenerate into a betrayal of the cause of Communism altogether. The purity of the Marxist world-view had to be preserved at any cost, in Lenin's opinion.

* * *

Up to now we have been relying on the reader's intuitive understanding of the notion of world-view. It is appropriate at this point to introduce some conceptual clarifications and show explicitly why materialism is in principle incompatible with religion.

Any world-view, the Marxist-Leninist one included, can be analyzed as a system of ideas, beliefs and tacit assumptions about the nature of reality. The elements of the world-view have for man the status of firm convictions. They are perceived as the truth about the world. In fact, the world-view is only a historically concrete, time- and culture-bound way of rationalizing our limited experiences and attempts to understand reality. Marxism-Leninism suggests what it believes to be the true alternative to the religious outlook. This includes at least these three major facets of the world-view:

(1) A certain vision of the relationship between man and nature.
(2) A concrete understanding of the relationship between man and society or groups of men and society.
(3) A certain understanding of the meaning of life, of human nature and its destination.

Dialectical and historical materialism serves as the theoretical core of the Marxist-Leninist world-view. Dialectical materialism, being a philosophical ontology (that is, a theory about the true nature of reality), has taken upon itself the task of elaborating an alternative to the religious view of creation. Marxism views human beings as natural products of the interplay of material forces, where there is no place whatsoever for any supernatural involvement. The ontological model of materialism posits the existence of an objective, self-sufficient world in which laws regulate the order of things. The contingent interaction of the forces of evolution produces the human species, the latter being but another element of the grand scheme of the unconscious universe.

Epistemologically speaking, Marxism considers human experience as cognitively unreliable. Knowledge is viewed as a reflection upon the natural world. Causal relationships between human beings and their physical reality are objective and independent of preferences and desires. Marxism views thought processes as emergent from and based on material practice, the prime form of which is economic. Those thought processes are believed to be bound directly or indirectly to the concrete, practical activities of men. Hence they represent, ideally, the content and the form of those activities. Even logical forms and the rationality of the moral and the aesthetic goals of humankind are derived, for the dialectical materialist, from the historical content of *praxis*. Cognitive illusions and fantasies comprise, from the point of view of Marxism, a distorted, an exaggerated vision of the otherwise objective material experiences of individuals. The latter simply interact with nature and society and create fantasies as a by-product of daily life. Marx writes with pride:

> Communism as fully developed naturalism equals humanism; and fully developed humanism equals naturalism; it is the genuine resolution of the conflict between man and nature and between man and man.[14]

The second major aspect of Marxism, the so-called historical materialism, aims at extending the materialist approach to the sphere of culture and society. A materialistic interpretation of history was indeed something that had never been suggested before.

Marx views the development of the human race as a law-like, objective process. It follows that basic economic activities determine the structure of sophisticated socio-political and intellectual achievements. Human culture is the result of economic production. The history of civilization is seen as a pattern of more or less rigid socio-economic formations. The latter are composed of a specific production base and an institutional and spiritual superstructure related to this base. Immersed in the context of a specific socio-economic formation, generation after generation are toiling relentlessly, in Marx's view, to produce and sustain the prosaic fact of human existence. In this sociological model, the human race is motivated by material necessity. The higher products of the human spirit are merely a direct or indirect representation of the bitter realities of life.

The history of mankind is understood by Marx to be a history of the exploitation of the labouring classes. The vested interest of the rulers, spread in the form of different ideologies, serves to reinforce and gloss over the existing order of inequality and injustice. Religion, which according to Feuerbach and Marx emerged initially as an illusory escape from daily tragedies and frustrations, is to be treated, according to Marx, as a Utopian form of compensation and consolidation for the disappointments of life. It had been taken over, however, by the ruling classes, says Marx, and gradually turned into a tool for the intellectual and emotional control of the masses. Marx insists on perceiving the history of Christianity as an enterprise for the preservation of the status quo, as an elaborate deception of humankind. Being a form of ideology, it has to be attacked with no degree of compromise by the purifying outrage of the revolutionary masses. As a materialist, Marx states:

> It is self-evident . . . that 'spectres', 'bonds', the 'higher being', 'concept', 'scruple' are merely idealist, speculative mental expressions, the concepts of apparently isolated individuals, the mere images of very empirical fetters and limitations, within which move the mode of production of life, and the form of intercourse coupled with it.[15]

In Marx's view religion has undergone an evolution from a spiritual protest against social and natural conditions of life to a false consolation for the desperate, and finally into a form of ideological subjection of the exploited classes to the social power of the exploiters. Actually, within the value system of Marxism-Leninism, this evolution is nothing but a deterioration of the initial goals of the whole movement in which the dominating social and cultural elite has perverted in the course of history the higher ideals of the early forms of religion.

Thus historical materialism provides the moral justification for the extremes of revolutionary action against Christianity. It theoretically substantiates and motivates atheism in its relentless pursuit of the destruction of Christian faith and practice.

Historical materialism, together with the dialectical teachings of Marx, Engels and Lenin, make an attempt to justify the educational and administrative offensive of Communism against religion. Humans, being themselves perceived only as a product of the socio-cultural environment of their time, have to undergo fundamental changes parallel to the changing social order. Early Marxism believed that the revolutionary reorganization of society would ultimately result in the quick decay and the eventual disappearance of religious forms of consciousness.

If humans are indeed ensembles of social relations, the reconstruction of these social relations will naturally result in the reforming of the human personality. Logically, therefore, it is to be expected that once Marx had elaborated an economic and socio-political doctrine of a society which should bring religion to its natural death, the preoccupation with the subject of direct struggle against religion would disappear from his writings. And indeed Marx's interest gradually shifted toward the areas of sociology and political economy. His initial enthusiasm for enforcing atheism through propaganda wars against theology and idealism gradually faded away. It seems that later in his career Marx began to believe that if economic and social change were to be carried out successfully, the new richness of ideas which emerged from a rationalized order of communistic social life would gradually replace the 'dream-world' of European Christianity. As shall be shown in later chapters, such relatively 'passive' attitudes to antireligious struggle would be picked up and promoted in the Soviet Union by the so-called 'mechanicists', causing Lenin's wrath, violent attacks on them by the main line of Soviet Establishment atheism and periodic destruction of that school of thought.

But even the mature Marx never consistently pursued this 'passive' attitude. Although in his later constructs of his future socialist state he only spoke about the necessity of separation of the Church from the State, 'the problem of religious belief continued to trouble him . . . throughout his life Marx persisted in a view that belief in God was . . . deeply wicked and anti-human'. When a silly, totally unscholarly, diatribe by a German atheist appeared, claiming that early Christians had been cannibals, ritualistically drinking human blood and eating human flesh, Marx was overjoyed, and said of the author: 'Daumer has proved . . . that the Christians really did slaughter people . . . offering human sacrifices. . . . Daumer's book . . . deals Christianity a death-blow.'

Aikman aptly concludes:

> That Marx believed that Christianity's days were numbered on the basis of a venomously critical explanation of Christian origins suggests . . . anything but total confidence that Christianity would pass away primarily through economic changes in society.[16]

Later in the development of the Marxist movement, not without the help of Engels and Plekhanov, the activist atheist sentiments grew stronger and stronger, once again becoming a top priority in the Leninist version of Marxism. Marx himself started with the following general view:

> Feuerbach resolves the essence of religion into the essence of man. But the essence of man is not obstruction inherent in each single individual. In its reality, it is the ensemble of social relations. Feuerbach, who does not enter upon a criticism of this real essence, is hence obliged to abstract from the historical process and to define the religious sentiment (Gemüt) regarded by itself, and to presuppose an abstract isolated individual. . . . Feuerbach, consequently does not see that the religious sentiment is itself a social product, and that the abstract individual that he analyzes belongs to a particular society.[17]

The Revolution in his view was still some distance away.

By contrast, Lenin developed a more pragmatic atheism, which later became the core of the Soviet attempt to annihilate Orthodox Christianity once and for all. It should be pointed out that while for Marx the critique of religion was but one of many revolutionary acts, for Lenin and the Soviet Marxists this critique was the first and most profound step towards Communist self-determination. The work of building up the world-view of the new socialist man had to start, in Lenin's opinion, with the conscious rejection of any affiliation to religious faith. Leninism turns Marxist atheism into a catharsis for awakening revolutionary souls, into a precondition and a test for the sincerity of any affiliation to the Communist Party. Communists, as the avant-garde of the working class, had to be devoted, and a measure of their devotion was to be introduced by a commitment to atheism.

Another issue that should be emphasized is the gradual shift to the present-day Soviet stand on religion, where a new transformation of ideas has taken place. Since the old view maintained that with the abolition of exploitation religion would surely die, and since this did not actualy happen after the act of expropriation, even after six decades of re-education, Soviet atheism felt compelled to introduce a convincing explanation. Ideological authorities did not give up the major principles of historical materialism, but they had to admit that religion is a much more enduring form of social consciousness than they had previously suspected. Communism could not possibly take upon itself the blame for any social malaise that according to the old theory produced the consolations of faith in God. Official ideologists therefore had to relate the existence of the tenacious religious world-view to the conditions of the pre-revolutionary world. Being deeply embittered by the endurance of the phenomenon of faith, they made the tactical move of proclaiming religion as the cause and not merely the symptom of social problems. Thus present-day religious practices became the scapegoat of the Soviet ideological machine, they became the only readily admissible reason for the failure of the complete re-education of the masses. The course of events did not quite follow the patterns predicted by the founders of Communism.

In the analysis to follow, we will review historically the sequence of measures and policies that emerged from the concrete interpretations of the Marxist-Leninist legacy.

2 Antireligious Policies, 1917–41

IN SEARCH OF A STRATEGY

A Soviet historian–religiologist, G. V. Vorontsov, distinguishes three phases in the assault on religion in the USSR in the period prior to the Second World War.[1] We shall follow his divisions but with some chronological alterations.

Phase One: 1917–20

This was a period of 'Storm and Push', in the words of Emelian Yaroslavsky, one of its leaders. The most lasting landmark of that period was Lenin's Decree of 23 January 1918 depriving the Church of the status of legal person, of the right to own property, or to teach religion in both state and private schools or to any groups of minors.[2] The deprivation of the Church of all property, income-generating enterprises and bank accounts was pursued by the regime in its youthfully dogmatic faith in the Marxian doctrine of materialistic determinism, according to which the Church should have collapsed once she had lost her material base. Not accidentally, therefore, the Eighth Department of the People's Commissariat of Justice, headed by Piotr A. Krasikov, was officially known as 'The Liquidation Department'.[3] These three years were marked by a brutal campaign by government representatives to take over the possession of Church properties (including religious temples and monasteries), encountering stubborn resistance from the faithful. Much blood was shed during these years. On 19 January 1918 (Old Calendar, henceforth O.S. for Old Style) Patriarch Tikhon anathematised Soviet leaders for their desecration of churches and for their campaign of bloody terror. The regime retaliated by arrests and brutal murders of dozens of bishops, thousands of the lower clergy and monastics, and uncounted thousands of lay believers.[4] During these years the first professionally atheistic journal began publication under the name *Revolution and the Church (Revolutsiia i*

27

tserkov'). It was then that the priorities for relentless struggle against religion were firmly established in fundamental party documents, as will be seen below. Lenin apparently soon lost confidence in the inevitability of the disappearance of religion when it was deprived of its material base, for he told one of his chief lieutenants for religious affairs, V. D. Bonch-Bruevich, that the education of the new Soviet man cannot be a spontaneous process. 'Propaganda "in the ranks of broad masses of all sorts of cultural, scientific, antireligious ... knowledge and achievements" will be of overwhelming importance.'[5] Towards the end of this period it was decided to consolidate atheistic work centrally under the Agitation and Propaganda Department of the CP Central Committee (*Agit-prop* for short, established in 1920), using the guidelines of Article 13 of the Russian Communist Party Programme, as it was then called (RCP for short), adopted by the 8th Party Congress, which stated:

> As far as religion is concerned, the RCP will not be satisfied by the decreed separation of Church and State [alone]. . . . The Party aims at the complete destruction of links between the exploiting classes and ... religious propaganda, while assisting the actual liberation of the working masses from religious prejudices and organizing the broadest possible education-enlightening and anti-religious propaganda. At the same time it is necessary carefully to aviod any insult to the believers' feelings, which would only lead to the hardening of religious fanaticism.[6]

This clumsily worded Article led to debates within the party and its press, to subsequent party congresses' resolutions on the correct strategy for atheism, to the setting-up of special periodicals of militant atheism and organizations of the same type, and even served the needs of power struggle intrigues behind the scenes.[7] The differences between the multiple resolutions on atheism then and now are directly related to the importance given to the cautious proviso contained in the last sentence of the above article, whether it was stressed or deliberately ignored. This is equally true of the waverings of the party line *vis-à-vis* religion: whenever the above warning is ignored, active persecutions mount; they subside when for some internal reasons the warning is suddenly remembered and reappears in a party policy statement.

But before we go on, it is necessary to clarify a Soviet euphemism: not every Soviet document which aims at combating religion mentions the word 'atheism'; political or scientific 'enlightenment', dissemination of 'scientific knowledge', 'socialist internationalism', are other euphemisms for atheistic propaganda. Thus, adoption of the 1919 Party Programme was preceded by the establishment in November 1917 of the People's Commissariat of Enlightenment, which in turn set up a month later (December 1917) the All-Russian Union of Teachers-Internationalists in order to overcome the resistance of the All-Russian Teachers' Union to the forced removal of religious instruction from the school curricula. It was to intensify the atheistic propaganda that in addition to these measures a Chief Administration for Political Enlightenment (*Glavpolitprosvet*) was formed in November 1920 as a special department of the Commissariat of Enlightenment. Lenin's wife, Krupskaia, became the first head of that department.

Phase Two: 1921–28

Phase Two, in accordance with Vorontsov's periodization, lasts from 1921 to 1926. More appropriately it should be extended to the end of 1928, that is, up to and preceding the April 1929 legislation 'On Religious Associations'. A vivid illustration of the atmosphere prevailing in the atheistic circles of those days is the fact that such publications as *Bezbozhnik* counted their years from the year of the Bolshevik *coup d'état*, 'The Great October Revolution' of 1917. Thus, for instance, the first issue of the newspaper for 1925 came out with the dateline '4th January, 8th year', instead of 1925. And it contained a cartoon with a priest inviting a young pioneer to serve a New Year *Te Deum*, but the pioneer responds: 'Our New Year is on 7th November. We live after Il'ich [Lenin]'.[8]

The 10th Party Congress, meeting at the height of the Kronstadt and the Antonov Rebellions, when Petrograd and many other industrial centres were practically paralyzed by the industrial workers' unrest and strikes and when Trotsky himself thought that the Soviet regime was on the verge of collapse, in addition to its resolutions 'On Party Unity' and 'On the NEP' also issued a resolution 'On Glavpolitprosvet and the Agitation–Propaganda Problems of the Party'. The resolution called for 'widescale organization, leadership, and cooperation in the task of anti-religious agitation and propaganda among the broad masses of the workers, using the mass media, films, books, lectures, and other devices'.[9] Only five months after the Congress a plenary meeting of the Party Central Committee (August 1921) issued an 11-point instruction on the question of interpretation and application of Article 13 of the Party Programme.

It established a clear differentiation between the uneducated and the educated believer. Any person performing any clerical duties in any religious association may not be a party member; neither may an intellectual who does not fully and completely subscribe to Article 13 of the Programme or evades direct participation 'in the cultural-enlightenment work directed against religion'. As for the uneducated peasants and workers, 'religious believers may in individual cases, as an exception, be admitted into the party if by their revolutionary struggle or work for the revolution and its defence in its most dangerous moments, they have proved their devotion to Communism'. The necessity to make such a compromise contradicts Trotsky's (and, a century earlier, Belinsky's) assertion that the Russian people are predominantly atheists or non-believers.[10] Its implication is the very reverse: religious convictions are so universal in the nation that even a militantly atheistic ideology has to make exceptions if it wants to have a mass party.

This provision does not mean the laying-down of arms by the party, for the decree then prescribes 'special re-education work' for such members, which would eventually turn them into consistent atheists. Moreover, this is the beginning of the New Economic Policy of pragmatic reconstruction of the national economy and temporary ideological retreat. Therefore the instruction warns against rash actions in regard to atheistic propaganda, against giving too much publicity to 'anti-religious agitation', and it stresses 'serious scientific cultural-enlightenment work, building up a natural-scientific foundation for a proper historical analysis of the question of religion', rather than the noisy antireligious public debates, which should continue but with less publicity that before. In

short, the directive suggests a 'constructive–educational'
rather than a 'destructive–negative' approach. Its aim was to
build up an educational system and develop a materialistic
Weltanschauung in the citizenry at large in which there would be
no room for religion, rather than to ridicule and attack. The
Central Committee Agitation Department and *Glavpolitprosvet*
were instructed to study the published antireligious output and
to improve it accordingly. The line and quality of *Revolution and
the Church* was to be subjected to the same scrutiny.

In conclusion, the Instruction requests that in all antireligious lectures and publications it ought to be 'systematically
emphasized that the RCP is struggling against all forms of
religious *Weltanschauung* and not against individual religious
groups'. This statement was very much in the line of
Lunacharsky who saw religion as a much more complex
cultural phenomenon, rather than a mere tool and product of
class interests in accordance with the classical Marxist legacy
shared by such theorists as the early Trotsky and the Bolshevik
radical left. I. Skvortsov-Stepanov, a leading Soviet theorist of
atheism, representing what would later be labelled 'the rightist'
position of 'mechanicism', began with the same premise as the
left, but placed the emphasis on religion as an expression of
ignorance of the 'laws of nature'. He believed that the mass
dissemination of natural sciences combined with the
withering-away of class difference would result in the gradual
disappearance of religion on its own – mechanically, as it were.
Trotsky's position is more difficult to define. In 1923 he
thought that the Russian masses were only superficially
religious, but a year later he warned that the struggle against
religion would be a long and arduous battle and spoke of
religion as a very powerful cultural phenomenon to be attacked
on all fronts and by every means except the *forced* closure of
churches. He differed from Lunacharsky in stressing the
advance of applied science in peasants' and workers' lives as the
panecea against religion: electrification, cinema, mechaniza-
tion and collectivization of work processes, communal kitchens
and outside work for women – these, according to him, were
more effective tools against religion than propaganda and
direct attack. Although the Soviets constantly used the labels
'leftists' and 'rightists' in attacking each other, I feel very
uncomfortable with these confusing terms, especially since

their position, at least regarding religion and methods of fighting it, varied quite pragmatically–opportunistically, more in terms of practical consideration than in theoretical principles. Lunacharsky, however, seems to have been quite consistent in opposing different policies to different religions. This was probably a Bonch-Bruevich policy. Lunacharsky allowed the tactic of attacking the clergy for allegedly diverging from Christ's teachings, from the Scriptures, only if the propagandist immediately followed this with an attack on the original teachings themselves – 'unmask' the 'myths' of the Scriptures.[11]

That instruction, although wholly in the spirit of Lunacharsky's writings, was quite incompatible with the practical antireligious policies of the time, which were directed particularly against the Orthodox Church, under the pretext that it was a legacy of the tsarist past. On the other hand, the sectarians were pampered and the Moslems even had their own People's Commissariat for Moslem Affairs after 20 January (O.S.) 1918, administered by a mullah, Nur-Vakhitov, the only clergyman ever to occupy high Soviet state office.[12] Nine months after the publication of this doctrine the Soviets gave active support to a schism on the Orthodox Church by granting legal recognition to and promotion of the schismatic Renovationists, while terrorizing the Patriarchal Orthodox Church and depriving her of all legal means of existence.[13]

Dr Joan Delaney Grossman is probably right in her opinion that this contradiction between the instruction and the practical policies implies serious disagreements in the top party echelons and represents an aspect of Stalin's power struggle and rivalry with Trotsky,[14] especially if Trotsky was correct in his memoirs when he said that in 1922 Lenin had entrusted the leadership of Soviet church policies to him. As mentioned before, Trotsky believed that 'religiosity was almost totally absent in the Russian working class', while in the peasants it was only a matter of habit and the absence of other entertainment to replace the singing and theatrical beauty of the service. His vision of the Church was so primitive that he thought the cinema could effectively replace it for the masses. As for books and journals, they would affect only the reading minority of the nation.[15] Logically Trotsky's simplistic view tallied with Lenin's epithet for religion as 'a moonshine' or Marx's 'opium for the people'. This notion, however, allows religion to be written off as a subordinate class phenomenon which would pass away mechanically with the passing away of certain classes.

Trotsky shows a particular contempt for Orthodoxy, which he sees only as a series of rituals – an attitude shared by Hitler's ideological adviser Alfred Rosenberg some years later.[16] But Trotsky's hatred for Orthodoxy must have gone deeper than that, for it was he who wanted the Patriarch arrested and shot, while Lenin was opposed, fearing the danger of creating such a prominent martyr. It was Trotsky who in 1922 presided over the *manoeuvres* pitting the Renovationists against the Patriarch and the regular Orthodox Church, thus contradicting his own assertion of the unimportance of the Church for the Russian people; perhaps he overestimated the possibility of permanently destroying the Church by these actions precisely because he failed to imagine the scale of the resistance of the nation to the party's antireligious actions.[17]

Returning to the issue of in-fighting, the Grossman thesis finds further support in the fact that Yaroslavsky, the future founder and leader of the League of the Godless (Militant Godless after 1929), was appointed a member of the all-powerful Central Committee Secretariat at the 10th Party Congress, already *de facto* in the hands of Stalin whom a year later Lenin would name its General Secretary. The above 1921 instruction, inspired by the ideas of Lunacharsky, the most prominent atheistic public speaker and the Commissar of Public Enlightenment at the time, was probably physically issued by Yaroslavsky. Yet it is difficult to see Yaroslavsky or anyone else there as a moderate. On the contrary, Lunacharsky's vision of religion as a complex social and cultural phenomenon could and would be used by the opportunistic Yaroslavsky as a rationale for the wholesale destruction of the Church despite his sometimes moderate language.[18] The 'moderate' Trotsky wanted to execute the Patriarch and unleashed a mad persecution of the Church in 1922; the hawkish Yaroslavsky issued a moderate decree on religion in 1921. And what about Lenin? His statement, 'On the Significance of the Militant Materialism', which would later be proclaimed as his philosophical testament, was worded in such 'dialectical' terms as to allow as hawkish or as moderate an interpretation as the needs of the party required at the time. He recalled for a close co-operation of all militant materialists, whether members of the Communist Party or not, and a wide use of the writings of the eighteenth-century French materialists, in a common promotion of 'militant materialism' and 'militant atheism', treating the two terms as practically synonymous. In particular, he stressed the function of the official Marxist philosophical monthly, *Under the Banner of Marxism* (*Pod znamenem marxizma*), where the article had first appeared, as the organ of 'an association of sorts, of the materialist friends of Hegelian dialectics' disseminating 'untiring atheistic propaganda and struggle', which, very symptomatically, he called 'the cause of our state' (*nasha gosudarstvennaia rabota*).[19] This made a mockery of the assertions that the state and the party ought to be seen as separate entities with different attitudes towards religion. This phrase also betrays the primary importance which even the 'liberal' Lenin of the NEP era gives to the subject of combating religion. A much more emphatic corroboration of the policy can be found in Lenin's secret instruction on how to react to the believers' resistance to the confiscation of church valuables, in general, and to a bloody incident in the industrial town of Shuia, in particular:

> The incident in Shuia must be correlated to . . . resistance to the confiscation of church valuables . . . here our enemy is committing a great error trying to involve us in a decisive struggle precisely when it would be particularly hopeless and unprofitable for them. Contrarywise, for us this is not only exceptionally beneficial but the only moment when we are given 99 out of 100 chances to gain a full and crushing victory over our enemy and assure for ourselves the necessary positions for decades ahead. It is precisely now and only now, when there is cannibalism in the famine stricken areas and hundreds if not thousands of corpses are lying along the roads, that we can (and therefore must) carry out the confiscation of valuables with fanatical and merciless energy and not hesitate to suppress any form of resistance. It is precisely now and only now that the vast majority of the peasant mass will either support us or at least will be unable to give any decisive support to those . . . who might and would want to try to resist the Soviet decree.

We must confiscate in the shortest possible time as much as

possible to create for ourselves a fund of several hundred million roubles. . . . Without this fund the government work . . . and the defence of our positions in Genoa are absolutely unthinkable. . . . With success we can do this only now . . . for no other opportunity but the current terrible famine will give us such a mood of wide masses which would provide us with their sympathies or at least neutrality . . . during the operation of confiscating the valuables. . . .

. . . Now our victory over the reactionary clergy is guaranteed. Moreover the main part of our enemies among the Russian émigrés, i.e. the S-Rs and the Miliukovites, will find it very hard to carry on their struggle against us . . . precisely because of the famine. . . .

Therefore . . . it is precisely now that we must wage a merciless battle against the reactionary clergy and suppress its resistance with such cruelty that it may remember it for several decades. . . .

One of the most efficient members of VTsIK [All-Russian Executive Committee] should be sent to Shuia . . . with an oral instruction given him by a Politburo member. The instruction should be that he arrest in Shuia as many people as possible, and by no means less than several dozens of local priests, craftsmen and members of the bourgeoisie on suspicion of direct or indirect participation in active resistance to the VIsIK decree on confiscations. Immediately on his return he makes an oral report to the Politburo. On the basis of this the Politburo also gives an oral instruction to the judicial authorities that the trial of the Shuia rioters, resisting aid to the hungry, be conducted in as short a time as possible concluding in the maximum possible number of executions in the ranks of the most influential local reactionaries in Shuia. If possible similar executions should be carried out in Moscow and other spiritual centres of the country.

I think we should not touch Patriarch Tikhon, although he is at the head of this rebellion of the slaveowners. . . . At the [next] party congress a secret session should be organized jointly with leading members of the GPU, the Commissariat of Justice, and the Revolutionary Tribunal. A secret decision of the Congress should approve a mercilessly decisive confiscation of church valuables. The more members of the reactionary bourgeoisie we manage to shoot, the better. It is precisely now that we must give such a lesson to these characters that they would not dare to think of any resistance for at least the next few decades. . . . Lenin. (TOP SECRET. NO COPIES TO BE MADE).

This document, addressed to the members of Politburo, although mentioned in the fifth edition of Lenin's *Complete Works*, remains unpublished and has become available through *samizdat*, but the style and tone of it leave little doubt as to its authenticity. The Shuia conflict took place in March–April 1922, just at the time of the publication of Lenin's article above. A detachment of soldiers with machine guns was brought to suppress the faithful. In the skirmish four civilians were killed and ten wounded. The subsequent trial resulted in the execution of eight priests, two laymen and one lay woman, and the imprisonment of twenty-five believers.[20]

As the document shows, the real aim was to find an excuse to unleash wholesale terror against the Church and to misrepresent the Church's stand to the population in such a manner as to antagonize at least a sizeable part of it against the Church.[21] The final 'catch' of the Church treasures, confiscations of less than 400 kg of gold and some 400 000 kg of silver, even in *Izvestia's* words was 'ridiculously insignificant'. As to the precious stones and pearls used to decorate icons, much was stolen by the chekists, nicknamed at the time 'pearl divers'. No foreign buyers were found for them, since they were of very inferior quality – the 'good Christians' had for centuries been donating to the Church only that which was of little use to them! Moreover the prices for precious metals stood very low on the world markets at the time.[22] Yet the propaganda effect was achieved, and that is all Lenin was interested in, as his secret instructions show. Thus began the first full year of the New Economic Policy era, the most liberal period in the whole history of the Soviet communist state.

It can be safely stated that although there were differences in the individual Soviet leaders' approaches to the antireligious struggle, it was not a question of moderation versus extremism as a matter of principle, but a choice of methodology, strategy, and the tactics of how to liquidate religion most effectively and 'safely'. Vorontsov is probably right when he says that a unified consolidated policy of combating religion was formulated only after 1926 and systematically pursued in the decade following that year.[23] Despite a relative crystallization and cohesiveness of attack (by divide and rule) in 1922, certain differences in the approaches to the subject can be detached at least until 1929–30.

The 11th Party Congress (1922) resolved to 'turn the publishing house of the *Glavpolitprosvet*, *Krasnaia nov*' and the journal by the same name into a special party publishing enterprise for popular Marxist and antireligious literature.[24] Following Lenin's appeal for consolidation of the efforts of Communist and non-Communist atheists, a non-party publishing house, *Ateist* (The Atheist), specializing in translating works of 'bourgeois' atheists, was founded in 1922. Moreover, the 12th (1923) and 13th (1924) party congresses continued to promote 'moderation'. A resolution of the former merely calls for the expansion of antireligious propaganda and warns against insulting religious feelings by 'primitive methods'. . . . of ridiculing the objects and ceremonies of a faith; saying that these methods only 'strengthen religious fanaticism'. Instead, it calls for more publication of antireligious literature of a popular-scientific nature, and more analysis of the origins and history of religion.[25]

At the same time, in accord with this resolution, a number of specialized antireligious periodicals began to be published in 1922, which, however, in the crudeness of most of their materials seemed to contradict the calls for moderation. A *Nauka i religiia* (Science and Religion), edited by a former priest Mikhail Galkin (literary pseudonym: Gorev) made its appearance in December 1922 and was soon replaced by the weekly Bezbozhnik (The Godless), edited by Yaroslavsky. Yaroslavsky then formed a Society of Friends of the *Bezbozhnik* newspaper (SFBN/ODGB) which less than three years later was transformed into the Society of the Godless (SB, renamed SVB or LMG, the League of Militant Godless in 1929), and along with its publications was marked from the beginning by rude and crude attacks on religion. A more sophisticated 'Society of Militant Materialists', renamed in 1928, 'of Militant Dialectical-Materialists', was founded in 1924, consisting predominantly (and, after 1928, apparently exclusively) of the Marxist philosophers grouped around *Under the Banner of Marxism*, and aiming at combating religious and 'idealistic' views among scientists, scholars and intellectuals in general.[26]

Concerned with the growth of 'religious sentiments' among scholars (especially natural scientists), teachers and the intelligentsia in general,[27] the Soviet government not only launched the above periodicals in 1922, but also began to interfere directly in the life of the Church. The Renovationist *putsch* in May 1922 was synchronized with the GPU's arrest of the Patriarch and immediately followed by the Renovationists' seizure of the Patriarchal chancery under false pretences.[28] As Lenin's letter above documents, clergy and laity loyal to the Patriarch were subjected to terror under the pretext of their resistance to the confiscation of sacramental vessels, often made of precious metals and adorned by precious stones, although of dubious commercial value.

With the conclusion of the church-valuables confiscation campaign it was decided to call off the physical assault on the Church for a while. On 15 May 1923 the Antireligious Commission of the CPSU Central Committee ordered the GPU 'to investigate all cases of closure of churches. Should these have taken place with abuse of the Soviet legislation on the cults, the guilty ones ought to be made responsible for their acts.' The Commission addressed a letter to the Central Committee suggesting immediate discontinuation of the closure of churches, and the publication of an article in *Pravda* condemning such acts. The CC followed with an internal letter to all local party organizations on 23 June, calling for a halt to such abuses which 'cause all sorts of dissatisfaction, made use of by anti-Soviet elements'.[29] But it is not clear whether any of those instructions were ever made public and thus could reassure the believers. A certain moderation in the policies towards believers, however, was obvious. Since at this stage of the state's confrontation with religion the 1918 Constitution promising freedom for religious as well as antireligious propaganda was still officially valid, lip-service had still to be paid to some semblance of 'equality' of opportunity for both camps. Hence the famous public debates between believers and atheists continued to take place, although from late 1921 the regime began to take steps to curb them. It was only after the 1929 legislation banning religious propaganda that the debates could officially be suppressed.

Among the most famous Communist participants in these debates was Anatoli Lunacharsky, the first Soviet People's Commissar for Enlightenment (education and culture). On the Christian side among the most famous and prolific debaters were Alexander Vvedensky and V. F. Martsinkovsky, in addition to the famous mathematician and priest, Professor Pavel Florensky, and the bishop medical doctors, Anatoli of the Archdiocese of Odessa (who would later perish in the camps like Fr. Florensky) and Luka Voino-Yasenetsky, one of the founders of the University of Tashkent and its first professor of medicine (who would pay with eleven years in prisons and camps for remaining a bishop). There were many other outstanding debaters defending the Church. The debates used to draw huge crowds. People had to spend hour upon hour in queues to purchase tickets to university auditoria or concert halls where the debates took place. According to the descriptions by religious authors, the debates often began in an atmosphere of hostility towards the Christian apologists, because a large part of the audience invariably consisted of Bolshevik and Komsomol activists brought to the hall in an organized fashion, but most often ended in applause for the religious speakers (particularly of the calibre of those mentioned above) who showed deeper conviction and greater erudition than their party-line atheistic opponents.[30] These observations may have been partial and subjective, but the fate of Professor Martsinkovsky seems to corroborate them. An Orthodox lay preacher of evangelization and a member of the Russian Student-Christian Movement who later joined the Evangelicals over the issue of adult baptism, Martsinkovsky in the years 1919–21 was a lecturer of ethics at the recently founded Samara University, where he attracted capacity audiences by his lectures on the inseparability of ethics from the concept of God. During the same period he toured the country participating in debates on religion and atheism with leading Communists. He described how after one public debate with Lunacharsky, the latter, having lost the debate, cancelled his appearance in another planned debate with Martsinkovsky. On one occasion early in 1921 a large Komsomol team of hecklers arrived and occupied the two front rows

with the aim of disrupting Martsinkovsky's lecture. Surprisingly, when their leader tried several times to heckle, he was not
supported by his boys. Later they explained their behaviour by
claiming that Martsinkovsky was not saying what their instruc-
tor had told them he would. It was in 1921 – that is, soon after
the adoption by the 10th Party Congress of the resolution on
Glavpolitprosvet and the Agitation–Propaganda Problems –
that Martsinkovsky and other religious lecturers and debaters
began to experience difficulties. On some occasions the
Communist organizers of the debates tried to limit the time of
religious apologists to ten minutes, but the audiences protested
and the organizers were forced to withdraw the limitation. On
other occasions an agreement to rent a university auditorium
for a religious public lecture would be cancelled at the last
minute. In the same year, in the wake of the Kronstadt
Rebellion, Martsinkovsky was arrested and held in prison
without trial for half a year. At the end of 1922 he was arrested
once again, and told quite openly by his prosecutors:

> We know you are not a political enemy. . . . We know you as a
> sincere man dedicated to your ideas . . . of God. But your
> work is harmful to us. You attract the intelligentsia. . . . In
> about three years, when our workers have become wiser, you
> may return with your religious preaching [to Russia]. . . . But
> the main harm of your work is that you attract university
> students.

Martsinkovsky was expelled to Czechoslovakia. Apparently,
the workers have not grown 'wiser' to the present day, because
Martsinkovsky was never allowed to return to the Soviet
Union,[31] and public debates on religion with speakers representing the Church are still not allowed, more than sixty years
later. Such has been the fate of the earliest Christian–Marxist
dialogue in a country of 'triumphant socialism'.

The other attempt to implement this 10th Party Congress
Resolution was made in the form of various Komsomol, and
later LMG, activities: attacks, parades, theatrical performances, journals, brochures and films.[32]

The Komsomol engaged in crude blasphemous 'Komsomol
Christmases' and 'Komsomol Easters' with mock processions
headed by hooligans dressed as Orthodox priests, Protestant
pastors or Jewish rabbis. These carnival processions often

included the burning of icons, religious books and mock images of Christ, the Virgin, and so on. According to one Soviet author, these were not local Komsomol initiatives but they corresponded to relevant instructions of the CPSU Central Committee. As always with Soviet official campaigns, first reports from the provinces were enthusiastic about the success of these parades with allegedly thousands of participants. But soon the truth emerged that they were a failure, that people were not eager to join cells of atheist activists attached to the Komsomol; for example, in the city of Smolensk with a population of 173 000 only 35 people joined them. At the same time they rallied the believers around the Church. The Church, not deprived of the right to organize Christian youth groups until the legislation of 1929, responded by organizing religious study circles, as well as women's church societies, choral societies, religious retreats, and other religious activities. A 1924 Leningrad Orthodox clergy conference was largely devoted to these subjects. The cited official Soviet author admits, with a hindsight of almost forty years, that the whole enterprise was a failure.[33] This is a tacit admission that atheism had failed in its competition with religion on more or less comparable terms, hence the 1929 legislation banning 'religious propaganda', effectively depriving the Church of the means to counter atheistic attacks against her.[34]

Phase Three: 1929–40

The third phase in the pre-war antireligious offensive, which Vorontsov places under the heading 'The Communist Party as the Organizer of the Mass Atheistic Movement in the USSR' and into the period 1926–37, needs several correctives.

First of all, the factual accuracy of Vorontsov's title is questionable. The era begins with the 1929 Soviet laws on 'religious associations' which forbid all forms of public, social, communal (let alone educational, publishing or missionary) activities for religious believers. Second, the closing of churches, mass arrests of the clergy and religiously active laity, and persecution of people for attending church reach unprecedented proportions after 1929. Third, participation of schoolchildren and teenagers in the actively antireligious Pioneer and Komsomol organizations, and through them almost automatically in the League of Militant Godless, as well as the coercive pressure exerted by the trade unions and local party cells to induce industrial workers and employees to join the League, give a very peculiar ring to the terms 'organizer' and 'mass movement'.

On the intellectual Marxist level the four-year polemics between the mechanicists and the dialectical materialists led by *Under the Baner of Marxism*, the philosophical flagship of Soviet atheism launched with this purpose in 1922, concluded in 1929 with what the chief editors of the journal (Deborin and his associates) had thought was their victory over the mechanical materialists at the Second All-Union Conference of Marxist-Leninist Institutions. The gist of the argument was: whether human conscious life, man's intelligence and ideas were entirely derivatives of the material world and environment surrounding them, as the mechanicists argued; or whether there was 'a *relative* autonomy of the life processes in nature', which was asserted by the dialectical materialists. In fact, James Thrower, a contemporary British scholar, argues that the dialectical position stems from Engels, while Marx's ideology was a naturalistic materialism, but at least ever since Plekhanov the two classics became a collective person, 'Marx-Engels', and Soviet scholars have simply been denied the choice of being Marxists *or* Engelsians.[35] Now, what has this 'abstract' debate to do with atheism and religion? Very much, in fact. The mechanicists argued, or more often implied, that since human thought, emotions, and life depended on the material environment, there was no point in spending so much effort on antireligious struggle. As the building of socialism–Communism progressed, so religion would die away. Moreover, some of them went so far as to claim that since Marxism-Leninism was scientific and materialistic, it merged with the natural sciences, the latter superseding the former as *the* philosophy of Marxism, the latter having no independent philosophy; therefore, instead of atheistic propaganda people should simply be taught natural sciences, and religion would die away.

As Lenin had indicated in his programmatic–'philosophical' article on militant materialism in the March 1922 issue of *Under the Banner of Marxism*, he and his 'dialectical materialists' were simply pragmatics who had realized that religion was anything but dying out; hence more active means had to be used against it, and in order to justify them, room had to be made for the autonomy of the intellectual and emotional life of man within materialistic philosopy. This could be done only by resorting to the all-saving manoeuvres of dialectical thinking.

But the events that followed that 1929 conference, in which 'all the most significant research institutions of the proletarian dictatorship' had participated, soon showed that the triumph of Deborin and his 'dialectical materialists' was premature. Stalin thought otherwise. There were to be no supreme ideological–philosophical spokesmen in *his* Soviet Union but himself. And so, *Under the Banner of Marxism* was withheld from publication from October 1930 to February 1931, when at last a triple issue of the journal (no. 10–12) dated *October–December 1930* appeared with the text of the Soviet Communist Party's Central Committee Resolution in the journal, dated 25 January, *1931 (sic)*. The resolution condemned the mechanicists and also attacked the Deborin group for having become too philisophically abstract in argumentation, too detached from the needs and interests of 'politics ... *partiinost*' and natural sciences'. The editorial that followed the resolution attacked the journal for failing to become 'the organ of militant atheism' as directed by Lenin, having published only twelve articles in nine years directly related to antireligious struggle; even then most of them dealt with abstract philosophical issues pertaining to religion and atheism, rather than aiding the party in unmasking religion's 'vilest counterrevolutionary role'.[36] Hence, as far as the 'philosophical front' of Soviet atheism was concerned, the role of the Communist Party as 'organizer' was in fact to disorganize and discontinue all genuine philosophic discussion even within the extremely narrow confines to which it had been limited prior to 1930. Thus, as the details that follow will indicate, it would be more accurate to call the decade between 1928 and 1938 not only the decade of the institutional destruction of the Church, but also the decade of transformation of all Marxist institutions into bureaucratic branches totally subordinated to the orders and policies of the CPSU Central Committee (actually Stalin) and its daily needs.

Of course, on all other levels of the 'antireligious front' 'readjustments' closely reflected this policy.

An 11 February 1929 CPSU Central Committee Resolution

'On the Party Leadership of the Komsomol' calls on the Komsomol to raise the political–ideological level of its membership which often suffers 'from social ailments (alcoholism, moral license) and alien ideological influences (religious prejudices, anti-Semitism, nationalism)'.[37] A little over a year later, the 16th Party Congress mentions the struggle against religion twice: (i) in the resolution on the Central Committee political report it mentions the duty of the party to help 'the emancipation of the masses from the reactionary influence of religion'; and (ii) in its resolution on the trade unions where the latter are obligated to 'correctly organize and strengthen antireligious propaganda', again in combination with 'anti-semitism, chauvinism, narrow-minded nationalism'.[38] The chairman of the League of Militant Godless (LMG), Yaroslavsky, in his published comments emphatically alleged that religion was akin to anti-Semitism, and stressed that the document called religion the number-one prejudice. Nevertheless, the published antireligious attacks of the 1930s were not as conspicuous as in the preceding decade and did not at all reflect the unprecedented magnitude of the actual persecutions of the last pre-war decade.

The Church was treated as a private enterprise, and with the liquidation of the New Economic Policy and introduction of forced mass collectivization taxes were deliberately raised to such levels that hardly any private peasant or shopkeeper could pay them. The same levels of taxation were imposed on the churches and the clergy, as illustrated by the USSR Council of People's Commissars Decree of 21 May 1929, which stated that the criteria for qualifying someone for tax purposes as a *kulak* were:

> participation in trade, usury . . . or having any other income obtained not through labour (included in this category are members of the clergy).

In the rural areas the taxes were levied mostly in quantities of agricultural produce, but priests had had no fields to till since 1918, and, in addition to all other problems, with the liquidation of the wealthier peasants as *kulaks* they lost those parishioners who had had the means to help the church and the priest materially.[39]

As to verbal propaganda against the Church, which was the

most prominent manifestation of the atheistic policies aimed at the 'unarmed eye' of the naïve outsider, the party relegates this more and more to 'public organizations': first of all to local party branches, but also to such organizations as the Komsomol, the Young Pioneers, the League of the Militant Godless, Museums of Scientific Atheism, Workers' Evening Universities of Atheism under the auspices of the Trade Unions, and others. To be sure, special conferences on antireligious propaganda, under the auspices of the Central Committee Agitation–Propaganda Department, became almost an annual event (1926, 1928, 1929, etc.), but they were not widely publicized. Instead, they worked out directives to their participants, who then much more publicly implemented them on either a local party level or through one of the above institutions. More often than not they gave the impression that the resultant policies were of their own making rather than coming from the centre. This is the principle of Lenin's 'democratic centralism' in practice.

One of the major trouble spots for Soviet atheism was the school. The delegates to the first congress of Soviet schoolteachers (1925) refused to endorse the principle of separation of church and state and sought to retain the teaching of religion in school.[40] According to Lunacharsky, the majority of schoolteachers were still practising religious believers in the early 1920s; hence the final resolution of the Congress insists only on *non*-religious rather than *anti*-religious education in school, and the Commissariat of Enlightenment was forced to make this the official school programme.[41] During this time, and later with hindsight, Lunacharsky justified this policy as the only realistic one at the time, in view of the shortage of atheistic teachers and the danger that an actively atheistic school would cause a very hostile reaction on the part of the peasants (so much for Trotsky's thesis on religious near-indifference of the Russian peasant). The Orthodox Marxist historian and Lunacharsky's deputy at the Commissariat, Mikhail Pokrovsky, plainly said that antireligious education in the primary school was unnecessary. Lunarcharsky, however, called it merely 'premature' for the primary school, but as early as 1925 he actively supported antireligious education in the secondary school, mainly through classes on culture, in addition to setting up branches of the League of the Godless (LG) in schools. It was only in 1928 that he and his Commissariat, under the pressure of attacks from the LG and particularly its leftist-radical Moscow branch, came out in favour of an entirely antireligious school from the first grade up, and issued relevant directives in 1929. Yet, even then, Lunacharsky warned against a general expulsion of teachers with personal religious beliefs, for fear that this would deprive the Soviet school of 30 to 40 per cent of the educational cadres – this after particular efforts, especially after 1925, to replenish the school with atheistic Soviet teachers.[42]

A 1929 *Agitprop* conference likewise resolved to intensify antireligious work in all educational establishments on all levels. Let us keep the priorities straight here: whatever the precedence in dates, it is the *Agitprop* line that is crucial; the Commissariat of Enlightenment only reflects and fulfils the party line. This led to the setting-up of antireligious sections the following year at all research and higher education teaching institutions. A special antireligious faculty began to function at the Institute of Red Professors in 1929. In the same year a massive purge of the Russian Academy of Sciences occurred, during which most of its non-Marxist scholars and almost all of those who were practising members of the Church were arrested, most of them subsequently perishing in the camps and prisons.[43] One of the aims of the purge was to decapitate the Church intellectually in order to clear the way for the propaganda that only the backward and the obscurantists believed in God.

The toughening of the assault against religion reflected the general line of the time. Not only the specialized atheistic press, but also *Pravda* and *Komsomol'skaia pravda* began to publish a huge volume of truly threatening antireligious articles in 1928. In 1929 not a single week passed without several highly aggressive articles against religion in the latter paper; often whole pages of it were entirely devoted to the 'unmasking' of the Orthodox, the Moslems, the Sectarians or Judaism. The tone seems to have been set by the editorial in the central *Pravda* of 25 December 1928. It stressed that there could never be any peace between a Communist state and any form of religion, and it scolded party members, the Komsomol, and even the LG for their passive attitudes to religion; and, 'worse: there are still unexpelled party members . . . who fulfil religious rituals and in their activities support the clergy'. It stated that the majority of party members, instead of supporting and encouraging the League of the Godless, avoided antireligious activities, wrongly believing that religion would die on its own as a consequence of gradually changing economic and class relations.

What was new in this article was, first, that religion as the enemy was being mingled, probably for the first time, with internal party factions; and that co-operation of the Trotskyites with the sectarians was being alleged. Second, no distinction between the Orthodox Church, the sectarians, and the Moslems as enemies of the socialist society was being made. On the contrary, it was stressed that the sectarians 'had particularly advanced since the revolution in fooling the backward working masses and peasants . . . making use of the freedom of religious preaching granted to them by the revolution'.[44] The editorial requested the banning of the open sale of Christmas trees as well as traditional feast foods in state stores during religious holiday seasons. Finally, the school on all levels was urged to become an active fighter against religion.

Although the article warned against the extremes of 'revolutionary anarchism' in attacking religion, and called for the dissemination of antireligious literature and education along with antireligious films and plays, it nevertheless discussed and defined religion only as a class enemy. Thus it was contradicting its own attack on the 'mechanicists' who made the withering-away of religion dependent on changes in class relations, which a year later was criticized as an oversimplification and 'a leftist-anarchist deviation'. This shows that the line of attack was not yet entirely crystallized, even in late 1928. The article reflected to some extent a left-radical trend of the Moscow branch of the LG, whose members often published their articles in *Kom. pravda* and were engaged in a war of words with Yaroslavsky throughout 1928 and 1929.[45]

Playing down the barbarity of these attacks, Vorontsov mentions only in passing an unpublished circular letter of the CPSU Central Committee of 1929 which 'pointed out that the mass character of the decisions to close churches was closely connected to the strengthening of the atheistic movement among the toilers', commenting that it was therefore 'not a coincidence that the movement to close the churches had reached its peak in 1928–29'. He then cites the figures of 532 religious establishments of all denominations closed in 1928 and 423 in 1929, which, of course, is a pittance in comparison with what happened during the following decade. The year 1928–9 was far from the peak. What is important here, is that he discloses the fact that most of the religious persecutions were carried out on the strength of *secret* internal memoranda emanating from the Central Committee, while *openly* the same Central Committee issued resolutions like the one 'On the Struggle Against Distortions of the Party Line in the Collective Farm Movement' (1930), which demanded 'categorically *to put an end* to the practice of shutting churches administratively'.[46] This, in fact, was a follow-up to Stalin's March 1930 *Pravda* article 'Dizziness From Success' which had called for moderation in the drive for the collectivization of agriculture.

It is interesting that Soviet 'religiologists' excuse the half-admitted assault on the Church in the 1930s and even the ban on religious propaganda in the legislation of 1929 which had been made on the grounds of alleged anti-Soviet attacks by church leaders, both inside and outside the Soviet Union. They cite such instances as: counter-revolutionary Orthodox sects ('Fedorovites' and 'Name-glorifiers') who allegedly hid in their midst leaders of former anti-Soviet peasant rebellions who appealed to the population to boycott the Soviet regime and its decrees. Trials of their leaders and members took place in Voronezh, North Caucasus and other places in 1929 and 1930. Another example most often cited by Soviet authors is the Ukrainian Autocephalous Orthodox Church (UAPTs), which they deliberately associated with the Orthodox Church as a whole, concealing the fact that the former was born in 1921 with the blessing and support of the Soviet Government as a rebellion against the regular Patriarchal Orthodox Church.

The official excuses for the attack on the Church usually cited by Soviet sources were many. They included the establishment in Rome of the Jesuit centre *Russicum* for the study of Orthodoxy with the aim of preparing clerical cadres for a future Roman Catholic mission in Russia, the Vatican's 1930 ecumenical prayers for the persecuted Christians of the Soviet Union and its appeal for a Christian 'Crusade' against the Bolsheviks, and, in addition, the activities of a Russian émigré 'Fraternity of Russian Truth' which appealed for subversive acts inside the Soviet Union in the name of God, and the financial support of the Russian Evangelical sects by the US Evangelical Churches who planned building 'a multi-storey Gospel House' in Leningrad. So vulnerable was 'the mighty Soviet State' which claimed consolidation of the whole people with the government, that these activities, which were but a fraction of the Communist subversive activities in the non-Communist world, were seen to be such a serious threat to its security that the government decided to deprive the main-stream Churches of an autonomous public voice forever. But the legislation depriving the Church of all rights except liturgical services within church walls preceded the above events, and was not their consequence. The legislation occur-red in two stages. The laws on 'Religious Associations' were published in April 1929, the relevant amendment was added to the 1924 Soviet Constitution on 18 May 1929 at the 16th Congress of Soviets; while the anti-Soviet appeals of the Pope and the Russian émigrés belong to the following year. They were a reaction to the above legislation, not vice versa. Secondly, Vorontsov himself stated that the Orthodox Church had moved to the position of unquestionable civic loyalty to the state after her locum tenens Metropolitan Sergii's 1927 Declaration of Loyalty. There was no reason why a loyal Church should be punished for the activities of the Vatican, sectarians, émigrés, or Ukrainian separatists, nor any reason for these discriminatory laws remaining in force to the present day, since the mainstream religions (the Orthodox, Moslems, Baptists, Lutherans, and the Roman Catholics of Lithuania, to name but a few) had proved their full loyalty and civic obedience to the State by participating in and even launching mass international peace campaigns and rallies on behalf of Soviet foreign policy objectives.[47]

But let us return to the late 1920s and the rising central role of the League of the Godless.

THE LEAGUE OF THE MILITANT GODLESS

'Struggle against religion is the struggle for socialism' was the official slogan of the Second Congress of The League of the Militant Godless (LMG). Ironically, this also proved to be its last All-Union congress. As *Pravda* indicated, it was to this 'public organization' that the Communist Party relegated the leadership role in the antireligious struggle, 'achieving direct control over the League via the CP faction of the League's Central Council, as well as through the CP cells in the League's local councils'.[48]

The journal *Bezbozhnik* (The Godless), edited by Yaroslavsky, appeared in December 1922. The following year a Moscow monthly for industrial workers *Bezbozhnik u stanka* (*The Godless at the Work-Bench*, henceforth *Bezbust*), an even cruder publication than the former, with insulting cartoons on God and the saints, formed the Moscow Society of the Godless. Two years later the *Bezbozhnik*'s ODGB (or SFGN: Society of Friends of the *Godless* Newspaper) merged with the former group to form the All-Union League of the Godless at its First Congress in 1925. Henceforth, at least until the 1929 Second Congress, there raged a power struggle between Yaroslavsky and his boys and the Moscow League of the Godless leadership (Galaktionov, Polidorov, Kostelovskaia, Lunin, and others). The latter were fighting a losing battle against Stalin's aide in the CC Secretariat, his obedient sycophant Yaroslavsky, one of the founding editors of *Kommunist*, which in the 1930s became the official ideological organ of the Communist Party Central Committee. The Moscow organization tried to retain its autonomy from the All-Union organization by betting on the old horse of left-wing 'anarchist' radicalism. It gained the support of the communist youth daily, *Kom. pravda* (which regularly published the militant articles of Galaktionov and his friends).

In addition, they were supported in the early period by the Moscow CP organization, in whose organ, *Sputnik kommunista*, a *Bezbust* spokesman, Polidorov, attacked Lunacharsky, Bonch-Bruevich and Yaroslavsky for preaching anticlericalism and a partisan attitude to different religions, instead of genuine godlessness. It is interesting that in his response Yaroslavsky first of all protests against being placed in the same category with the other two ideologists, stressing that he does not share any of Lunacharsky's concepts of antireligious struggle nor has anything in common with B.-B.'s sympathy towards the sectarians. This assurance did not prevent a close alliance of Yaroslavsky with Lunacharsky in years to come, between 1925 and 1930, and after 1930 it became safer for the opportunistic

Yaroslavsky to avoid and later even to criticize his former mentor.

Returning to 1924, Yaroslavsky's main points against Polidorov were that first the question is not anticlericalism *or* godlessness, but both. Second, all religions are ideological enemies of socialism, even the Renovationists who claim to be socialists; but arrests, imprisonment, and physical compulsory destruction is possible only of those Churches which oppose and actively resist the Soviet State, like the pre-1923 Orthodox Church. The methods of struggle must be different when a Church declares and practices civic loyalty, because it includes in its flock dozens of millions of perfectly loyal workers and peasants, who should be re-educated by the atheists but not attacked as outright 'class enemies'. Thus, in contrast to Polidorov and the *Bezbust* editors Kostelovskaia and Galaktionov, Yaroslavsky, Anton Loginov (both members of the CPSU CC apparat), Lukachevsky and their associates from *Bezbozhnik* argued that seeing religion only in terms of a class phenomenon and only as a class enemy represented a partial and oversimplified vision. Religion is also 'a certain system of *Weltanschauung*, ethics, emotions and behaviour.... You forget the believer if you approach religion only as a tool of class exploitation.' Antireligious propaganda will be ineffective if the propagandist is not aware of the personality, emotions, ideas, and thoughts of his listener. Although the CPSU Central Committee was obviously on the side of the Yaroslavsky–Loginov school, the debate was not resolved at the first Congress in 1925. Although the 1926 All-Union Conference on antireligious propaganda called by the CC *Agitprop* threw its weight in Yaroslavsky's favour, the debate still continued.[49]

Even, as we have seen, the central *Pravda* as late as December 1928 reduced the whole problem of religion to the issue of a mortal class enemy of the proletariat and socialism. In the following year Stalin gained full control over the 'left' and 'right' deviations, making way for vicious attacks on both. Yaroslavsky followed suit on the religious front (the term 'front' was symptomatic), by attacking the class-centred stand as a 'left-anarchist' deviation. He also attacked 'mechanicists' and 'right-deviationists'. Skvortsov-Stepanov and others were arguing that religion should be countered by mass compulsory education in the natural sciences, contending that then it would die of its own accord. Quite consistently, Yaroslavsky and his ilk saw a logical link between the class-attack position of the left and the do-nothing position of the 'mechanicists'. If the whole religious phenomenon could be explained away in terms of a class phenomenon, then there would be no need to combat it if one genuinely believed that a classless society was being constructed. Attacking Skvortsov in 1930 at the conference of the All-Union Society of Militant Dialectical Materialists, Yaroslavsky stressed that an active all-sided assault on religion was inseparable from the building of socialism. One of the slogans of the second LMG congress became: 'Struggle against religion is a struggle for the Five Year Plan!' And the LMG press from then on published masses of reports of LMG's participation in the Plan fulfilment, subscribing and recruiting subscriptions for the state loan. At the same time, emulating the Party, LMG conducted a purge in 1932–4, of the 'rightist' elements in its ranks criticizing Bukharin in its press.[50] Stalin's words at the 16th Party Congress (1930) that religion was 'a brake on the building of socialism', were immediately picked up by the LMG and reiterated many times in its speeches and writings. One of them, Lukachevsky, even criticized the above *Pravda* article for *de facto* minimizing the threat of religion by reducing it to the status of a class enemy. He ridiculed the early Marxist belief (shared to some extent, as we have seen, by Trotsky, very much in vogue in the early *Bezbozhnik* and throughout the lifespan of the *Bezbust*) that the appearance of a tractor would kill religion. In contrast, Lukachevsky pointed to the popularity of religion among the émigré and nationalistic intellectuals, and said that although its roots were socio-economic this was not the only source of religion, and could not alone explain the current growth of the sectarians, for instance.[51]

The vision of religion as a complex social and cultural phenomenon, as we have seen, appeared to be establishing a kinship between the ideas and policy of the LMG, especially after 1929, and Lunacharsky, who made several far-reaching statements, when he said for example that 'Freedom . . . may be cut . . . when it is abused for the direct class struggle against the proletarian dictatorship.'[52] He said this while speaking on religious freedom and its limitations, which could and would be used as a green light for the total onslaught against religion from 1929 on. Even as late as 1929 Lunacharsky was still warning against the use of direct force and persecutions, not on principle but only in as much as it was strategically unwise and counterproductive. He argued that, on the contrary, 'church is an infection' and its physical suppression is acceptable but only when the majority of the population is on your side or when the clergy can be accused of breaking the law. What subsequently happened in the following decade was the worst possible combination of Lunacharsky's theories with the 'leftist practices' (which he personally attacked at the second LMG Congress, when he accused Lunin of the *Bezbust* of proposing a *general* physical persecution). The result of this sort of law issued in 1929 was that any pursuit of the true pastoral duties by a clergyman became punishable by law.[53] Lunacharsky's words perfectly rationalized such persecutions. Is it possible that this 'abuse' of Lunacharsky's line played a role in his retirement from his post as commissar later in the year?

In the typical Leninist–Stalinist tradition Trotskyite and generally 'leftist-deviationist' roots in the subsequent antireligious holocaust were not acknowledged. Neither had Lenin acknowledged his debt to the Socialist-Revolutionary agrarian programme, nor did Stalin acknowledge the Trotsky–Preobrazhensky source of his programme of forced collectivization.

Although the scene for the 'final' and complete assault on religion was set at the second LMG congress (June 1929), and although the victory of Yaroslavsky's line there was a foregone conclusion, the Moscow opposition gave a few rearguard battles during that year. One of the most colourful was I. Bobryshev's attack on Yaroslavsky in the latter's own *Antireligioznik*. He accused the LMG of minimizing the class-enemy thesis in attacking religion, of having scarcely any workers and peasants in its ranks, of engaging in antireligious archaeology instead of aggressively combating religion, of having been indifferent to the issue of transforming the school into a militantly antireligious institution, and of opportunistically using the writings of non-Marxist Western bourgeois atheistic authors in its publications. Yaroslavsky refuted all these accusations, stating that the LMG began a concerted struggle for the *anti*religious school as early as 1927, but that in contrast to the leftists who simply wanted physically to destroy religion and churches, the Yaroslavsky policy was to replace the religious *Weltanschauung* with that of dialectical materialism. This, he said, was Lenin's purpose in addition to his position that the works of the French encyclopaedists and any bourgeois atheists should also be used for the dissemination of atheism in the USSR. He admitted, however, that the effect of the LMG work was much more modest than they wished, because the League had remained decentralized until the second Congress (a hint at the 'heterodox' behaviour of the Moscow organization), and therefore it could not consolidate its actions and policies. Also, it was the poorest of all Soviet 'public' organizations, almost without any full-time branch activists. Furthermore, neither the CP nor the Komsomol local branches supported LMG activities, and in the Ukraine they were banned 'for tactical reasons', according to the Ukrainian Government. All this apparently changed at the Second Congress. Its resolutions taking up seventy-seven tightly printed pages leave no doubt that the CPSU Central Committee delegated to it full powers to unfurl a sweeping attack on religion with the aim of its near-total destruction and with the right to mobilize all 'public organizations' of the country. Otherwise it would not have dared to dictate to schools, universities, the armed forces, the trade unions, the Komsomol, the Organization of Young Pioneers, and the Soviet press in general, as it did in its resolutions addressed to each of these institutions. It criticized each of them separately for poor organization of antireligious activity in their particular fields, and arrogantly instructed them how to become more effective.

It even gave commands to the Party regarding the antireligious front. Paraphrasing the Congress decisions, Yaroslavsky writes:

> The Komsomol must obligate all its members to join the League . . . the Party must direct its party organizations and all its members to further the very work of the LMG as well as directly participate . . . in the LMG. . . . We must turn . . . to a systematic recruitment of toilers . . . there ought not remain a single Pioneer troop without a junior LMG branch.[54]

What was in store for religious groups in the context of the mounting terror and the 'enemy within' mania of the time was clear already from the following descriptions of religions and Churches:

> All religions, no matter how much they 'renovate' and cleanse themselves, are systems of ideas ... profoundly hostile to the ideology of ... socialism. ... Religious organi-zations ... are in reality political agencies ... of class groupings hostile to the proletariat inside the country and of the international bourgeoisie. ...

> Special attention must be paid to the renovationist currents in Orthodoxy, Islam, Lamaism and other religions. ... These currents are but the disguises for a more effective struggle against the Soviet power. By comparing ancient Buddhism, and ancient Christianity to communism, the Renovationists are essentially trying to replace the commun-ist theory by a cleansed form of religion, which therefore only becomes more dangerous.

It is important to look at the historical background of this resolution. This was the period when the Soviet Government changed its policy towards the Renovationist schismatics in the Orthodox Church. Whereas in 1922–3 they were actively fomenting the schism, in 1924–7 they were actively pressing both sides for reconciliation in the belief that they would get agents and informers from the Renovationist leaders *within* a reunited Church. They still continued to recognize only the Renovationists as the legitimate Orthodox Church. From the end of 1927 they recognized both groups; and there appeared signs that the Soviets feared that the more modern, 'progres-sive' and socialist Renovationists, shaved and wearing secular dress, were a dangerous challenge to the regime. And from 1934 the persecution of the Renovationists began to reach the proportions of the persecution of the traditional Orthodox Church.[55]

As for the second Congress resolutions, they admitted that there was 'some growth of sectarian groups', but claimed that this represented local rather than national tendencies. The resolution warned, nevertheless, that lay religious activists exceeded one million (over 50 000 communities of all faiths with at least twenty lay activists in each) and that lately all of them ('even the Orthodox') had begun to adopt modern,

'American', methods of mass work and were attracting youth via special services, study circles, choral societies and the like. Therefore, opposition to religion must be pressed; and it approved the change from non-religious to anti-religious education in the school system.[56] This, together with 'the constitutional change on the rights of religious organizations represents one of the greatest victories of the atheistic movement'. The resolutions, then, despite their militancy, warn against antireligious 'ultra-left anarchistic phrase-mongering'.

The general resolution 'On the Immediate Aims of Anti-Religious Struggle' and the resolution 'On Schools and Work With the Children' demanded that no school or work days-off be allowed on religious feast days and that days of rest should not coincide with Church feasts.[57] The same year saw the official replacement of the seven-day week by a six-day one – five days of work, the sixth off. The antireligious propaganda believed this would be a most effective means of preventing believers from attending the Sunday liturgy. In addition, the 25th and 26th of December were proclaimed the Days of Industrialization with obligatory presence at work. Yet, high work absenteeism on religious feast days is reported as late as 1937.[58]

The resolutions further proclaimed that local LMG branches should aim to effect total public ostracism of the clergy. They ordered that priests should not be invited to private homes. Soviet citizens should discontinue all donations to the churches and pressure should be brought to bear 'on the trade unions to refuse to perform any work for the churches (for example, printing of religious literature, building of religious temples, and so on)'. This LMG resolution preceded the relevant Party decisions by one year. This was unquestionably devised in order to boost the prestige of the LMG as the leader in atheistic affairs and in order that the 16th Party Congress (1930) resolution on the trade unions should appear as a response to the will of the toiling masses. It called upon the unions:

> to pay particular attention to socialist education . . . to the systematic struggle against petty-bourgeois prejudices . . . to organize correctly and boost anti-religious propaganda, struggle against anti-Semitism, narrow nationalism.[59]

The Young Pioneer organizations were urged to participate actively in antireligious struggle. 'Groups of the young Godless must be formed at schools.' Children must be prevented by Soviet authorities from serving as acolytes and from being drawn into groups for home religious instruction.

In May 1930 the First All-Union conference of the godless young pioneers took place in Moscow. As a consequence of the CP Central Committee resolution calling off 'administrative measures' against religion, during 1930–31 antireligious work at the school in a number of places was weakened. But 1931 saw the 5 September 1931 CPSU CC resolution calling for a full-scale 'communist upbringing in the Soviet school', which was immediately interpreted as active antireligious 'education'. By the end of 1931 the LMG boasted that out of the total of 20 000 000 school-children 2 000 000 were LMG members,[60] a rather modest proportion, hardly substantiating the claim that the majority of school-children were atheists.

Meanwhile, the main LMG congress of 1929 had gone further and took the armed forces to task for ignoring the antireligious instruction of soldiers. One of its longest resolutions (consisting of fourteen pages), 'On the Work in the Red Army', details a programme of a most active and intensive antireligious re-education of draftees and other military personnel. Three years later the LMG was boasting of its successes in the armed forces, where its cells began to be set up on a systematic basis in each unit after 1927. However, the only figure the author cites belongs to 1925 when a survey of one army unit produced the following data: 28 per cent of the recruits remained religious believers at the end of their service term, 32 per cent had lost faith as the result of antireligious education in the army; that is, 60 per cent of the recruits had been believers at the time of their recruitment. The author claims that thanks to the atheistic re-education work in the armed forces 10 000 demobilized soldiers went back to the villages as propagandists of collectivization and industrialization and as atheistic village culture-club organizers (that is 10 per cent of the 100 000 such propagandists sent in that year to the villages).[61] Quite a different picture was presented some nine years earlier by a communist publicist and sociologist, Ya. Yakovlev, whose book, *The Village as It Is*, was highly acclaimed at the time in the Soviet press and widely quoted. He describes how ex-Red Army soldiers who had joined the Communist

Party while in the army, were now concealing their past party membership from their neighbours as well as from the author, only on occasion admitting that the idea was being abused by the Soviet reality.[62] It is not certain whether this contrast is evidence of improvement or of changed police and censorship regulations, but judging by the opportunistic zig-zags in the LMG propaganda lines, the latter is more likely. For instance, in the 1920s the propaganda against the Church was that she had supported the 'Imperialistic War' of 1914, preached unqualified patriotism denying the importance of class differences, and thus was the enemy of the working class. It was likewise asserted that the sectarians had supported the Tsarist war efforts and had served in the army, but under the Soviets declared themselves pacifists, refusing to bear arms not out of religious principles but out of hostility to socialism. In contrast, by 1938–9 the line of the antireligious attack was that a Christian could not be a reliable soldier because Christianity is fundamentally anti-war, preaches love of one's enemy and turns the other cheek, instead of resisting the enemy.[63] So much for the principles; but let us return to the second Congress once again.

The general resolution ends with an instruction to the trade unions, the Komsomol, the departments of education and consumer co-operatives to treat 'anti-religious propaganda as an inseparable part of their work and to provide regular funding for it'.

A separate resolution 'On the Sectarian Movement' rejected the earlier preferential treatment for the sects and declared unrelentless war against them on the same terms as any other religion, stressing, however:

> the necessity to distinguish the mass of rank-and-file sectarians from the top strata who are fully conscientious class enemies of the Soviet power, and counterrevolutionaries.

There is a characteristic statement at the end of the resolution that 'religious temples should be shut only with the agreement of the majority of the working population'. There is no qualification that this majority must consist of or at least contain religious believers, let alone members of the given religious confession. Henceforth, many churches and temples of all religions were closed by means of organizing a meeting at a local club or factory where an open vote was taken under pressure. Genuine believers who were willing to risk their social and employment status by defending the church often found themselves in the minority. A characteristic case in point was a huge plant in a suburb of Moscow, the Trekhgornaia Factory, where of its 8000 workers, 3000 fought for the retention and reopening of the factory settlement church. The reports on the case were at variance with each other: some publications emphasized the 'revolting' situation of 3000 workers being still in the nets of the obscurantist clergy while others boasted that 5000 were in favour of transforming the church into a factory club (without elaborating whether this was a case of a genuine vote or just a mathematical subtraction of 3000 active believers from the total, and the subsequent assumption that all the others wanted the church closed).[64] Even in cases where the vote for the closure of a church did take place, part of the reason may have been the result of antagonism between the sectarians and the Orthodox. At least one Soviet author wrote that in some cases the sectarians voted with the atheists to close an Orthodox church.[65] The reverse could also occur, particularly as long as there was preferential treatment of the sectarians by the Soviets; hence the Orthodox often saw them as 'pink'.

The resolution 'On Youth' expressed concern with the passive attitude of the Komsomol to the campaign against religion. It stated that in some areas Komsomol branches had fallen apart under the impact of the activities of the Orthodox Church and the sectarians or:

> become a tool of anti-Soviet policies at the hands of local religious organizations ... members of the Komsomol participate in religious feasts. The percentage of young people expelled from the Komsomol for religious convictions has increased in some areas (the Urals, Vladimir).

> Most Komsomol organizations ignore anti-religious work ... only 2½ per cent of the Komsomol membership have joined the SVB.

and conversely: 'the majority of SVB organizations ignore work with the youth'.[66] This is a very strange admission. Does it mean that as early as 1929 Soviet atheistic activism was already mostly represented by the older generation?

The resolution 'On the Press' took the general Soviet publications to task for paying too little attention to active atheism. It declared that it was their duty to join the front of active attack on religion, because 'struggle against religion is a political struggle'.

In the resolutions on education the Congress urged the most active antireligious education of children from the very first grades and the establishment of antireligious departments in all institutions of higher learning.[67]

Two years later a leading antireligious propagandist and theorist, N. Amosov, added that antireligious education at grade schools was not enough: 'All LMG councils must fully participate in the development of anti-religious work among pre-school children.'[68]

As we have already seen, the Second LMG Congress was obviously allowed to mobilize all public organizations for the struggle against religion, with special emphasis on the Komsomol. Indeed, the Komsomol Programme adopted at its 10th Congress in 1936 stipulated the following:

> The Komsomol patiently explains to the youth the harmfulness of superstitions and of religious prejudices, organizing for this purpose special study circles and lectures on antireligious propaganda.

The Statute adopted at the same Congress stipulated that it was the duty of every Komsomol member 'to struggle against the remnants of religious prejudices'.[69] The remarkable growth of the LMG between 1929 and 1932 was evidently mostly due to the imposition of LMG membership on the Komsomol. However, its subsequent decline and its admission that 'only 45 percent of the LMG membership dues were paid during the first quarter [of 1933] and even less in the next quarter' and that in a city boasting several thousand members only seven persons turned out to be genuinely interested in the work of combating religion[70] – all this indicates that the new recruits to the mass membership of the Komsomol were a rather unreliable and unenthusiastic lot, although the formal statistical growth figures are remarkable indeed. The All-Union League of the Godless grew from 87 000 members in 1926 to half a million in 1929. Although it officially aimed at 17 000 000 members in 1931, it seems to have peaked in 1932 with 5 670 000 members (at least on paper). Thereafter the membership began to decline to under two million in 1938, rising somewhat again to about 3.5 million in 1941, its last year of prominence. The League put out masses of publications in most languages of the USSR. During the peak year, 1941, it published ten atheist newspapers and twenty-three journals. Here are some of the circulation figures for its periodicals. The weekly *Bezbozhnik* newspaper reached 500 000 copies per issue in 1931. The circulation of the illustrated monthly journal by the same name (except for 1928–32, when it appeared fortnightly) and also edited by Yaroslavsky, published since 1925, grew from 35 000 in 1928 to 200 000 in 1931. After 1932 the circulation dropped to 150 000. By 1938 the circulation of the monthly grew to 230 000, declining to 155 000 again in the following year. Meanwhile, *Bezbozhnik u stanka* grew from a monthly with 70 000 copies per issue in 1924 to a fortnightly journal in 1929, but its circulation continued to waver between 50 000 and 70 000 until its final closure in 1932. Yaroslavsky's 'scholarly-methodological' monthly of the LMG Central Council *Antireligioznik* (The Antireligious) appeared in 1926. By 1929 each issue contained about 130 pages and had a circulation of approximately 17 000, climbing to 30 000 in the following year, but declining to 27 000 in 1931. In those years efforts were obviously being made to publish some theoretical and scholarly material in it. But by the late 1930s its contents became hopelessly dreary, primitive and repetitious. Its size was reduced to sixty-four pages by 1940, but many issues appeared as double issues for two months at a time and consisted of eighty pages. The circulation varied between 40 000 and 45 000 in the last two years of its existence, and it folded up in 1941.[71] An *Antireligious Textbook for Peasants* was issued in six editions between 1927 and 1931, with a circulation of 18 000 for the first edition and 200 000 for the sixth. A similar textbook for the urban reader appeared in 1931, followed by a universal-amalgamated textbook. One of the most aggressive pioneers of LMG, I. A. Shpitsberg, began publishing a journal of 'atheistic scholarship' in the late 1920s called *Ateist*. Its editor in 1931 became P. Krasikov who changed the name to *Voinstvuiushchii ateizm* (Militant Atheism), a strange name for a scholarly journal, and its publisher was the LMG Central Council. Its 'scholarship' obviously did not fare very well, for the following year it was swallowed up by *Antireligioznik*. From 1928 to 1932 a journal for peasants *Derevenskii bezbozhnik* (The Rural Godless) was published. There is a glaring contradiction between the claim that peasants loved it so much 'that each issue would be literally read to tatters' and the fact that it ceased publication by the end of 1932. More probably the religious persecutions and the forced collectivization, together with the artificially induced famine designed to break the peasants' resistance (1932–3), antagonized them so much that the regime thought it wiser to discontinue this 'popular' publication. Vorontsov also mentions cases of lynchings of atheist propagandists in the villages, and speakers at the second plenum of the LMG Central Council (1930) openly admitted cases of the murder of antireligious agitators by the population.[72]

To sum up the post-1929 publications of the LMG, the non-serial antireligious literature alone grew from a total of 12 million printed pages in 1927 to 800 million in 1930. In 1941 sixty-seven books and brochures of antireligious propaganda were printed with a total circulation of 3.5 million copies.[73] There is no information available on the numbers of these publications actually bought by the public.

From 1926 to 1937 the League 'trained a whole army of antireligious propagandists and organizers of anti-religious work among the masses'. Their work differed from the 1921–5 period, according to Vorontsov, in the following respects:

> First, their work became more systematic and of a mass character. Secondly . . . more varied means of ideological influence were used . . . e.g. the cinema and the network of anti-religious museums. Instead of anti-religious carnivals at Easter and Christmas, special campaigns of lecture cycles were practised.
>
> [Thirdly] . . . no debates between the atheists and believers were practised any more, as a rule, after 1929. Instead, there were mass meetings at which former clergymen who had broken with religion, gave talks.[74]

Why were public debates discontinued? To answer this question we have already cited the case of Martsinkovsky, which disproved the official Soviet claims, that the religious apologists were invariably beaten at such debates. Soviet practice is generally to suppress that which does not serve their cause – for example, crime statistics or, much more recently, child mortality rates since 1974 when they began to rise.[75] An excellent admission of this policy is contained in a 1930 publication by one of the top three LMG leaders. It advised that social surveys of believers in school classes where the majority of pupils 'are religious believers, is harmful',[76] and that questionnaires should be used only where the results would be predictably favourable to the Soviet cause. Therefore it may be safely concluded that by the end of the 1920s Soviet leaders were convinced that the atheistic orators generally failed in open and public confrontations with religious apologists. As to the reliance on clergy-renegades, a Soviet source claimed that from the ranks of the Orthodox clergy their total number had run into several hundreds in the 1930s; that is out of a total of forty to fifty thousand – not a very impressive achievement in the face of the tremendous pressures and persecutions the clergy was enduring as the only alternative to reneging.

An illustration of the real worth of Soviet social surveys based on the principle of 'surveying' only that which serves their interests, was the well-publicized survey of 12 000 Moscow industrial workers in 1929 on their attitude to religion. Although the questionnaires 'were completely anonymous' (the Soviet author does not say how anonymous was the method of distribution and collection of the questionnaires), in a climate of gathering clouds of persecution only 3000 returned the questionnaires completed. Predictably the vast majority of these respondents, in fact 88.8 per cent, turned out to be atheists. Consequently the press and propagandists hailed the results as demonstrating that nearly 90 per cent of the Moscow industrial proletariat were convinced atheists.[77]

No better and no more reliable was the leader of LMG. In the Lunacharsky vein adopted by the LMG at the time, a 1934 textbook on atheism for the peasants, approved and prefaced by Yaroslavsky, admits that religion is not only the domain of illiterate masses, but that there are sincere believers among the intellectuals as well. Three years later in a brochure in English for American readers the same Yaroslavsky asserted that scholars and scientists who claim to believe in God are simple deceivers and swindlers; none of them is sincere.[78]

We may remember that by that year a new wave of religious persecutions including mass arrests and closure of urban churches was sweeping the country after the 1930–33 lull, which followed Stalin's 1930 article 'Dizziness From Success' and his secret instruction of the same year. Immediately thereafter antireligious printed propaganda, particularly in the pages of *Kom. pravda* was toned down and reduced in quantity to a fraction of its 1929 volume. This says much about the independent policy stands of Soviet public institutions.

Soviet authors now ridicule those Western scholars who claim that a secret five-year plan was adopted at the time to annihilate organized religion in the USSR. Yet the antireligious press officially stated in 1930 that an 'antireligious five year plan was adopted by the Second Plenum of the LMG Central Council'. Although officially it only set LMG membership goals (17 million members in five years) and concentrated its propaganda on the LMG's assistance to the government in fulfilling the economic Five-Year Plan, subsequent events suggest that the annihilation of religion was one of their unpublished aims.[79]

The atmosphere in, and the prerogatives granted to, the LMG are vividly reflected in the report on its Central Council Second Plenum cited above, when the Peoples' Commissariat of Enlightenment spokesman was heckled for the insufficiently active attack on religion through the school system. Particularly singled out for criticism was *Glavnauka*, Chief Administration for Science and Scholarship. The spokesman assured the audience that the institution had been reformed and, as praiseworthy evidence of this, stated that it had reduced the total number of historical buildings under its protection (mostly ancient churches and monasteries) from 7000 to 1000. 'This is a measure of considerable progress,' he said, the logical implication being that the destruction of all monuments of past culture would be a triumph of total progress.[80]

And yet two years later we find Soviet press criticism of the LMG for allegedly reducing antireligious struggle. Moreover, at the height of Stalin's 'final solution' of the Church question, antireligious museums were closing down, chairs of 'scientific atheism' were closed even in such institutions as the University of Moscow. Indeed, even the figures for atheist lectures and publications suggest a decline in 1940–41. Although 239 000 antireligious public lectures were delivered to a total audience of 11 million in 1940, this adds up to an average audience of under fifty per lecture. Even the combined total circulation figure of 6 million for the three Russian antireligious periodicals in 1941 was considerably smaller than the 1931 total; moreover, the mass circulation weekly *Bezbozhnik* seems to have ceased publication altogether, having been absorbed by its namesake monthly. The League's membership, as we have seen, declined from 5 760 000 in 1932 to 3.5 million nine years later.

Did the terror morally alienate sincere atheists from the ugly persecutions of believers? It is more likely that the centralized terror of the 1930s could not tolerate any forms of autonomous organizations, even the atheistic ones, and simply destroyed everything that was in any way prominent in its wake, including organized atheism. These may have been factors. But another, and more important, factor must have been the changing of Stalin's mood. On the one hand, he must have lost patience with the LMG when its leader admitted in 1937 that a third of the urban and two-thirds of the rural population were still practising religious believers despite the flood of antireligious propaganda and persecutions.[81] On the other hand, the 'campaign' may have achieved its purpose in Stalin's opinion: organized religion had practically ceased to exist, and this for Stalin's totalitarian frame of mind was more important than the faith of an individual citizen, pushed by the terror system into isolation and thus less likely to congregate into communal expressions of religious life. Finally, war clouds were gathering on the horizon, and Stalin needed some consolidation, patriotism, and unity of the nation in place of the divisive onslaughts of Marxist purism and atheism. It was no coincidence that the leading official Soviet history journal published an article in 1937 on the meaning of Russia's conversion to Christianity in the tenth century. The author, a very respectable historian Bakhrushin, praised that event as having opened Russia to contemporary universal European culture by way of the most advanced state and centre of learning and art of the time, which was Byzantium.[82] Henceforth, this attitude to Russia's Christianization became official Soviet doctrine. Yet, wild attacks on the contemporary Church and believers continued well into 1938. In line with the Great Purges, Yaroslavsky declared that a purge of 'several hundred reactionary zealots of religion' among the millions of believers was necessary. The clergy were attacked as foreign spies, and several trials of bishops with their clergy and lay adherents were reported as 'unmasked nests of foreign spies' and 'subversive terroristic gangs'. It was only in 1939, when the likelihood of a major war appeared on the horizon, and especially after the annexation of the territories in the west (1939–40),that the tone changed. The same Oleshchuk who a year earlier 'reported' the 'unmaskings' and spoke about the clergy and religious laity as enemies, was now claiming that:

> Only an insignificant minority [of people] in the ranks of religious organizations consists of hostile-class elements. . . . tha majority of believers are our people, backward workers and collective farmers.

A year later he reprimanded the antireligious activities and activists in the recently annexed western Ukraine and Belorussia for being overzealous and too aggressive, saying this only foments religious fanaticism. From the 'lofty' rostrum of the chief ideological mouthpiece of CPSU, he even advised not setting up LMG cells in those areas for the time being.[83]

This changing climate is well reflected in what was probably the last of Yaroslavsky's programmatic statements before the factual discontinuation of the LMG's work and the closure of its last periodicals in September 1941. Addressing the All-Union conference of the officials of antireligious museums on 28 March 1941, Yaroslavsky warned against the tendency of the 'simplifiers of anti-religious propaganda' to condemn all believers as:

> blind ignoramuses and total idiots. . . . It is wrong to think that the dozens of millions of religious believers are all . . . idiots . . . pitiful cowards and spiritually empty individuals. . . . There are many completely loyal Soviet citizens still possessing religious beliefs and superstitions.

And he called for patient, tactful, and mostly individual person-to-person work, without offending the believer, but re-educating him, and suggested a differentiated methodology, depending on the area and region. In some areas, he said, religion has almost wholly withered away; in others, particularly in the recently annexed western provinces and new Soviet republics (the Baltics and Moldavia), where religion is still powerful, there ought not to be a brutal offensive. Indeed, in the part of his speech where he boasted about the achievements of atheistic work in these newly Sovietized regions, he cited only one figure: a mere seventy-five attendants at the first-ever course for atheistic propagandists in Estonia; that is in a population of 1 200 000. Granted, the course was organized in Tallin's Russian Workers' Club, but he stressed that the students came from the whole 'republic'; and even if only Russians attended, there were over 150 000 Russians living in Estonia at the time.

He called for moderation, and yet when he says there were very few attempts to reopen, let alone build new churches, he presents this as evidence of the total decline of religion in the Soviet Union, as if he did not know by what means the number of churches across the whole Union was reduced from over 40 000 in 1929 to considerably less than 1000 a decade later. He called for moderation, and yet when he cites the few examples of renewed petitions to reopen a church, he brands the initiators of the campaign as former *kulaks* and falsifiers of figures. In one case he claims that there were only between ten and fifteen *kolkhoz* peasants who really wanted to reopen a church but that they fraudulently reported there were 533; yet he does not explain how eleven to fifteen collective farmers could muster 10 000 roubles for repairing the church![84] All his assurances do not tally with his own admission only four years earlier, that over 50 per cent of the population still believed in God; nor do they answer the question why 50 per cent of the population were left with only a handful of temples to serve them? A revealing answer to these contradictions arrived less than five months after Yaroslavsky's address, when the Soviet population occupied by the Germans and Rumanians reopened and rebuilt thousands of churches and rushed to them in their millions.[85]

Three months after the Nazi attack on the USSR, in September of 1941, the last antireligious periodicals were closed down. The reopening of churches in the German-occupied territories required the Soviet Government to make some concessions to the believers at home, in order to rally them to the defence of the country. The liquidation of the LMG itself took place very discreetly somewhere between 1941 and 1947.[86]

The result of a decade of LMG activities with the full co-operation of the OGPU-NKVD was the reduction in the number of all overtly functioning religious communities of all faiths, according to official Soviet data, from more than 50 000 in 1930 to 30 000 by 1938, and 8000 in 1941, on the eve of the German attack. This last figure, however, includes the annexed western territories with at least 7000 religious temples of different denominations (Orthodox, Roman Catholic, Protestant, Jewish). In other words, the 1938–9 holocaust resulted in the closing (and very often destruction) of some 30 000 temples, despite Soviet admissions in 1937 that 'the number of believers in some areas ... exceeds that of the atheists', and that on the average some 66 per cent of rural and 33 per cent of urban dwellers were practising religious believers.[87]

With the outbreak of war the 'unemployed' Yaroslavsky decided to seek a more lucrative *métier*: 1942 saw the publication of his article on the Orthodox Christian writer and Russian nationalist Dostoevsky. The subject was Dostoevsky's alleged hatred of the Germans.[88]

This metamorphosis of one who is still being hailed in the Soviet atheistic press as one of the country's most dedicated Marxist ideologues, is a fine comment on the ideology and its adherents. However, a true Marxist-Leninist might explain this in terms of dialectics: the historical moment of the time necessitated the upholding of rational traditions and non-Marxist values so that the Marxist state could survive and return to the promotion of world Communism and antireligious struggle in the more secure times to come.

3 The Post-War Atheistic Scene: A Renewal of the Offensive

FROM THE WAR TO KHRUSHCHEV

The lull in atheistic attacks against the Church did not last very long. Already in September 1944 when victory was beyond doubt, the Central Committee issued a decree calling for renewed antireligious efforts through 'scientific-educational propaganda'. Party members were reminded of the need to combat 'survivals of ignorance, superstition, and prejudice among the people'. Another Central Committee resolution, calling for the intensification of atheistic propaganda by the mass media, was issued in 1945, soon after the end of the war.[1] As long as Stalin lived, the renewed atheistic propaganda was mostly limited to words, and was only rarely accompanied by direct harassment or acts of vandalism. The main target of verbal attacks was the Roman Catholic Church and the Vatican in particular; although on the local level Orthodox bishops, parish priests and believers had to fight for the survival of churches opened during and immediately after the Second World War. Here and there local officials of the Council for the Affairs of the Orthodox Church did close some parishes and made life difficult, particularly for the bishops, by trying to prevent any disciplinary measures that the bishops might take against immoral or otherwise unworthy clerics and church activists. Such actions by state officials were quite legitimate in terms of the 23 January 1918 Decree depriving the Church of the status of a legal person, and of the two latest Constitutions implicitly denying the Church the status of a social organization. Such deliberate undermining of church discipline was further facilitated by the 16 March 1961 Instruction of the Council for the Russian Orthodox Church Affairs (CROCA) and the Council for the Affairs of Religious Cults (CARC), which explicitly forbade 'Religious centres, religious associations and the clergy ... to apply any measures of force or punishment.'[2]

Although no centralized brutal attacks against the Church occurred under Stalin in the post-war period, the year 1947 was marked by a definite escalation of the antireligious campaign. For the first time since the end of the war the Communist Youth daily, *Komsomol'skaia pravda*, emphatically declared that membership in the Young Communist League (*Komsomol*) was incompatible with religious belief; *Uchitel'skaia gazeta* (The Teachers' Newspaper) said the same thing about the teaching profession, and again called for a resolute struggle against the 'false' theory of a merely non-religious education: it had to be actively *anti*religious.[3] The first antireligious attacks in the CPSU chief ideological organ *Bol'shevik* (renamed *Kommunist* at the 19th Party Congress, 1952) appeared in 1947 in one article on education. Attacked, among other things, were Western influences, weakness of the ideological content in the post-war school and non-socialist attitudes to labour. They appealed to a combination of Stalinist post-war Soviet-Russian nationalism, Marxist ideology (Lenin's article on 'The National Pride of Great Russians' being interpreted as the proper form of nationalism), and Stalin's leadership. The official interpretation is that this type of patriotism is opposed to religious survival. The latter must be combated.[4] But although this was followed in the course of the next three years by numerous ideological articles containing implied attacks on the religious *Weltanschauung*, most of them avoided mentioning religion by name, or did so in the context of attacks on the 'pernicious influences of the imperialistic reaction ... [its] idealism, mysticism, clericalism [which] have become widespread in the contemporary bourgeois natural sciences'.[5] One of the early exceptions is a 1950 article which, *inter alia*, praises the formation in 1947 of the All-Union Society for the Dissemination of Political and Scientific Knowledge, or *Znanie* (Knowledge) for short, very much in the vein of the late Skvortsov-Stepanov:

> In contemporary conditions the propaganda of natural sciences becomes particularly important. It helps ... to overcome the capitalistic survivals in the mentality of people, to overcome superstitions and prejudices [i.e., religion – D. P.].[6]

The 'USSR' volume of the *Great Soviet Encyclopaedia* re-affirmed the CPSU's resolute and unwavering negation of any religion. Just as before the war, it was the *Komsomol* and its periodicals which took a leading position in the active offensive against religion.

As a Soviet publication later admitted in just so many words, the above *Znanie* society was formed as heir and successor to the defunct LMG. But its diversified lecture and publications programme, and its 'mass education' activities which become the forum for its attacks on religion, made it a much cleverer and more devious institution than the one it had replaced. Already in 1950 it was claiming 243 000 full and associate individual and 1800 institutional members. The very fact of diversity allowed genuine scholars, even non-atheists, to belong to it, and there was the added attraction that giving popular lectures through the *Znanie* network paid well and gave some fringe benefits. This did not mean that a scholar who was a practising believer would be forced to deliver a lecture on atheism, but it added extra prestige to an atheistic *Znanie* lecturer who could boast that he belonged to the same society as, say, Academician Kapitsa. The society began to grow by leaps and bounds after the CPSU Central Committee resolution of 20 June 1949, 'On the State of and Measures to Improve the All-Union Society of . . . Knowledge', which took the society to task for the following reasons: (1) its membership to date was only 34 000 full members and 16 200 associate members, with only 10 per cent of all scholars participating; (2) 'The Society does not pay sufficient attention to the propaganda of scientific atheism'; (3) 'The Administration of the Society shows insufficient supervision over the quality and ideological content of the lectures.'

The resolution then formulates the tasks of the Society: (1) 'The Society is to be transformed into a mass voluntary organization of Soviet intelligentsia' ('voluntary' in the Soviet Union ought to read 'compulsory-voluntary'). (2) The Society is to concentrate in its lectures on such topics as: the communist upbringing of the toilers; struggle against various expressions of bourgeois ideology; the materialistic explanation of phenomena of nature and of social life . . . (5) The administration of the Society is to supervise more closely the 'ideological content of the lectures'. 'All lectures are to be submitted to the

administration for approval prior to their delivery.'[7] There is
no evidence that this 'Stalinist' instruction on close control and
pre-censorship of every word uttered in public by a Soviet
lecturer was ever abolished or amended, even in the subsequent post-Stalin 'liberal' years. Be that as it may, the resolution
was obviously implemented effectively, for by 1972 the society
grew to 2 457 000 members, including 1700 members of the
Union and Republican Academics of Sciences and 107 000
professors and doctors of sciences. In many cities the society
runs 'Houses of Scientific Atheism'.[8]

The year 1950 seems to have been important for the renewal
of some form of attack on the Churches, but there probably
continued to be divisions in the ideological establishment camp
on how to do it. On the one hand, it was in 1950 that the first
post-war issue of an academic atheistic periodical began to be
published by the USSR Academy of Science; on the other hand,
after the appearance of this first issue under the title *Voporosy
istorii religii i ateizma*, four years went by and Stalin was dead
before the next issue came out.[9] Either Stalin himself did not
like the content and blocked its further publication, or else he
felt that pressure against religion could be increased by the
well-tested administrative measures without too much intellec-
tualizing about it in highbrow volumes of some 300 pages. The
latter is more likely, because the increasing pressures on the
Church in the last five years of Stalin's reign do not indicate any
liberalizing intentions on Stalin's part regarding religion. As
the above illustrations show, in 1950 the Soviet press summed
up the results of the three preceding years of cautious renewal
of antireligious propaganda, maintaining that religion would
not wither away on its own, therefore antireligious activity and
propaganda should be stepped up.

This is the conclusion that Khrushchev inherited, and he
unleashed the attack on religion on a scale which the post-war
Stalin (bound by the 1943 'concordat') had not dared to do.

Joan D. Grossman believes that it was the aged Bonch-
Bruevich who was the architect of Khrushchev's assault against
religion. But this is very unlikely. Indeed, Bonch-Bruevich was
one of the editors (and perhaps the founder) of the antireligious academic periodical mentioned above, and was active in
the revival of atheistic propaganda until his death in 1955. His
last major publication stressed the rights of religious believers

in Soviet society, the principle of the separation of Church and state, and the alleged freedom of conscience under the Soviet constitution. In his arguments in favour of religious freedom he cites whatever communist authorities he can find (Stalin in 1913, Malenkov in 1952). Just before his death he rewrote in 1954 his 1929 article on Lenin and religion in which he emphasized Lenin's warnings against using force to suppress religion. Moreover, when B.-B. was important in shaping the Bolshevik antireligious policy he was in favour of courting and 'domesticating' sectarians and Old-Believers, whereas under Khrushchev and even after his time the Protestant sects have sometimes been attacked even more severely than the Orthodox.[10]

It is interesting that next to the B.-B. article *Voprosy ist. rel. i at.*, No. 2 (1954), published Oleshchuk's highly aggressive antireligious article, quoting passages from Lenin, which, in contrast to those cited by B.-B., support a general attack on religion. In 1954 there were also two controversial Central Committee resolutions on religion. That of 7th July stated that both the Orthodox Church and the sectarians were successfully attracting the younger generations by the high quality of their sermons, charity work (illegal since the 1929 legislation), individual indoctrination, and the religious press. This 'activisation of the Church has resulted in an increase of the number of people . . . participating in religious services'. The resolution called on the Ministries of Education, the Komsomol and the trade unions to intensify antireligious propaganda. Lack of unity in the Soviet leadership after Stalin's death was made evident by the fact that four months later (10 November 1954) the other CPSU Central Committee resolution appeared which criticized arbitrariness, the use of slander and libel against the clergy and the believers, and insulting epithets in the antireligious campaign.[11]

Therefore if B.-B., the old veteran of atheism, who certainly had direct access to Khrushchev and was a very influential Old Bolshevik, was the architect of any antireligious policy of the time, it would have been the one reflected in the November, not the July, resolution, while Khrushchev's antireligious assault, finally unleashed in 1959, was a realization of the July resolution. Oleshchuk and the other surviving veterans of the pre-war LMG were more likely the spirits behind the July resolution and the subsequent persecutions. However, ideological strategy disagreements delayed the attack; 1955 to 1957 were probably the most liberal years for religious believers since 1947. But the offensive was not called off and an early foreboding of an intensification of the antireligious campaign to come could have been seen in the 1957 re-publication of Yaroslavsky's pre-war book *On Religion (O religii)*. As to the 1954 resolutions, the November document called only for the eradication of errors in the antireligious propaganda, not for its abolition, while the July 1954 resolution had called on the Academy of Sciences to participate prominently in the atheistic offensive. Duty-bound, the Academy accepted a role in the campaign in its decisions of 30 October 1954. Less than three years later it began to publish its *Yearbook of the Museum of History of Religion and Atheism*; but a mass-circulation *Znanie* Society monthly, promised in the July Resolution, had to wait until September 1959, when it appeared under the title *Nauka i religiia* (Science and Religion), with an abundance of slanderous antireligious material not unlike its pre-war predecessor, Yaroslavsky's *Bezbozhnik*. In circulation, however, it never matched the latter, growing from 100 000 copies per issue to a peak of over 400 000 in 1981–3, subsequently declining to 340 000–350 000.

Significantly, the editorial in the very first issue of *Science and Religion*, setting the tone for the publication and its aims to aid in the intensification of 'militant atheism' until 'the complete eradication of religious superstitions' has been achieved, refers to the then recent XXI CPSU Congress and its proclaimed aim of 'the over-all construction of a communist society' as its point of departure. This is an indirect confirmation of the never-refuted rumours at the time that a secret resolution was adopted at that congress to annihilate religious institutions in the country during the implementation of the Seven-Year Plan adopted at the congress. Yet, contradicting its promise of militancy, the editorial warns against insulting believers' feelings and the use of arbitrary force, and refers only to the 10 November 1954 Resolution.[12]

Although the more aggressive July 1954 Resolution mentioned the Church press as a dangerous threat to atheism in the USSR, at that time it consisted of only one Russian Orthodox monthly with a circulation of no more than 15 000 copies,[13] one Baptist journal and a Ukrainian Orthodox journal – both published six times a year, each with a circulation of perhaps ten thousand copies or less. The Church publications appeared in open sale in a few churches in the major cities for no longer than an hour or two per issue and were very difficult to subscribe to, while the number of atheistic pamphlets alone in 1950 equalled forty, with a total annual circulation of 800 000 copies, not to mention the atheistic monopoly in the education and mass media. In addition, the Resolution ordered that:

the teaching of school subjects (history, literature, natural sciences, physics, chemistry, etc.) should be saturated with atheism . . . the anti-religious thrust of school programmes must be enhanced.

Indeed, every subsequently published school textbook became even more emphatically assertive of atheism than before, with such declarations as:

Religion is a fantastic and perverse reflection of the world in man's consciousness. . . . Religion has become the medium for the spiritual enslavement of the masses.[14]

Predictably, it was the tougher July 1954 document rather than the milder one of November that led to much greater repercussions some five years later and proved to have been a trial balloon for the persecutions of 1959–64. One looks in vain for any printed pledges to stamp out religion or similar statements in the official state and party documents. The antireligious hints in them are even flimsier than in the pre-war decade. For instance, the Central Committee report at the 20th Congress (1956) merely mentions 'survival of capitalism in people's minds' which it will be 'impossible to stamp out . . . without the participation of the masses'.[15] This was followed by a more explicit hint of things to come in Khrushchev's 1958 Theses on Educational Reform which emphasized the need to develop a materialistic world-view in youth. Finally, the euphemisms in the resolutions of the 21st Party Congress (1959) leave very little doubt of a forthcoming toughening up of antireligious policies, particularly in the following passage:

in the ideological sphere: strengthening of the ideological-educational work of the party, raising of the communist consciousness in the toilers ... struggle against bourgeois ideology.[16]

An article in *Pravda* (21 August 1959) took the 'ideological workers' to task for holding the mistaken view that now, once the deepest roots of religion have been eliminated, the social base of religion liquidated, the consciousness of the Soviet people raised, the necessity for patient daily efforts to overcome religious prejudices has allegedly disappeared.[17] The pre-war line that religion will not disappear on its own, for 'religious survivals possess exceptional vitality owing to the stagnant and conservative nature of religious ideology',[18] is restated once again. And, as in 1929, it is admitted that 'the degree of religiosity ... has increased in some areas of the country'. We are told that between '1954 and 1960 the CPSU Central Committee ... has emphatically restated the importance of intensifying the atheistic work', although not a single one of the published CC documents since the above two of 1954 ever mentioned atheism by name. Thus the context of this assertion must be found by reading the party documents between the lines, and understanding clearly that 'struggle against the bourgeois ideology, reactionary ideas, capitalist survivals', and so forth, stands for struggle against religion. Again, as in the pre-war era and as mentioned in relation to the secret Seven-Year Plan, there were secret instructions about which the poor churchmen could only guess.

For the first time since 1941 the pre-war LMG veteran, Kryvelev, reappeared in *Kommunist* of that year, although the thrust of his attack was directed to contemporary trends in Western theology, especially its allegedly reactionary, anti-Soviet, anti-scientific character. All the other ideological antireligious articles which by 1959 were appearing in almost every issue of *Kommunist* attacked religion mostly by using such euphemisms as: survivals of the old ideology, superstitions, prejudices, petty-bourgeois ideological survivals and the like.[19]

In 1959 there was introduced an obligatory course of 'The Foundations of Scientific Atheism' in all institutions of higher learning.[20] But it was the 9 January 1960 Central Committee

Plenum Resolution 'On the Tasks of Party Propaganda in Modern Times' which openly and emphatically called for the escalation of an antireligious attack in terms much closer to the July than the November 1954 Resolution. It took local party organizations to task for a 'passive, defensive attitude to the idealistic religious ideology, hostile to Marxism-Leninism', and called for 'an active offensive struggle against bourgeois ideology, hostile to Marxism-Leninism'. There were no instructions to avoid offending believers or anything of that kind in this resolution, which emphasized in terms reminiscent of the 1928–40 era that religion was hostile to the official ideology of the Soviet state and remained incompatible with it.[21] This resolution set off a flood of antireligious articles in *Kommunist* and other Soviet periodicals in 1960 and the following year; for example, the chief philosophical monthly of the Academy of Sciences, *Problems of Philosophy* (*Voprosy filosofii*) published thirteen major antireligious articles in 1960 under its new rubric of 'Marxist-Leninist Ethics and Scientific Atheism'. This is in contrast to the absence of any major militantly atheistic articles in that journal in 1959, only two or three in 1958 (including one by the LMG veteran Oleshchuk), none in 1957 and one by the leading Soviet ethnographer Tokarev in 1956. The programmatic editorial for this 'new' course appeared in the March 1960 issue of the periodical under the title 'For the Creative Development of the Issues of Scientific Atheism', which in its turn referred to the above CPSU Central Committee Plenum Resolution of 9 January 1960. The editorial also mentioned a 15–17 June 1959 All-Union conference on atheism organized jointly by the Academy of Sciences and the *Znanie* Society, in which 800 scholars and propagandists of atheism participated. The report of the *Znanie* Society board to its III Congress mentioned fifteen inter-republican and republican, and 150 provincial, conferences and seminars dedicated to the question of 'improving the ideological and scientific contents of atheistic propaganda' which had occurred in the course of 1959, with the total participation of over 14 000 propagandists. The report criticized the illiteracy of many propagandists, lecturers and authors; for example, a cartoon in *Science and Religion* (subsequently *NiR*) depicts Adventists as praying before an icon, and an article in the same publication calls the Hebrew Talmud 'a prayer book held by believers in their hands' during services in synagogues. And it called for immediate publication of a basic textbook on scientific atheism, which in fact soon appeared. Its third edition in 1964 was issued with a circulation of 50 000.[22]

Leonid Il'ichev, who then headed the CC Ideological Commission (formerly *Agitprop*), in his 1959 *Kommunist* article had still used language of euphemisms; but in 1960 he attacked the Church unequivocally in a most aggressive manner. He admitted that the new line was born at the XXI Party Congress, which proclaimed the communist society as inseparable from an atheistic upbringing of the toilers. He also hinted why suddenly it was necessary to renew and escalate the attack on religion, when he said religious concepts were being disseminated 'particularly [by] the sectarians and the Roman Catholic clergy. Hence . . . the struggle against religious ideology must be escalated . . . particularly the educational work with individual believers.'[23] The latter phrase was menacingly reminiscent of the late 1930s. This policy was endorsed by a plenary session of the Komsomol Central Committee in 1961. Communist party cells at places of work or study, similar Komsomol branches, local sections of the *Znanie* Society and trade-union branches appointed atheist members as personal tutors in atheism to known religious believers, in most cases their workmates. They visited these believers at their homes, and tried to convince them. If this did not work, they would bring it to the attention of their union or professional collectives, and these cases of 'religious backwardness' and 'obstinacy' were aired at public meetings.[24] Should all these efforts prove fruitless, then followed administrative harassment at work or school, not infrequently culminating in lower-paid jobs, blocking of promotion, or expulsion from college if the believer was a student. Physical harassment of believing schoolchildren by their teachers was also common.[25] There was a concerted campaign in the early 1960s to induce priests and theologians to defect to the atheist camp; this reaped a harvest of over 200 such defectors, including two theology teachers, one priest and one layman.[26] These efforts, however, were soon abandoned after it was realized that the defections and their loud publicity had little effect on believers, for most of the defectors had not commanded the love, devotion and faith of their parishioners to begin with.[27]

In 1960, as in 1929, the general school was criticized for insufficiently active antireligious education. A collective open letter to the RSFSR Minister of Education, citing instances of practising believers among school pupils, accused the school of ignoring its duty to wipe out religious 'superstitions'. Characteristically, it described believing parents in pejorative terms as 'fanatics', and active believers and clergy as 'swindlers' who fool and cheat people in order to catch them in their nets. Responding to this letter, the Minister stated that one of the aims of Khrushchev's 1959 educational reform of polytechnisation of the secondary school was to make education more effectively atheistic. A special instructional letter from the Ministry of Education of February 1959 obliged school administrations to take measures to make education truly antireligious, wherefore in the course of 1959–60 Darwinism and 'the origins of life on earth' began to be taught intensively, and all natural sciences were subordinated to the purpose of 'developing a scientific-materialistic attitude in students towards nature'. A whole series of books with a Marxist-materialistic interpretation of life and nature were issued at the same time as additional school readers. Both the letter and Minister's answer treat expressions of religious belief as a very serious social epidemic.[28]

The 1960 CC Plenum resolution called for the introduction, beginning in 1961–2, of special courses of basic political education in senior highschool grades, because 'It is indispensable . . . that in the process of education students master the materialistic *Weltanschauung*, the communist ideology.' And a 1961 report on the work of the Leningrad Museum of History of Religion and Atheism boasts some achievements along the lines of the 1960 resolution and the above articles. In the field of individual work with believers, special schools training such individual agitators were set up in Leningrad in 1958, proving that there must have been secret instructions to this effect long before the above plenum resolution. Two special 'universities of atheism' were formed in Leningrad and several in its province. One of the city 'universities' was run by *Znanie*, the other by the Museum. They trained lecturers, propagandists and agitators for individual atheistic work. Clubs of atheism were formed for the masses at the local 'Palaces of Culture', followed by the formation of special atheistic film clubs.[29]

The 1961 22nd Party Congress, the one which publicly denounced Stalin more broadly and fundamentally than the 20th Congress and which was hailed by many at the time as launching a new era of liberal communism, escalated the antireligious attack to new levels of intensity and intolerance when it issued the new Communist Party Programme proclaiming the construction of Communism within twenty years. Khrushchev followed closely Marx's imperative, 'Communism begins at the outset with atheism',[30] when he declared:

> It is impossible to take a man into communism who is covered with a mass of capitalist prejudices. We must first emancipate him from the burden of the past. . . . Man cannot develop spiritually if his head is crammed with mysticism, prejudices, false ideas. . . . Communist education presupposes the liberation of the mind from religious prejudices and superstitions.

Although none of the Congress resolutions spelled out religion in so many words, Khrushchev in that Congress speech called for the intensification of 'scientific-atheistic' education to prevent the 'dissemination of religious ideas, especially among children and adolescents'. This was sufficient for the Soviet authors to interpret the 22nd Party Congress as having drawn the attention of communists and of all progressive humanity to the necessity for struggle against religion – for the complete eradication of religious prejudices of all Soviet people, who must be brought up in the spirit of a scientific materialistic *Weltanschauung*.[31]

The 22nd Party Congress's antireligious line was followed by a militantly antireligious resolution of the 1962 14th Komsomol Congress, which called for a more 'concrete' attack on religion, 'revealing its reactionary essence'. It also adopted a new Komsomol Statute which declared that the duty of each Komsomol member was 'the conduct of a resolute struggle against . . . religious prejudices'.[32] *Kommunist* and *Vop. is. rel. i at.*, not to mention the daily press, followed with a series of very militant articles against religion in 1962 and 1963, calling it a hostile phenomenon and ideology which must be eradicated by every means. One of the most militant was written by our 'old friend' Oleshchuk calling for an even more intensive attack.[33]

The militancy of the antireligious campaign definitely gained momentum after the 'liberal' 22nd Party Congress. The CPSU Programme adopted at the Congress declared that 'the current generation of Soviet people will live under Communism';[34] this was officially interpreted by the Academy of Sciences as an imperative 'to emancipate the consciousness of Soviet citizens from all and every kind of survival of the old exploiting society, including the religious survivals'. The authors argued that this requirement gave paramount importance to a decisive antireligious struggle and propaganda of atheism.[35]

Two CPSU Central Committee resolutions were issued on 6 July 1962. One was addressed to the party leadership of Belorussia, the other to the provincial party administration of the Kuibyshev Province. Both party administrations were taken to task for insufficient activity in antireligious struggle. It was decreed, for instance, that 'the population be persistently educated in scientific atheism. An end must be put to the dissemination of religious ideas, especially among children and youth.' The instruction is definitive and categorical. Its obvious meaning is that religion must be eradicated by any means possible, even including direct persecution. In Soviet practice such resolutions addressed to two or three individual party administrations are always meant to be read as addressed to the whole country and to be followed by all other party administrations. And this was precisely how *NiR* interpreted the resolutions.[36] During the same year the journal declared editorially that it was the duty of every member of Soviet intelligentsia to be a propagandist of atheism.[37] The period was rife with all sorts of conferences on antireligious propaganda, on methods of combating religion.[38] All this led up to the June 1963 ideological plenum of the Central Committee with its mammoth speech by Il'ichev.

Il'ichev linked religion with Western 'ideological subversion' of Soviet society and called the people who were still 'in the hands of survivals of the past', 'amoral'. He stated that 'the religious opiate' is 'one of the extreme forms of bourgeois ideology', and advised 'a merciless war against all those who stand in the way of building communism', that is, a merciless war against religion. Although he treats religion almost exclusively as a class phenomenon, a survival of the hostile classes and their mentality, almost in the style of the left wing of the LMG of the late 1920s, he admits that its vitality is such that 'where we don't work, the influence of the Church and the sects grows'; and he calls for a militant, aggressive assault on religion, although he uses the term 'scientific-atheistic propaganda'. Stalin, he says, had a wrong interpretation of the class struggle and its progression, the interpretation being that his ceasefire with respect to religion after 1943 may also have been wrong. No mercy or respect for believers' feelings is ever mentioned in that speech, which came after four years of direct and brutal persecution. On the contrary, Il'ichev scolded the atheistic front for being too passive. This was soon followed by his massive article in *Kommunist* in which he blamed the relatively tolerant 1943–53 Soviet policies towards religions on Stalin's abuse of the 'Leninist legality'; that is, the mounting persecutions were being presented as a 'return to Leninist principles', return to Soviet 'legality' (*sic*).[39] Thus Khrushchev and his staff not only approved direct persecutions of religious faith, but by presenting them as constitutionally legitimate further helped to debase the concept of the rule of law in the eyes of the population.

STREAMLINING FOR PERSECUTIONS

In preparation for the intensified campaign against the Church, the Soviet Council of Ministers issued three instructions, none of which is to be found in the published Soviet codes, aimed at the suppression and liquidation, wherever possible, of monasteries and convents. One of them (of 16 October 1958) cancelled the tax exemptions on monastic properties granted on 29 August 1945. The second one (of 6 November 1958) introduced a very high tax on land lots belonging to the monasteries of 40 r. per 0.01 ha. (4 post-1961 roubles). And the third one (also of 16 October 1958) instructed republican ministries and local government to cut the sizes of land plots under monastic control and to study ways and means of reducing the number of open monasteries.[40] The reason for starting the campaign with an attack on monastic institutions must have been twofold.

First, there are no clear laws in the Soviet codes regulating the legal status of monasteries and there are no groups of twenty laymen to represent the monastic institutions (officially) to the civilian authorities. In fact, each monastery is registered as an affiliate of the Moscow Patriarchate directly, in a special resolution of the Council of Ministers of the USSR.[41] But since the Church and all the ecclesiastical institutions and dignitaries do not enjoy the status of full legal persons in Soviet law, while the lay members of the 'twenties' do, it is easier to suppress those church bodies which have no 'twenties' to represent them (legitimately).

Second, monastic institutions perform an extremely important spiritual function in the life of the Orthodox Christians, as centres of pilgrimage, as centres for soul-searching confessions and spiritual consultations with the recognized elders, and as institutions reaffirming laymen in their religious commitment, in strengthening the faith of the nation.

Thus, by closing the monasteries or aiming at this, the regime was killing two birds with one stone by attacking the Church's legally weakest link and depriving the religious masses of one of the most essential parts of the spiritual diet. The tangible five-year-long antireligious holocaust began in 1959, developing along the following lines: (i) mass closure of churches, reducing their total number from some 22 000 to about 7000 by 1965; (ii) closure of monasteries and convents accompanied by the reinforcement and reiteration of the 1929 legislation banning organized or any other group pilgrimages either to monasteries or to locally revered holy places, many of which commemorated closed and destroyed monasteries or sites where large groups of monastics had been executed in the 1920s or 1930s; (iii) closure of five of the then still existing eight seminaries, accompanied by bans on the short intensive pastoral courses periodically run by some bishops in the 1940s and 1950s, thereby acutely intensifying the problem of clergy replacement; (iv) strict banning of church services, even private ones, outside the church walls, accompanied by an order to record the personal identities and identification documents of all adults requesting a baptism, church wedding or funeral. Non-fulfilment of these orders, which amounted to reporting the persons involved to the KGB, led to the deprivation of state registration of the offending clergy, without which no priest was allowed even to assist at a service without the special permission of the state plenipotentiary for religious affairs; (v) deprivation of parental rights for the religious upbringing of children; (vi) secret instructions banning the presence of children at church services and the administration of Communion to children four years of age and older; (vii) forced retirement, arrests, and prison sentences meted out to priests and bishops on trumped-up charges, but in fact for resisting the closure of churches, for sermons attacking religious persecution and atheism, for Christian charity and generally for making religion popular by personal example; (viii) oral, and in some places local written, orders, banning the ringing of church bells and the conducting of daytime services in rural churches from May to the end of October under the pretext of field work requirements, although cinemas and clubs were not required to cease daytime operations.[42]

In 1960 the closing-down of seminaries began with those of Kiev, Saratov and Stavropol, which either closed or ceased to accept students. Before 1965 the seminaries of Volhynia and Belorussia likewise ceased to exist. According to the former secretary of the Volhynia Seminary, it was closed in 1964 under the pretext of lack of students. In reality, the Volhynian CROCA representative had ordered the seminary to provide him with the lists of seminary applicants. He then instructed the local armed forces recruitment offices to block the candidates' de-registration at the recruitment points of their residence. Even those who somehow managed to overcome this obstacle were then refused residence permits in Lutsk where the seminary was situated. Thus, over a period of several years the seminary was literally drained of students. A similar method was used to close the Belorussian Seminary, and probably the others as well.[43] Yet the Soviet media misrepresented this as a natural decline 'of the numbers of those willing to enrol for theological studies', as a sign of the decline of religious beliefs.[44]

As had been the case thirty years earlier, all forms of mass media were now being called upon to consolidate their campaign against religion, and the process of atheistic re-education was not to be limited only to special subjects in the senior-school grades:

It is indispensable that the pre-school institutions and schools participate accordingly in the system of scientific-atheistic education, as well as higher education establishments, research institutions, museums and creative associations . . . houses of culture, clubs, libraries, etc.[45]

Like the League of the Godless before the war, so the *Znanie* Society was now leading to ideational onslaught against religion. In January 1960 there was a high-level *Znanie* conference on atheism with such important party bureaucrats as Brezhnev, Kosygin, Mikoian, Suslov and others participating.[46] Since within a few days after the conference two republican first party secretaries (from Moldavia and Belorussia) threatened to take measures to stop the violation of 'socialist legality' by churchmen, it is clear that the guidelines on tactics adopted at that conference encouraged attacks on the Church in the name of re-establishment of the Leninist legality. This was fully in line with Khrushchev's attack on Stalin as a man who had violated Leninism and the Leninist–socialist legality; because of the 1943 oral concordat concluded between Stalin and the surviving leaders of the Orthodox Church and the bye-laws adopted at the 1945 *Sobor* (Council) of the Russian Orthodox Church which flatly contradicted the whole volume of Soviet legislation regarding the Church from 1918 to 1929. The bye-laws reconstructed the strict hierarchical structure of the Church, in which the bishop was the leader of the diocese, and the parish priest of the parish, whereas the Soviet law knew only groups of twenty lay persons. The fact that the Soviet Government tacitly accepted the Church bye-laws without, however, amending its own laws on these matters must have meant that it viewed the situation as only a *temporary* compromise. Stalin was repeatedly accused by Soviet leaders and the press of having violated Lenin's decree on the separation of Church and State.[47] A Soviet law invalidating all legislation passed by the Nazi occupiers on Soviet territory held by them during the war was invoked to close most of the churches and monasteries reopened during the war on the territory occupied either by the Germans or the Rumanians (Moldavia and the Black Sea littoral from Bessarabia to Crimea). Since most of the church re-openings during the war had in fact occurred in the *occupied* territories, this law alone allowed the Soviets to

close some 65 of the 80-odd monasteries and convents and a
good many of the 15 000 Orthodox churches, which were
closed between 1959 and 1964. The fate of the religious
establishments of other faiths was very similar.[48] Many
churches during these years were liquidated in territory never
occupied by the enemy (for example, in the Kirov Diocese of
seventy-five churches functioning in 1950 only thirty-five
remained open in 1965). Here, other 'legal' means were used.
For instance, the law that a person's residence must be within
the area of his employment was invoked to ban missionary visits
by priests to parishes left without a priest.[49] At the same time the
local CROCA official ('plenipotentiary', as he is officially
called) would deprive a popular priest of a registration permit
on some pretext and then refuse to register any newly ordained
candidate for that parish, thus depriving the parish of clergy
services. Meanwhile, filling clerical vacancies was becoming
more difficult because of the closure of seminaries (only three
of the post-war eight remained by 1965) and of the special brief
pastoral-preparatory courses for mature candidates without
regular theological training, which used to be run periodically
by diocesan bishops until about 1957–8; but then they were
banned, apparently by some unpublished Soviet instruction.
After the parish remained without a priest for over six months
the local *soviet* would close it on the grounds that the church was
not being used.[50] Another common means of closing a church
was to refuse to let the parishioners make major repairs. Then
the appropriate state commission could rule the building
unsafe for use, and the very *soviet* which had refused the repair
permit could now close it on those grounds.[51]

Expanding on the law (1918 and 1929) banning religious
instruction for minors, children under 18 years of age were
forbidden to attend Baptist worship services in 1961, and by
the fall of 1963 the ban was extended to Orthodox churches as
well. In 1963 the Central Committee of the Komsomol urged
that services not be allowed to begin if children were present in
the church.[52] There is evidence that this stipulation was applied
under state pressure and threats until after the fall of
Khrushchev. Furthermore, the 14th Komsomol Congress
(April 1962) declared that 'freedom of conscience does not
apply to children, and no parent should be allowed to cripple a
child spiritually'. The top Soviet professional legal journal,

Soviet Justice, added legal grounds on which parents could be deprived of parental rights over their children by the state, since that right is granted to the parents by the state to begin with.[53] This could henceforth be applied to individual religious families. And fifteen years later this practice was legalized implicitly in the Constitution of the USSR of 1977 which makes it a duty of each Soviet citizen 'to educate the children so . . . that they become worthy members of the socialist society'. Since the Communist Party is the 'vanguard of the whole people' of the Soviet Union whose 'socialist society is . . . on the road to communism', and since one of the main aims of the socialist state is the 'upbringing of members of communist society', the above passage on parental family duties can be easily interpreted (whenever the authorities might decide on the desirability of such an interpretation) as a duty to bring up their children as Communists, that is, as atheists.[54] Thus the deprivation of parental rights on the grounds of religious beliefs becomes quite legal. This shows that, if not in practice, at least in terms of their legal status the situation of believers has not improved since the fall of Khrushchev.

But let us return to the early 1960s. In March 1961 the USSR Council of Ministers issued a decree 'On the Strict Observance of the Laws on Religious Cults'. Four months later the Church was forced to change her bye-laws radically in order to bring them in line with Soviet laws. This decree deprived the priest of all control over the parish: he became simply a hired employee of the 'twenty' for the performance of religious rites. The party thought it was easier to infiltrate groups of laymen associated with the Church than the clergy, for in addition to depriving the clergy of administrative powers, special 'Administrative Commissions Attached to the Executive Committees of the City Soviets of Workers Deputies' began to be set up in 1962 in the context of Khrushchev's idea of involvement of public organizations in state administration in preparation for the future Communist society. But these commissions, made up of members of local *soviets* and of representatives of other public organizations were apparently meant mostly as disciplinarian supervisors primarily over religious bodies, because their instructions and prerogatives were included in an internal manual on Soviet laws on religion for Soviet administrative personnel; as from 1966 they began to be transformed into

'Commissions-in-Aid to the Executive Committees of the Soviets of Workers Deputies on the Observance of Religious Cults'. As they are meant to be set up locally and the above manual contains only a 'Model Statute', there seem to be multiple variants of the regulations of their work, make-up and functions. One of such later regulations reads in parts:

3. The commissions are to be made up of politically literate persons who can keep the religious societies under completely close observation ... Their membership should consist of deputies of local *Soviets*, employees of cultural and education establishments, financial organs ... propagandists ... and other local activists.
  ...
  Commissions function on the approval of city and county *soviet* executive committees

4. The functions of the commissions include:
  (a) a systematic study of the religious situation ... the contingent of people who frequent churches and participate in religious rites, ... and the degree of influence of the religious societies and the clergy on the involvement of youth and children in the church. ...
  (b) continuous study of the ideological work of the church, sermons ... Ascertain who are the young people whom the priests try to prepare for church work ...
  ...
  (d) study of the membership of religious societies (parish organs) exposing their most active members. ...
  (e) ... expose all attempts by the clergy to violate Soviet laws and immediately inform the state organs.
  (f) help the financial organs to expose those priests who perform religious rites illegally in private homes and apartments. ...
  (g) expose ... unregistered priests who illegally visit towns or villages and perform religious rites there.[55]

One of the main purposes of the commissions is the finding of ways ... to limit and weaken activities of religious societies and the clergy.

The second part of the instructions deals with the groups of twenty laypersons and is addressed to a county or village *soviet* executive:

> the groups of twenty in existence today . . . are not reliable. They consist almost entirely of . . . illiterate fanatics . . .
>
> Try to recommend the formation of new twenties made up of . . . non-fanatical persons, who would sincerely fulfil Soviet laws and your suggestions, instructions. When such a twenty has been formed and its membership satisfies you, only then sign a contract with it. . . .
>
> Let the group of twenty . . . elect its executive body. . . . It is desirable that you . . . take part in the selection of members of such an executive body and that [they be] . . . those who carry out our line. . . .
>
> It is recommended that you not include priests, choir directors, church watchmen . . . and other people working for the church into the groups of twenty.[56]

The aim of this document was to divest the clergy of all direct control over the parish and to make certain that the control was entrusted to people who cared little, if at all, for the spiritual life of the parish. Such personnel of the 'twenties' bred discontent in the parish, often resulting in direct conflicts between the priests and the executive organs of their parish, and turned the latter into a tool of control of the clergy by the atheistic government, as testified by many *samizdat* documents.[57] The smooth transition and evolution of these bodies from Khrushchev's into Brezhnev's era, while many secular institutions were changed, indicates once again the essential continuity of the antireligious policies of these two periods.

The March 1961 decree emphatically reiterated the 1929 stipulations expressly forbidding the parishes to engage in any form of charity, and forbidding religious centres to 'offer financial aid to those parishes and monasteries which do not enjoy the support of local population'. This was then used to close many smaller parishes under the guise of their amalgamation with others, having made the barely solvent parishes insolvent by such measures as, for instance, a ban on profit from the sale of candles. The argument used here was that this was a disguised form of soliciting obligatory payments to the church, forbidden by the 1929 legislation (as if anyone was being forced in the church to buy candles).[58] The process was further facilitated by depopulation of rural areas, particularly in central and northern Russia, the Urals and Siberia, owing to intensive urbanization. Logically this should have led to the proportional reopening of churches in urban areas. But this did not occur, because of the authorities' resistance to the opening of new churches.

The ban on aid to monasteries was very timely from the Soviet point of view, for as early as 16 October 1958 a decree of the Council of Ministers reintroduced a tax on monastery buildings and land-holdings, abolished by a decree of the same Council of Ministers in 1945, as discussed above.[59] Thus once again, as in 1918, an attempt was made to squeeze much of the Church out of existence by trying to starve her monasteries and many of her parishes. This did not work; the Church and the faithful came to the monasteries' aid. So the government's next step in 1961 was to ban all charity to monasteries, but still most of the monasteries survived until the direct administrative closures of the following years. To justify this process it was accompanied by a massive anti-monastic campaign in the press, where monasteries were depicted as parasitic institutions, with fields and gardens tilled by exploited peasants while the monks and nuns were enjoying the proceeds. Monasteries were accused of black-market operations, and monastics of lechery with nuns and female pilgrims, and of drunkenness. Monastic administrators were accused of collaboration with the enemy during the war. And the actual expulsion of monks and nuns from the monasteries accompanied by the forced closure of the emptied monasteries was presented as a voluntary process. Photographs of former monastics as happy workers and peasants, accompanied by appropriate interviews and statements confirming the alleged satisfaction of the monks and nuns to be once again among the productive and toiling Soviet masses, appeared in the Soviet media.[60] Similarly attacked and 'exposed' were secret hideaways and underground monasteries of the Old Believer sects of True Orthodox Wanderers. These were often accused of harbouring criminals or deserters from the war.[61]

To effect a stricter control over the Churches the two state councils — one on the Affairs of the Orthodox Church, the other dealing with all the other religions – changed their functions during the period between 1957 and 1964. Set up originally by Stalin in 1943 allegedly as mere liaison bodies between the given religious institutions and the state, they now appropriated for themselves the functions of highly dictatorial and despotic supervisors and controllers over every aspect of church life. Professor Igor' Shafarevich, a famous Soviet mathematician and an Orthodox Christian, observed that although two official Soviet collections of party and state documents on religion published in 1959 and 1965 made no mention of CROCA, in fact during these years it had become 'an organ of unofficial and illegal control over the Moscow Patriarchate'.

The two councils were amalgamated in 1965 into a single Council for Religious Affairs (CRA). Ten years later the 1975 revisions of the 1929 legislation for the first time officially and overtly legislated the CRA, raising its status to the position of arch-supervisor over the Church. But Shafarevich believes that a secret instruction of 19 October 1962 had in fact given these prerogatives to the Council (or rather, to its two predecessors).[62]

REVIVAL OF THE 'GOD-BUILDING' HERESY

An interesting aspect of the antireligious campaign was revealed at the February 1962 'All-Union Conference On Scientific-Atheistic Propaganda' held in Moscow. It discussed concrete suggestions for the development of a streamlined, well-thought-out system of atheistic upbringing. The view prevailed that even such measures as the multiplication of 'Houses of Political Education', creation of atheistic 'Houses of Culture', additional atheistic publications, and obligatory courses of scientific atheism in schools and colleges, would not be enough.[63] What was needed was a complete integration of disciplines, all with an atheist ideological content, and a presentation and solution of problems taken from all aspects of social life in the context of atheistic *Weltanschauung*:

> Religious people should be educated in the principles of communist morality and ethics, religious customs and traditions are to be replaced by religious feasts and rituals to satisfy the aesthetic and emotional needs of believers.[64]

There is nothing new in this idea. The very popular Russian-Soviet writer V. Veresaev, a medical doctor by profession, as early as 1926 argued in lectures and articles in favour of developing beautiful and standardised rituals at least for such occasions as name-giving (to an infant), weddings and funerals. To those who saw rituals as signs of reactionary backwardness and clericalism, he pointed out that the secular life of Soviet atheism was already full of rituals (parades, demonstrations, 'red weddings', secular requiems), only they were 'depressingly untalented and miserable'. He and hundreds of his correspondents argued that people were often turning to church rites after being disappointed in the bureaucratic indifference and ugly poverty of the Soviet ritual of marriage or birth-registration. One correspondent, a Communist, cited a friend, a rural teacher, who had told him he would not preach atheism to peasants 'because you'll make the man an atheist, will deprive him of all rituals along with his religion, but give him nothing to replace them with'. Indeed, although the official propaganda (beginning with Lenin) compared the faith with moonshine-vodka and alcoholism, at least one of Veresaev's correspondents, a Komsomol activist, describes how a person whose wife had just been buried by means of the cold and indifferent secular-communist ceremony, empty and unreconciled, found satisfaction only in consuming a full bottle of vodka and crying his soul out, so that vodka came *in lieu* of a religious rite, not with it.

Veresaev's appeals met with stern attacks from positivist intellectuals 'of the Pisarev type': 'Soviet office workers, responsible party officials, and the majority of university students'. Veresaev argued that these 'stooping people with protruding foreheads, short-sighted eyes and thick spectacles' had no sense of beauty and therefore needed no colourful rituals and feasts in their lives. But he warned that, should they prevail, 'life would become a bore and man would turn into an empty container'.[65]

As we know, they did prevail. Whether or not this was one of the reasons for the survival of religion and its admitted new growth in the late 1950s to early 1960s, Veresaev's appeals were finally echoed many years later. The reluctance to plunge too deeply into the subject is associated with the fear of resurrection of the whole 'god-building' deviation of Russian Marxism, represented by such figures as Gorky, Lunacharsky, A. Bogdanov, V. Bazarov, Yushkevich and other outstanding Marxist intellectuals. They argued that Marxian materialism on its own was too mechanistically determinist in its approach to the human person and its role in history. Its materialism would not be able to inspire the masses to any voluntary action, let alone revolution. Man needed religion to act, to develop the necessary energy for action and for creativity. Inspired by such authors as the Austrian *Naturfilisof* Mach and his *Empiriocriticism*, as well as by Feuerbach and Nietzsche more than by Marx *per se*, these early Russian revisionists argued that freedom of will reigns supreme in the world, while the Marxian notion of necessity is a product of this freedom. They interpreted the term 'religion' after Feuerbach, namely as a link, any link, not necessarily between man and the Supernatural, but as a link between individual men, between man and the nation in the past and present, between man and a personified history, as it were. Yushkevich argued that the destructive element is much more strongly represented in Marxism than constructive and positive harmony of emotions and elation. Lunacharsky wrote:

> For the sake of the great struggle for life . . . it is necessary for humanity to almost organically merge into an integral unity. Not a mechanical or chemical . . . but a psychic, consciously emotional linking-together . . . is in fact a religious emotion.

Gorky defined religion as 'a sense of connection with the past and future', and saw the emotions of friendship and mutual respect linking people together as potentially religious, and believed that they would form a religion in the future.

Lunacharsky in his essay on atheism argued that a consistent regular atheist is a pessimist, because life becomes meaningless, ruled by death. The only optimistic way out is to plunge into a life of pleasure. He saw in the context of atheism the only non-pessimistic solution in turning to a Feuerbachian religion of Man-godhood: idolation of man as an autonomous agent of history and carrier of the historical mission of the progressive class of the given period of history. His freedom is expressed in joy that his intellect has recognized historical necessity and agreed to subordinate itself to it, and participate in it. This he called *religious atheism* where matter is deified, because 'matter stands above all intellects'. The commandment 'Love God over everything else' may be translated into the social-economic language as:

> You must love and deify matter above everything else, [love and deify] the corporal nature or the life of your body as the primary cause of things, as existence without a beginning or end, which has been and forever will be.

'God has been found,' says Lunacharsky: 'You must love and deify the material world', because 'it is the primary cause of things'. In the final analysis, he says:

> God is humanity in its highest potential. But there is no humanity in the highest potential. . . . Let us then love the potentials of mankind, our potentials, and represent them in a garland of glory in order to love them ever more.

He follows this with excerpts from *Our Father*, interpreting each verse in terms of his atheistic religion of deified mankind. This atheism, he says, 'is full of light, life struggle'.

Lunacharsky saw Marxism as an atheistic religion, its religious component being its belief in the victory of socialism, its belief in science and its ability to transfigure man and his human and social relations. He interpreted the mass events of the 1905 revolution as an expression of the religious forces of the nation. Even a god had to be created ('built', hence 'god-building') for this new religion of the future, a god as the personification of the social ideal of socialism, because in the notion and image of a god 'all that is human is uplifted to the highest possible potential'.

Like Leo Tolstoy, the 'god-builders' rejected the divinity of Christ but deeply respected Him and interpreted Him as a revolutionary leader and the first Communist on earth. Rather inconsistent, in view of their rejection of God as a real person, was their acceptance of the institution of prayer, which in the god-building cult would be addressed to progress, humanity, the nation, and to the human genius. As the whole cult was primarily meant as a means to achieve a collective frenzy of sorts for a common revolutionary action, the god-builders placed the stress on the communal or collective prayer, and wrote that Marxism as a new religion must lead to the erection of new temples, new rituals and new prayers. According to Lunacharsky, the new revolutionary theatre with its symbolic plays would create the necessary religious frenzy in the viewers.[66]

These ideas were vehemently attacked by Lenin. Although his attacks on the movement amounted to a simple name-calling containing no rational arguments,[67] party discipline, and particularly Lenin's victory in 1917, put an end to this school of thought, except in the case of Bogdanov, a medical doctor and a philosopher, whose empiriomonism was inspired by Avenarius's *Naturfilosofie* and Mach's empiriocriticism.[68] Gorky and Lunacharsky had caved in to Lenin's reprimand even before the revolution. We saw that, as the Commissar of Enlightenment, Lunacharsky would represent all Scriptures as evil and wholly unacceptable; he rejected Christ even in the above context. In fact, in his later writings he called Jesus a mythical personality in the classical Marxist tradition, rejecting Him as a historical figure.[69]

From the Orthodox Christian viewpoint this attempt to create a Communistic counter-church, a mystical anti-Christian cult, belongs to the category of false prophets predicted by Christ, and to the black mass of Satanism. A Soviet author, Laskovaia, quite appropriately points to a similarity of the god-builders' ideas with the 'Death of God' concepts of later Western agnostic or atheistic theologians, such as D. Bonhoeffer, or Bishop J. Robinson.[70] She ignores, however, the revival of only slightly camouflaged god-building ideas among Soviet atheists, especially after their recognition in the course of 1965 of the failure of Khrushchev's wholesale attack on religion. Then more and more suggestions appeared in the Soviet press for the introduction of pseudo-religious rites which would use symbols to create a mystical link between the people and the promised Communist society of the future, glorified in the Communist-orientated labour of the present. These rites or services would have a future orientation like Communism itself, would venerate and celebrate the Communist promise of an ideal society. To this end there would be celebrations of events and days for glorifying Communism. Special temples with symbolic artistic ornamentations should be built to glorify Communism as the greatest achievement of man's mind; oratorios should be composed and performed in these temples. Paradoxically, these articles were printed in the mid-1960s in the Communist youth daily in a section under the heading of 'Reason against Religion'.[71] Thus Soviet Marxist atheists were returning to the days of the French Revolution with its religion of Reason.

But since the idea of a structured, institutionalized and philosophically based religious cult of Communism had already been categorically rebuffed by Lenin, its new protagonists did not go as far as the earlier 'god-builders', nor was it permitted by the ideological watchdogs to so blatantly challenge Lenin's authority. Therefore, the theoretical discussion of the establishment of a more or less institutionalized cult soon petered out, reducing itself to the suggestions and introduction of some isolated rights in connection with events in personal or collective life. Since 1966, for instance, an 'All-Union Day of the Agricultural Worker' has been set up when the completion of harvest is marked by some locally devised rites, often based on such semi-pagan, semi-Christian rituals as those connected with St John the Baptist's Day. The celebration of the day of the Agricultural Worker is supposed to 'inspire . . . to call people to labour feasts', to extol 'the social, political, and ideological unity of society under socialism'. Apparently this holiday is celebrated differently in various parts of the country. In some parts of the Ukraine, where it bears the name of the Holiday of Hammer and Sickle and takes place in December, it is celebrated thus:

> On an early December morning tractor drivers [from the surrounding region] converge in Zhitomir. At the entry to the city they are met by representatives of the city factories who report to them on the progress of the socialist competition and invite the drivers to their factories, where the peasants and the workers engage in heart-searching and business like discussions. Then a parade of agrarian technology takes place at the Lenin Square. Solemnly, accompanied by an orchestra, the best workers and peasants receive their prizes and diplomas. Then all of them make public production-quota pledges for the forthcoming year at the city theatre.[72]

Special rites and ceremonies were devised in the 1960s to celebrate the granting of passports on the occasion of the sixteenth birthday of a Soviet citizen when he or she receives the internal passport, which thereafter becomes the means to control every movement, act, and job of a Soviet man or woman. 'Initiation into the ranks of workers and peasants' involves another rite. To compete with the Church, the Soviets have been introducing since the late 1950s a more ceremonious form of civil marriage, solemn rites of giving a name to a baby, civic burial rites, the so-called 'secular requiem'.[73]

Soon after Khrushchev's fall, Soviet authors engaged in the atheistic campaign cautiously began to question its actual effectiveness. Their general conclusion was that it had misfired. It antagonized the believers against the Soviet system instead of converting them to atheism. It merely pushed the religious life underground where it is more dangerous than if it is in the open. And it has drawn the sympathies of many unbelieving and indifferent people to the sufferings of the believers. Generally, after the fall of Khrushchev direct mass persecutions stopped, although very few of the closed 10 000 to 15 000 churches were reopened for worship.[74]

On 10 November 1964 the Central Committee of the CPSU issued a resolution 'On Errors Committed in the Conduct of Atheist Propaganda . . .' The resolution reaffirms that actions which offend believers and the clergy, as well as actions of administrative interference in the affairs of the Church, are unacceptable. As we have seen, such decrees and resolutions are a regular feature after every wave of particularly harsh persecutions or at the time of change of leadership. In all cases they are a testimony that the ideological leadership of the Soviet Communist Party had once again admitted defeat in its head-on attack on the Church.

4 Antireligious Policies after Khrushchev

A RETREAT? 1964 TO EARLY 1970s

The fall of Khrushchev resulted in an almost immediate toning-down of the antireligious attacks. Moreover, the two main antireligious academic serials, *Yearbook of the Museum of History of Religion and Atheism* and *Problems of History of Religion and Atheism*, soon ceased publication as well.[1] They had been published by the Academy of Sciences where, even in the overpoliticized humanities and social sciences, genuine scholars are still to be found. Hence, such a rapid end to the serials could have reflected the negative attitude of the genuine scholars towards such scholastically questionable publications emanating from their institution, taking advantage of the first opportune moment to have these publications discontinued.

However, events would soon show that no major changes of principle in the antireligious policies of the post-Khrushchev establishment occurred. All that happened was a recognition that the crudeness and brutality of the persecutions of 1959–64 did not pay. The attack continued, but the strategy changed. Hardly any of the churches that were closed under Khrushchev were subsequently reopened, and the few that did were almost matched by those closed by local authorities from the early 1970s to the early 1980s.[2]

Under Brezhnev (or more exactly, under the KGB chief Andropov, for the KGB and its predecessors have been the *de facto* curators of the Church since the first years of the Soviet power), many of the secret, and therefore unofficial, temporary instructions aimed at suppressing the Church were made into laws and published, thus legitimising many aspects of the persecutions. The Institute of Scientific Atheism, established in 1964 as the main Soviet research and co-ordination for antireligious work and attached to the Academy of Social Sciences of the CPSU Central Committee, was raised in status and importance when the function of publishing major studies on religion and atheism was handed over to it from the regular

Academy of Sciences, which was not under such tight control by the party as the Academy of Social Sciences. In place of the defunct *Problems of History of Religion and Atheism*, a new irregular serial, *Problems of Scientific Atheism*, began to be published in 1966, now under the auspices of the CPSU CC ASS. Whereas its predecessor occasionally contained serious scholarly articles by such outstanding historians as the late A. A. Zimin and other Russian medievalists on social aspects of religion in Russian history with little atheistic content, *Problems of Scientific Atheism* has had a more partisan and militant profile. In short, atheistic propaganda after Khrushchev became more centralized and co-ordinated, and its research more politically engaged and hence less scholarly and reliable than it had been under the Academy of Sciences.[3]

It was in 1965 that for the first time a statute of the CRA was published, simultaneously amalgamating the former Council for the Russian Orthodox Church Affairs and the Council of Religious Cults into the single organization of the Council for Religious Affairs. The prerogatives granted to this body included decision-making powers on such matters as whether to permit or to close a religious association. This changed the body from being an intermediary between the government and the Church, as was allegedly claimed by Stalin at his fateful encounter with the Orthodox Metropolitans in September 1943,[4] into the virtual super-administrator over the Church. V. Furov, the CRA deputy head, several years later boasted in a report to the CPSU Central Committee:

> The [Patriarch's] Synod is under CRA's supervision. The question of selection and distribution of its permanent members is fully in CRA's hands, the candidacies of the rotating members are likewise co-ordinated beforehand with the CRA's responsible officials. Patriarch Pimen and the permanent members of the Synod work out all Synod sessions' agendas at the CRA offices ... and co-ordinate [with us] the final 'Decisions of the Holy Synod'.[5]

So far the state has successfully resisted the reopening of any of the seminaries closed under Khrushchev (let alone opening additional ones); but giving in to the pressure both of the church leadership and of growing numbers of student-applicants, it has allowed considerable expansion of the existing three seminaries and two graduate academies. By the early 1980s their student numbers have grown to some 1300 day and over 1000 extramural students, from less than 300 day and some 500 extramural students at the end of Khrushchev's reign. The numbers have continued to rise in the 1980s, although only about 20 per cent of the applicants gained admission owing to lack of space.[6]

Table 4.1 shows that there had been no noticeable decrease in the number of atheistic lectures delivered in the immediate post-Khrushchev years. One suspects, however, that the 1966 to 1970 decrease either continued or at least was not reversed, because we failed to find any such statistics in the Soviet press for subsequent years. Even *NiR* editorial dedicated to the 30th anniversary of *Znanie* and to its seventh congress does not mention any statistics on the numbers of antireligious lectures.[7]

Table 4.1 No. of lectures on atheist themes annually, 1954–70

Year	No. of lectures across the whole USSR
1954	120 000
1958	303 000
1959	400 000
1963	660 000
1966	760 000
1968	679 000
1970	650 000 (approx.)

As to the publication of books and articles, Figures 4.1 to 4.5 indicate the dynamics of the antireligious printed propaganda from Khrushchev's onslaught to the early 1980s.[8] They show a sharp decline from 1964 to 1970 in the total numbers of books and articles printed, but not in the number of copies per title. The publication figures after 1970 are uneven, showing clearer growth tendencies again roughly from 1980, which coincides, as will be shown below, with the renewed toughening of the general line towards religion, and comes as a response to the growth in the numbers of people turning towards religion.[9] As to the total number of books (titles) printed, it had stabilized at 160 to 180 per annum from 1967 to 1980, declining somewhat thereafter, while their total circulation has been steadily growing from the lowest point in 1970 of 2 500 000

Figure 1.1   Antireligious articles in the Soviet central press (excluding the literary and other professional monthlies and the professional atheistic press)

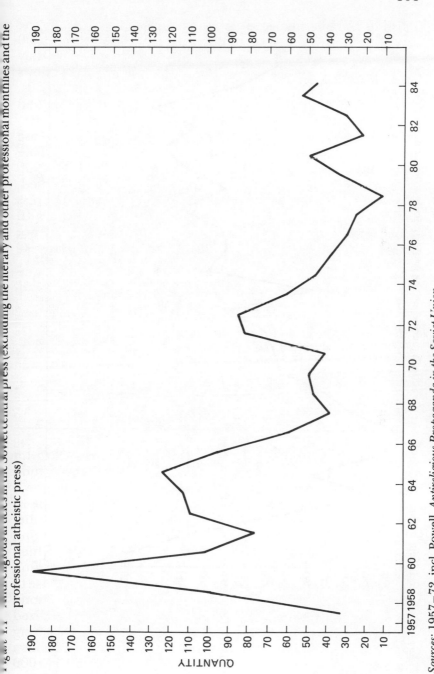

Sources: 1957–72, incl. Powell, *Antireligious Propaganda in the Soviet Union.*
1973–84, *Letopis' gazetnykh statei* (1973–78, section 'Ateizm, Nauka i religiia, Religiia') (1978–84, section 'Ateizm, Religiia').

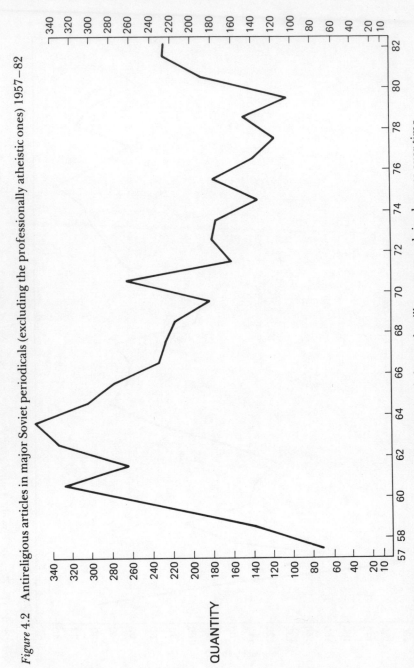

Figure 4.2   Antireligious articles in major Soviet periodicals (excluding the professionally atheistic ones) 1957–82

Note: These figures are approximate and should only be used to illustrate trends in changes over time.

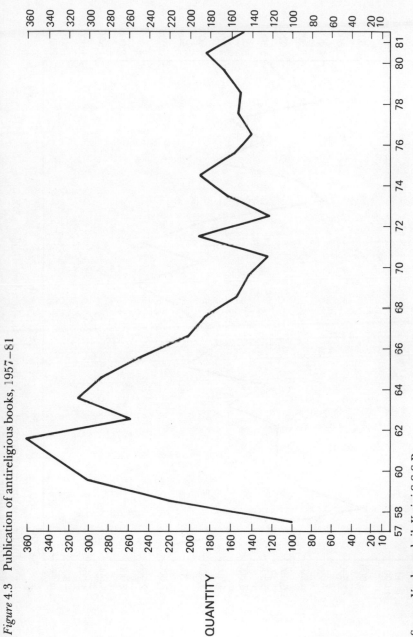

Figure 4.3   Publication of antireligious books, 1957–81

Source: Yezhegodnik Knigi S.S.S.R.

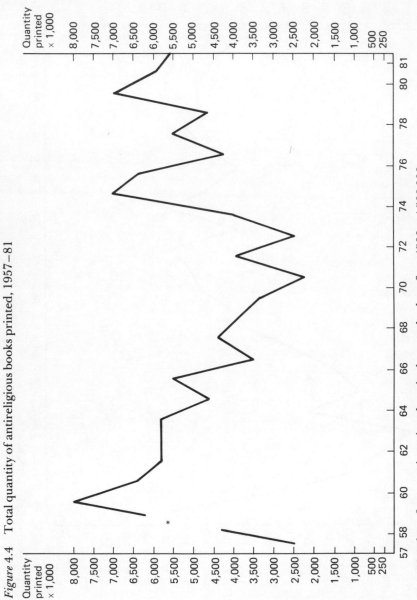

Figure 4.4   Total quantity of antireligious books printed, 1957–81

Note: Numbers for quantity printed are in thousands, therefore 4500 = 4 500 000;
*no data available for 1958.

Figure 4.5   Average circulation (no. of copies printed) per book, 1957–81

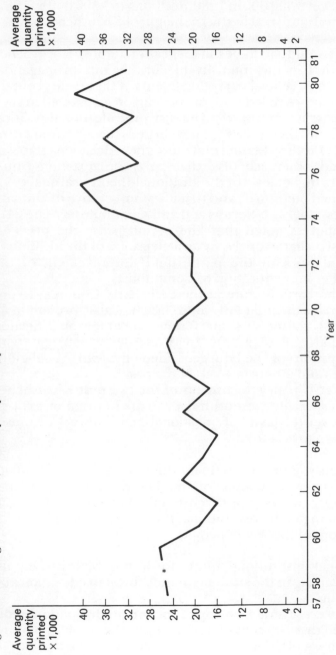

Note: Numbers for average quantity printed are in thousands, therefore 36 = 36 000;
* no data available for 1958.
Source: Yezhegodnik Knigi S.S.S.R.

copies to over 6 500 000 in 1980, declining to 5 500 000 by 1982, equal to the figure reached at the height of Khrushchev's attack in 1962.

Thus, it would hardly be fair to speak of the post-Khrushchev era as a lull in the intensity of antireligious propaganda, although most central party documents of these years contain less direct, more veiled criticism of religion, expressed in such language as: 'it is necessary to intensify the ideational-political work among the toilers'. They urged the importance of 'teaching Marxism-Leninism at the higher education establishments and other schools'; that party organizations must 'ascertain a higher level of the ideational-theoretical quality . . . of published literature', and that it was imperative to 'unmask the professional anti-Soviets and anti-Communists'. The 24th Party Congress noted that 'the period [since the previous Congress] is characterized by an activization of the ideational-theoretical work of the party, [and] improvement of the Marxist-Leninist education of Communists.'

Only the Party Statute at the 24th Party Congress (April 1971), retains the militantly antireligious clause present in all RCP–CPSU statute versions. It states in Paragraph 2, Section 'd' that a party member must 'carry on a decisive struggle with any expressions of the bourgeois ideology, with . . . religious prejudices and other survivals of the past'.

Most CPSU policy documents of the two post-Khrushchev decades, especially those addressed to the Komsomol, express concern over the laxity of 'ideational-political work'. Komsomol is taken to task for:

> frequently ignoring the main thing, namely: the development in young people of the Marxist-Leninist *Weltanschauung*, the class approach to all phenomena of life, its upbringing in the revolutionary, working class and military traditions of the Soviet people.

Educational institutions must 'form the Marxist-Leninist *Weltanschauung* in the students' minds through education and upbringing'[10]

There were several Komsomol documents that undoubtedly stimulated these directives: for example, the resolution of the 15th Komsomol Congress (1966) which complained that:

Imperialism leads a massive ideological offensive against Soviet youth. Its main aim is to disseminate in its midst individualism and social passiveness, replace the class solidarity . . . by greed for a petty-bourgeois prosperity; [to replace] ideological convictions by skepticism and critical attitude.

The resolution then elaborated on the necessity for renewing the ideology of Soviet youth. It resolved to set up special 'republican and district Komsomol schools', on the model of the party schools.

A Komsomol central document of the following year complained that members of the Komsomol working with the pioneers did not pay enough attention 'to ideational-political activities', and in the 1968 resolution, on the Komsomol's 50th anniversary, the usual appeal to follow the directives of the CPSU in inculcating in the young generations the Marxist-Leninist revolutionary ideas of class struggle, was included.[11]

Although atheism and antireligious struggle were not mentioned in these documents by name, terms like 'Marxist-Leninist ideas' or 'scientific *Weltanschauung*' were the usual euphemisms used in antireligious attacks and atheistic propaganda. An excellent illustration of this is the special ideological resolution of the CPSU Central Committee of 26 April 1979. Its main point of reference is the 25th Party Congress of 1976, the key documents of which do not mention atheism by name, but speak about a relentless progress towards Communism and call for ideological vigilance. Yet it is precisely in elaborating on these points that the Central Committee resolutions is explicit:

work out and implement concrete measures for the escalation of atheistic education. Raise the responsibility of communists and Komsomol members in the struggle against religious superstitions.[12]

It may be remembered that in the 1930s even when documents of the LMG complained that Komsomol were not giving sufficient support to the League, many acts of physical destruction of churches were committed by Komsomol brigades; similarly when the above documents called upon the Komsomol to participate more actively in ideological and antireligious campaigns, Komsomol hoodlums again harassed the Church and its adherents.[13]

There is a marked difference in style and militancy between the documents of the 1970s and those adopted by the Komsomol under Khrushchev, for instance the resolution of the 14th Komsomol Congress (1962):

> It is imperative to arm the young generation with the knowledge of scientific atheism and with the methods of work with those young people who have fallen under the influence of religion, to protect children and teenagers from the tenacious fetters of churchmen.

Or take the Komsomol Central Committee Resolution 'On the Improvement of the Scientific-Atheist Work Among Youth' of January 1957. When the party was still using only euphemistic references to religion and antireligious struggle in its documents, the Komsomol did not mince words.[14] The lack of direct attacks on religion in the Komsomol documents of the late 1960s are evidence that the party was revising its antireligious strategy and finding that former methods of attack had been ineffective.

There are obvious signs of uncertainty in the post-Khrushchev antireligious policies. On the one hand, the direct persecutions of the Khrushchev era on a mass scale were discontinued, on the other, the Soviet media boasts of the decline of religious rites (particularly weddings, funerals, baptisms), of the numbers of seminarians and, allegedly, of practising believers, in the early 1960s, as if this was a natural process and not a result of terror, harassment, threats, and physical closures of temples and seminaries. These claims were often substantiated by selected spot sociological field surveys of believers and non-believers, of which there was a large number in the 1960s and up until the early 1970s. Apparently, soon after it had become obvious that the persecutions had not been achieving the desired results, it must have been decided to make a thorough study of the believers in order to work out a more effective antireligious policy. Yet whatever the published data of such surveys, those in charge must have known they were unreliable. In fact some Soviet publications have partly admitted as much when describing the methodology of such census-taking and the use of local Komsomol activists and antireligious lectures for the purpose, and the collection of the information via personal interviews rather than anonymously.[15] The doubtfulness of the survey indicators, particularly those showing the decline of religious conviction and practices, is further corroborated by the near-absence of printed reports on any detailed and informative surveys since approximately 1973. A source who had worked as a *NiR* staff journalist from 1975 to 1980, informed this author that a team of sociologists led by Pivovarov (not to be confused with the priest Alexander Pivovarov) had carried out several detailed surveys in the late 1970s, but their findings were apparently classified, as none of them were ever published or even made available to the *NiR* staff.[16] Apparently the data so blatantly contradicted the earlier claims that no semi-officially tolerated level of rigging could save the situation. This is an illustration of how cautious one must be when using Soviet data, especially when it relates to such a touchy subject as religion and atheism.[17]

There seem to have been at least two quite different policy stages in the post-Khrushchev era, indirectly paralleling that suspect field survey. At first, it seems, the party leadership wanted to avoid direct attacks on religion, having recognized the negative effect of Khrushchev's onslaught. One of the early signs of this change of direction was an article in *Kommunist* published only a few days after Khrushchev's demotion. The author was taking up the old Bonch-Bruevich's line when he protested against wholesale condemnation of all movements arising 'under a religious form' as being reactionary. He argued that progressive movements have continued to arise from within certain religious movements and often 'millions of believers . . . and honest ministers of religion sincerely believe that their faith . . . stimulates progressive movements'. The duty of Marxists, he says, is to co-operate with such movements.[18] He was referring to the leftist religious movements of the West and the Third World. This was quite a change from Khrushchev's blanket attack on all religions.

Altogether, antireligious articles in the general Soviet press were considerably scaled down in quantity and tone in the years 1965 to 1979 (see Figures 4.1 and 4.2). *Kommunist* for 1965, for instance, contained only two directly antireligious articles by professional 'religiologists' and even they took the form of analyses of the methodology of antireligious propaganda and criticized its primitivism. Most general ideological articles were not concerned with religion. Even the hardline N. Egorychev, Secretary of the Moscow City Party Committee, in his article on the Komsomol does not mention struggle against religion as a target of Soviet youth education.[19] *Science and Religion (NiR)* at this period painted religion as the resort of old people, mainly old peasants, who find in religion their last consolation after the horrors and losses of the Second World War. The tone of most of the articles is that of a patronizing tolerance of the old and the harmless, unlike the vicious and contemptuous attacks of the recent past. However, the party would not tolerate for long this revival of the 'mechanicist' passive approach towards religion as an institution doomed to die on its own.

On 27 July 1968, *Pravda* came out with an editorial condemning this approach to religion and to antireligious propaganda. Once again, 'the Party, Komsomol and Trade Union organizations may not take an indifferent attitude to religious views which fog over the thinking abilities of a certain part of the population'. Referring to the April 1968 Central Committee Plenum's resolution on the need for the improvement of ideological work, the article called for a flexible antireligious propaganda, for more initiative on the local level, with different approaches depending on the place and situation. It criticized *Znanie* for having reduced its annual volume of antireligious lectures from 760 000 (in 1966) to less than 650 000. Another article criticized the work of the Moscow *Znanie* section in which most of the 369 professional antireligious lecturers were of the old generation and failed to communicate effectively with the mostly young and well-educated audiences. The *Pravda* editorial signalled the coming re-intensification of antireligious attacks by stressing that 'the formation of the Communist *Weltanschauung* is impossible without antireligious struggle, without an active scientific-atheistic upbringing'.[20]

This sudden re-activisation of the antireligious front was actually a logical follow-up of the Central Committee resolution of 14 August 1967, 'On the Measures of Further Development of Social Sciences and in Increasing Their Role in the Building of Communism'. It was the most important ideological party document during this relatively 'soft' era. It avoided direct reference to atheism and antireligious struggle, in contrast to similar documents of the 1958–64 era. Yet it came closest *to naming such tasks*, especially when dealing with educational establishments, the Komsomol, and the *Znanie* Society. It called for a radical improvement in the teaching of Marxist-Leninist philosophy and broader participation of scholars and social science teachers in 'people's universities, schools of communist labour, lecture- and cine- lecture-series of *Znanie*'.[21]

One of the direct results of the 1967 resolution and of the commotion which followed was the formation in December 1971 of the 'Philosophic Society of the USSR' with a declared aim, not of pursuing the truth as expected of philosophers, but of leading:

> an untiring atheistic propaganda of scientific materialism and . . . struggle against the revisionist tolerant tendencies towards religion, against all concessions to the religious *Weltanschauung*.[22]

As in the years immediately preceding 1962, the most antireligious activity was being relegated to social organizations, the Philosophic Society, Znanie, and Komsomol. Meanwhile, the CROCA/CRA assumed supreme authority over the Church, effecting discreet but direct and increasing oppression of the Church, of individual parishes and of whole dioceses.[23]

RENEWAL OF THE ATTACK

The second, more aggressive stage seems to have begun roughly from the mid-1970s, following upon the 1975 amendments to the 1929 antireligious legislation and the 25th Party Congress; it found its most explicit formulation in the 1979 CC resolution. Great importance is attributed to this document by the most authoritative Soviet atheist publication.[24] But the resolution, as well as the 25th Party Congress, was preceded by the 1974 Leningrad conference dedicated to 'The Topical Problems of the History of Religion and Atheism in the Light of Marxist-Leninist Scholarship'. During the same period, from 1971 to 1975, over 30 doctoral and some 400 magisterial dissertations were defended on the subjects of atheism and critique of religion.[25] This is evidence of the intensification of antireligious activities by the *Establishment* during the whole decade of the 1970s.

Even as physical harrassment declined after Khrushchev, the quantity and aggressiveness of antireligious publications was again on the rise, especially from the early 1970s.[26] The main mass-circulation *Znanie* periodical, *Science and Religion* (*Nauka i religiia*) since 1972 has shown signs of nostalgia for the defunct LMG,[27] implying perhaps that *Znanie* does not compare with its predecessor. The press and special conferences have continued to complain about insufficient action taken against religion and to appeal for the *activisation* of atheistic propaganda.[28]

Despite the fact that 'Foundations of Scientific Atheism', a course for students in all fields of studies in all establishments of higher education, introduced in 1954 and made obligatory in 1959, was being taught in over 500 establishments of higher education in the USSR by 1975, complaints continued that there was much laxity and little enthusiasm on the part of both students and instructors.[29] Since the early 1970s more concern has been expressed over the growing attraction of young people (presumably mostly young intellectuals) to religion via the art, architecture and music of the Church. Recognition of such non-material motives as causes of behaviour and ideas contradicts the materialistic doctrine of Marxism, causing divisions among Soviet religiologists. While one of the most prestigious religiologists, the late P. Kurochkin, continued the refrain of 'interdependence of the atheistic work with the problems of national economy' (and he is not a lonely figure in Soviet religiology), others began to point out that, deprived of political and material power by the Soviet system, and thus of the negative associations inseparable from such functions, religion has gained greater attraction for contemporary young Soviet persons. They now see the beauty of its temples and frescoes; and in their eyes the cultural–historical role of the Church is not blemished by the politico-economic aspects which now have retreated into the nebulous past. In conclusion, at least one Soviet philosopher suggests that a 'constructive cooperation of Soviet philosophers and atheists' is absolutely necessary for the success 'of militant atheism' and 'atheistic education'. In this conclusion he is supported by his apparent opponent, Kurochkin, who likewise sees a threat to Marxist atheism from the Orthodox Church's 'ever more intensive propaganda that precisely she drove Russia onto the broad track of global social development'. Contradicting his own assertions of materialistic determinism, he warns against nihilistic tendencies and results in antireligious propaganda. Often, he writes, a break with religious ethics without their replacement by a Communistic morality leads to moral decline, consumerism, lechery. When breaking with religion, writes Kurochkin, the most important thing is not the break itself, but the necessity to fill the subsequent vacuum with a new Communist moral education. The neo-god-building implications in these writings are quite obvious: in order that atheism and materialism replace the religious moral fabric in society they must acquire the properties of a religion, become a pseudo-Church.[30]

The new line of antireligious propaganda distinguishes between the alleged loyal majority of believers and the enemies of the Soviet state on the fringes of the Churches. This is the subject of the CRA secret report to the CPSU Central Committee, according to which the only commendable behaviour of a bishop or a priest is complete subordination to the local CRA plenipotentiary and absence of any pastoral activities on his part outside the routine performance of religious rites. If a certain bishop is criticized for 'high religious activity', he will be moved about all the time from one diocese to another on CRA's orders. In the same report the CRA boasts of having gained control over the Patriarch's Synod, which was forced to co-ordinate in advance the sessions' agenda and decisions to be reached with the CRA.[31]

There is a similar divide-and-rule policy toward the Baptists. Whereas persecutions were stepped up during the 1970s against the Initiative Baptists, a faction which had broken away from the official Baptist Church in 1962 in protest against a latter's subservience to the regime's antireligious orders, and whose congregations refused secular registration, the official Baptist Church was practically pampered by the regime during the same period. The treatment accorded it was much better than the one given the Orthodox Church. Its congresses were allowed genuine debates and even to cast negative votes on decisions adopted and candidates promoted by the administration, at least once succeeding in electing a person from the floor to the central administration in place of the official candidate. According to Kuroedov, the late CRA chief, since 1977 the official Baptists were allowed to open 300 additional churches (mostly by attaining registration for formerly unregistered communities); the Lutherans, 129; the Muslims, 69 mosques; the Roman Catholics, 40 churches; the Orthodox, only 33. Extrapolating his figure of 2000 Baptist and Adventist churches serving an estimated four to six million fundamentalist Protestants in the USSR and juxtaposing it with his 8500 temples serving 40–50 million Orthodox believers, we discover that the former have 50 per cent more churches per capita than the Orthodox (plus many hundreds of unregistered Baptist churches).[32] The reason for this preferential treatment of the official Baptists is quite clear: to convince the schismatic Baptists that they gain nothing by remaining in opposition.

Similarly, there is a marked difference in the treatment of believers, depending on their educational and professional levels. For instance, 'party members, administrative personnel of the high and middle executive categories, teachers and professors of all types, army officers and personnel of the Ministry of Internal Affairs, and so forth were subjected to direct persecutions for baptizing their children', and therefore had to look for priests who would agree to perform these services secretly.[33]

Peasants and workers rarely suffer serious consequences for the same acts. The uneducated and the elderly, in contrast to Khrushchev's times, are generally left alone. The young, particularly those with higher education, have been actively persecuted for practising religion, particularly if they do so openly or take part in Christian study groups or form church choirs.[34] Many members of such groups have been arrested and imprisoned, some in psycho-prisons. In the latter case the Snezhnevskian extension of Marxist materialistic determinism into psychiatry has been implied, namely, the doctrine that man's behaviour is determined by his material and social environment. Consequently, anyone who had gone through Soviet atheistic education all the way from kindergarten to university and yet remained a religious believer or, even worse, became one in mature age, is seen as a split personality or a plainly psychotic case.[35] Whereas under Khrushchev there was a general campaign of intimidation and terror against the clergy, now it is only the most dedicated priests, particularly those who attract young people and offer missionary pastoral guidance, who fall foul of the secular authorities.[36]

Another aspect of this renewed attack on religion is a regional differentiation and decentralization of tactics and methods, in accordance with the 1968 *Pravda* editorial mentioned above. Only reports on Latvia speak about the so-called KVAT clubs (Clubs of Militant Atheists) at its institutions of higher learning. Although there was an attempt by the Soviet press around 1971 to popularize the idea of these clubs, the name of which is so reminiscent of the LMG, there is no evidence that they took root anywhere except Latvia, where they have been in existence since approximately 1960. The Latvian clubs of atheistic students run schools for young lecturers of atheism and organize antireligious theatrical presentations. In western Ukraine a similar function is performed by Yaroslav Halan Clubs, which seem to specialize in fighting against the remnants of the banned Uniate Church. Special emphasis is apparently applied to antireligious propaganda in the areas which had missed Stalin's antireligious holocaust of the 1930s since they were outside his empire at the time. These clubs of militant young atheists are also active in devising and implanting the new secular rites, in an attempt to replace the church-related rites.[37]

The issue of these neo-god-building rites was not abandoned after Khrushchev's fall, but was revived as an alternative to the churches to avoid suppression by direct force. This movement can also be seen as a revival of neo-paganism, similar to Hitler's attempts in Nazi Germany. Indeed, a god-building idolisation of the people as builders of a future communistic paradise on earth becomes idolisation of the nation state. It is argued that because the state is engaged in building Communism, it must be mighty. This leads to idolisation of the physical might, power and military prowess of the socialist state. The result is an aggressive chauvinism, promoting a climate which justifies any aggression by such a state in terms of its ideology and 'faith'.

In their conventional expressions of religion the Soviets have preferred pagan revivals to Christianity. This can be illustrated from examples of official Soviet literature and from *samizdat* documents which show attempts of subversive Soviet agencies to penetrate the genuine *samizdat* in order to sow distrust among the dissidents.[38] Soviets have reported with satisfaction the re-emergence of paganism in areas without churches (which is as much a reflection of a need for religious faith as a potential for communist god-building).[39] As for the god-building rites, official Soviet atheistic literature has claimed great success in the 1960s and early 1970s in tearing people away from the Church.[40] But the accuracy of these claims is doubtful. In fact, lately they appear to have been toned down. Instead, there has been more anxiety shown regarding the survival of the church and especially the increasing participation of young people in the life and rituals of the established religions. Soviet claims of a steep decline in baptisms and marriages performed by the Church after the introduction of relevant secular ceremonies may have simply meant that more people asked their priests to perform the former secretly and privately. The point is that the State stipulated in 1962 that persons requesting church burials, weddings and baptisms must submit all their passport data to the church register. All this information must be given to Soviet officials who may harass people involved, at their places of work or education. Consequently, people began to make private arrangements with trusted priests who made no record.

Articles began to appear in the Soviet press as early as 1972 expressing great concern that Communist Party and Komsomol members were not only participating in religious rites but even initiating them. Several districts in central Russia and Siberia were named where such 'heresies' were occurring, despite the new Soviet rites and rituals. In line with the regionalist differentiation in antireligious work, it was stated that in the Moscow, Leningrad, Lipetsk, Gorky regions and in the Tatar ASSR, 'faculties and departments for training atheist lecturers have been created in the evening universities of Marxism-Leninism; in the Ukraine, Moldavia, and Lithuania seminars exist on a permanent basis' for the same purpose. Yet the Party ideological department found all of this insufficient to counter the influence of religion, especially on the younger generation, finding the media atheistic material unconvincing and of very low quality, and pointed out that in some areas, for instance Uzbekistan, the quantity of antireligious lectures actually declined. It appears that the Establishment's main concern was with the increasing amount of indifference to atheism and atheistic propaganda, a kind of agnosticism as it were, in the ranks of Soviet youth.[41]

The most important formal events in the state's policies towards religion of the post-Khrushchev years have been in the area of codification (discussed in the second chapter). The latest Soviet Constitution implied a right to remove children from actively religious families. This was spelled out much more clearly in the new family legislation of 1968 and in the laws on national education of 1973. Both maintain that it is the duty of parents or guardians to bring up children in the spirit and morals of Communism, which means active atheism. Another article of the family code allows the courts to deprive parents of their parental rights if they 'do not fulfil their obligations as to the upbringing of their children', which presumably means if they fail to bring up their children as atheistic Communists.[42] Some laws passed between 1966 and 1975 dealt directly with Church–State relations, ending some of the ambiguities of the Khrushchev era. Predictably, the comments of the late CRA chairman, V. Kuroedov, were that the new laws represented a marked improvement in the status of the Church. But his own deputy, V. Furov, inadvertently admitted the miserable legal position of the Church and her hierarchy in his comments on the history of the Soviet laws on religion. He states:

> Not a single religious organization has the right of interference in the activities of another against the latter's will: appoint priests not wanted by that organization, take away a temple from it ... because these are leased by the Soviet executive organ exclusively to the local group of believers.

That is, the Church hierarchy has no disciplinary powers over its parishes, laity or parish clergy whatsoever in the Soviet law. Similarly, as Furov explains in so many words, the parish priest, being an appointee of the bishop, has no administrative or economic powers in the parish either. Moreover, although the Soviet law permits 'uncontrolled freedom' of sermons from the pulpit, they may only be 'of exclusively religious character'. Neither Soviet law nor Furov gives any definition of the above phrase; but Furov adds that any 'bourgeois- anarchic' content in a sermon is criminally punishable. Furov's secret reports to the CPSU Central Committee cited earlier give explicit illustrations of what is meant by these limitations when they mention persecution of clergymen for criticizing Marxist atheism and materialism in their sermons.[43] In fact, the aim of Soviet laws on religion, past and present, has been to make the Church as passive as possible.

An *Ukaz* by the RSFSR Supreme Soviet Presidium of 18 March 1966, 'On the Administrative Responsibilty for Violation of the Laws on Religious Cults', enumerates only violations by churchmen, such as evasion of registration of a religious community with the state organs, violation of the (state) rules on religious performances and carrying out of special services for youth. No punishments are mentioned for violations by the secular authorities.[44] The 1975 amendments of the 1929 legislation raised the status of the CRA from that of a liaison body between the Church and the Soviet Government to that of administrator over the Church and the bishops and greatly increased its authority. Every parish, including those in the process of formation, was now rendered powerless and placed completely at the mercy of the CRA which alone had the authority to grant them registration. One of the amendments states:

> A religious society or a group of believers may begin to function only after the Council of Religious Affairs . . . has arrived at a decision regarding the registration of the society or a group.

In other words, a group of believers applying for registration is legally deprived of the right to communal worship while waiting for the registration.

Other amendments stated that the CRA arrives at its decisions on the recommendation of the local government of the given town or district. The believers could only wait, pray (but not communally) and hope. They are permitted to submit their original petition to the local government, but not to begin to meet regularly or keep up the spirit of community worship of the parish-to-be. The local government must submit the petition with its comments and recommendations to the CRA within one month – the views and comments of the local government on the issue are not conveyed to the petitioning believers. Then the CRA may take any time it wishes to arrive at its decision, which is final. This weakens the position of the religious society. In the past it dealt with the local government where it could argue and appeal its decisions, or eventually present its case to the Patriarchate which could and often did take up its case on a much higher level with the CRA (CROCA in those days). But now the distant and lofty CRA in Moscow is the first and last authority, dealings with which for a provincial church group are clumsy, complicated, and expensive.[45] The CRA secret report to the CPSU Central Committee leaves no doubt that the purpose and function of the CRA is to strangle the Church or at least to demoralize her internally by using all forms of intimidation, blackmail and threats to the clergy.[46]

Yet the legislation comes one step closer to granting the Church legal status by permitting both diocesan or spiritual centres and religious societies and parishes to build and own secular buildings for residence or administrative use, or for the production of articles necessary for the given religious cult. The existing laws on religion are being revised at the time of this writing, apparently under the direct pressure of the Moscow Patriarchate.[47] The bits and pieces of these revisions have been appearing periodically in the *Journal of the Moscow Patriarchate*. One of the earliest revisions requalified the clergy's income for the purposes of taxation as of January 1981, from Article 19, meant for commercial private enterprise, to Article 18, equalizing the legal status of clergy income with that of medical private practice or that of private educators. The maximum income tax according to Art. 18 (that above 7001 roubles p.a.) is 81 per cent, according to Art. 19 it is 69 per cent of income.[48] Curiously, professors at the theological schools and all clergy and laity working for the Department of External Ecclesiastical Relations of the Church, although also paid from Church funds emanating from believers' donations, are taxed similarly to all Soviet employees, with the tax ceiling of 13 per cent, in recognition of their contribution to the Soviet image abroad, at least indirectly rewarding subservience to the state.[49] Other published bits of the presumably new legislation equalized the clergy with the rest of the citizenry as to property and inheritance rights, and as to the privileges granted to war veterans should a member of the clergy be a former Soviet soldier or officer.[50] But the most interesting innovations have extended the rights of religious societies – i.e. the parish lay organizations (of at least twenty persons) – considerably. The religious society has at last been officially granted the status of a legal person, with the rights of signing legally binding contracts with Soviet trade unions as well as independent workers for building projects and similar works. The new amendment does not specify any more the character of the building a religious society may build 'for its needs', but presumably it includes the right to build not only residences and administrative centres but also temples for worship; because a subsequent paragraph says:

> Should a house of worship . . . be state property in leasehold of a religious society in accordance with a contract, its insurance at the cost of the society is compulsory.

Presumably this means that henceforth temples may also be *owned* by religious societies when either built or bought by them; as the law spells out for the first time that buildings 'bought or built' by a religious society 'become a property of the religious society'. Judging by past precedents, the ambiguity left in the law by not specifying the right to own temples is there to leave the State room to resist 'uncontrolled' dissemination of new churches, especially those owned by the church bodies.

The atheistic State, however, continues to be well 'protected' for the time being. First, the religious societies may buy or build only 'in accordance with the existing regulations': meaning, they have to gain the CRA's permission first of all to legally exist, i.e. to be registered, and this remains, as we have seen, a totally arbitrary right of the CRA and the local Soviet government bodies. Second, although as a legal person the religious society receives full control over its bank account (also spelled out in the new legislation of late 1985), the body itself can be heavily infiltrated and controlled by state agents, owing to the right of the local government bodies to reject elected parish officials and to inject the body with their people. Thus, unless the legal-person status is also extended to the clergy, the latter's (i.e. the Church's) real rights and prerogatives may be even more effectively curbed *vis-à-vis* the lay parish organization now gaining the power that it lacked before.

What is an unquestionable gain for the Church *per se* though these amendments is that the rights of children and adolescents

to be in church have now been affirmed in the written form for
the first time in Soviet law. In the past clergy has often been
persecuted for involving minors in church services and in
1961–4 even for serving a liturgy in the presence of minors.
Children ten years of age and over may now actively participate
'in the ritual', i.e. serve as acolytes, psalmists or choir singers;
while children of any age may be present at church services and
receive communion.[51]

By this differential policy of 'carrot and stick' – the disparity
between the taxation levels for the clergy useful and useless to
the state, the threat of deregistration for a missionary zeal and
total devotion to Christ contrasted with a tolerant attitude to
lukewarm clergy, etc. – the regime seems to indicate that it has
reluctantly reconciled itself to the notion that religion is here to
stay. All the regime can hope to do is to minimize its 'harmful'
impact on the Marxian social structure by the above measures.

ATHEISM'S NEW OFFENSIVE . . . OR DEFENSIVE?

The authoritative *Problems of Scientific Atheism* (*Voprosy nauchnogo ateizma, VopNAt* for short) began to point out in the latter
half of the 1970s the inadequacy of explaining the persever-
ance of religious beliefs in the USSR solely in terms of the
'survivals of the pre-revolutionary past'. 'The vast majority of
members of religious communities are under sixty years of age
and were born and raised after the October Revolution, not to
mention the younger generations of believers,' says one article.
Another adds that although social conditions for the existence
of religion do not exist in a socialist state, the complexity of the
phenomenon of religion is such that not only does it continue to
survive, but 'reproduces itself and shows signs of new vitality'.
As in the debates of the 1920s, 1930s and 1950s, the article takes
to task those atheists who claim that religion will die away with
the disappearance of the last traces of a class society, that is
those who treat religion in a classically Marxist context. Such
people fail to notice the dynamics of religion, and the fact that
the new generations of believers are often well-educated Soviet
citizens, so their religiosity cannot be brushed aside as a sign of
intellectual ignorance and backwardness.[52] The Brezhnev
speeches at the 25th (1976) and 26th (1981) party congresses

and the 26 April 1979 CPSU Central Committee resolution 'On Further Improvements in the Ideological, Politico-Educational Work' called for a 'complex approach' to ideological questions, harking back to Lunacharsky and Yaroslavsky during the time of the Second LMG Congress. These remarks were immediately picked up by atheistic authors as being new directives for atheistic propaganda. Furov, the author of most of the secret reports on the Church, saw this 'newness' already in Brezhnev's 1977 Constitution − namely, in its Article 52 which had replaced the phraseology of Article 124 of Stalin's Constitution. Whereas the latter had spoken of the freedom of antireligious propaganda, the 1977 Constitution spoke of freedom of atheistic propaganda. Furov interpreted this as a difference between a negative approach and a positive one: replacement of the religious *Weltanschauung* with an atheistic one. Kurochkin added that the 1979 CC Resolution resulted in a more active antireligious propaganda, embracing all aspects of public life and culture, with a more intensive participation in it of CP organizations, the mass media, higher and secondary schools, as well as institutions of culture and scientific research.[53] Sophistry of the language aside, we ought to remember that there is nothing new in this; this was the crux of Yaroslavsky's arguments against the radicals from *Bezbozhnik u stanka* from 1928 to 1930.

What is more significant is that all these speeches and resolutions were clearly seen as signals for further escalation of the intensity of antireligious activities, as witnessed by the resolutions of the 1982 19th Komsomol Congress. While the 18th Congress, meeting only four years earlier, still avoided direct attack on religion, preferring euphemisms, the 19th one ordered all local Komsomol committees 'to perfect the atheistic upbringing of the young generation, to profoundly expose the antiscientific essence of religious ideology and morals':

> In order to improve the efficiency of atheistic upbringing, the struggle with religious survivals and traditions . . . it is recommended that the Komsomol organizations:
>
> − explain to the youth the antiscientific essence of religious ideology from the position of a class approach. More attention should be paid to the study of the foundations of scientific atheism in the system of Komsomol political

education ... intensify criticism of the clerical bourgeois propaganda, its attempts to use different channels for the revitalization of religious organizations in our country ...

– make a fuller use of the cinema, the theatre, institutions of culture and libraries for the scientific-atheistic propaganda ...

– improve individual atheistic work with children and teenagers, especially with those stemming from religious families; recruit young teachers, pioneer and Komsomol workers for this work ... Educate militant atheists, form active atheistic public opinion, do not leave without an exacting reprimand every case of the Komsomol members' participation in religious rites.[54]

As we see, there is nothing new in the warnings, in the methods of antireligious work, or in the complaints that Soviet Komsomol youth continues to frequent churches and, at least in some cases, to prefer genuine religious rites to the neo-god-builders' ersatz rituals. What is puzzling, however, is that it took the Komsomol fourteen years to reflect in its major policy document the above *Pravda* editorial's warning about 'the dissemination of religious views ... among children and teenagers'. Probably a clue to this puzzle is to be found in two ideological policy editorials in the two top ideological journals of the Soviet Union, *Voprosy filosofii* and *Kommunist*, marking the sixtieth anniversary of Lenin's 'On the Importance of Militant Materialism'. *Kommunist* in particular admits a growing apathy towards questions of Marxist theory and ideology on the part of the younger generation, including young Soviet intellectuals, and even 'philosophers' (*sic*). This trend is blamed on the 'bourgeois philosophers' who charge 'the Marxist-Leninist philosophy *per se*' with responsibility 'for the individual negative facts in the history of Soviet science connected with a nihilistic attitude towards the theory of relativity, genetics and cybernetics'. Consequently, 'some Soviet philosophers and representatives of other fields of scholarship' not only fall into the positivist trap of 'creeping empiricism', claiming that sciences are a 'philosophy unto themselves', but even treat every 'statement of principle by the party leadership on ideological errors ... in individual scholarly works as ...

diktat and violation of freedom of scientific research and of the autonomy of science'.

Turning directly to questions of atheism, the journal attacked 'certain god-seeking motifs ... mystical subjects ... aesthetization of religious images, church leaders, romanticisation of [the Orthodox monastic institution of] elders [*starchestvo*], identification of national traditions ... with the church traditions and rites' in the works of contemporary (mostly young) Soviet writers. 'Problems of atheistic education,' declared *Kommunist*, 'remain a topic for today.'[55]

This is seconded by *Vop. fil.*, which incidentally speaks not of an offensive but of a necessity 'to defend ... scientific materialism'. In its thesis on the topicality of Lenin's 1922 article for the present day, the journal sees historico-ideological parallels between the time of the writing of the article and today. Having lost the duel with Bolshevism in the open Civil War, the Russian bourgeoisie allegedly tried in the early 1920s 'to stifle the young Soviet republic' on the ideological front by setting up free religio-philosophical academies, study circles, and periodicals (the article passes over in silence Lenin's real method of dealing with these philosophers: by arresting and expelling all of them abroad and closing the institutions and their journals by force). Lenin's article was the Marxist-Leninist response and policy directive. Now the would-be bourgeoisie, having witnessed 'the catastrophe of traditional rationalistic values' has been turning towards the irrational, searching an escape from the scientific-technical revolution in Gnosticism and other forms of mysticism. All this adds particular topicality to Lenin's article and to the necessity to intensify antireligious struggle; which, according to the journal, is still qualitatively quite weak, lacking (after nearly seventy years and billions of roubles and millions of tonnes of paper expended on antireligious propaganda) 'fundamental work on the history and theory of atheism, criticism of religions, practical scientific-atheistic propaganda ... highly qualified cadres of atheists'.[56] In other words, the atheistic cart is still there where it was in 1922.

No wonder that after such an admission the CPSU Central Committee came out with another militant resolution a year later. The task set by the June 1983 Plenum for the party and its ideological workers was 'to form a scientific, Marxist-Leninist

Weltanschauung in all Soviet people'. The General Secretary Andropov (Gorbachev's 'godfather' in the Mafia sense of the term) promised that 'the ideological work is quickly becoming the first priority [of] the party committees on all levels'. Each citizen, said Andropov, must 'become an active builder of communism'; and Chernenko added, 'Communists are consistent atheists'. The Plenum Resolution avoided dotting the i's on this issue, leaving the interpretation to the ideological workers, who, as could be expected, stressed the direct bearing of the Plenum Resolution 'on the overcoming of the religious survivals in socialist society'.[57]

According to inside Church information, pressures against the Church have been on the rise once more in the 1980s. The Church sees it, however, as rearguard attacks of an ideologically bankrupt but physically powerful enemy. This opinion seems to be borne out by the ideological policy statements cited above. The preference of the top leaders themselves not to get directly implicated in this new offensive may have been guided as much by the uncertainty of gaining an ideological victory over religion and a desire to have some room for manoeuvrability, as by a desire not to antagonize the believers too much now, on the eve of the Millenium of Russia's Christianity.

THE MILLENNIUM AND THE SOVIETS

As 1988, the one thousandth anniversary of the official date of the beginning of Russia's conversion to Christianity, draws nearer, an undeclared duel between the Russian Church and the Soviet ideological sector over the meaning of the date and the role of the Church in Russian history and culture has been gaining momentum. Officially, the state expressed its formal if very modest gesture of goodwill towards the Church by returning to her the most ancient monastery of Moscow, that of St Daniel – in ruins to be sure, after decades of its use first as a prison for juvenile delinquents, then as a warehouse and factory, where church sanctuaries were deliberately turned into public lavatories. The rebuilding of the monastery will cost the Church over 5 000 000 roubles.[58] Believers' requests to return the most ancient monastery of Russia, that of the Kiev Caves, for the same occasion, and several other most revered

monasteries and churches, have fallen on deaf ears. Nevertheless, the return of St Daniel's monastery was a gesture of
positive recognition of the Church as a historical phenomenon.

At the same time, throughout the 1970s and 1980s, attacks of
the Soviet media upon the Church as a cultural and historical
phenomenon have been mounting. The Church is accused of
having no legitimate claim to having been the source and the
champion of Russian culture, of the development of the
Russian national-historical consciousness and of the struggle
for the survival and unity of the Russian nation. This harks
back to the themes of the LMG, particularly of its Second
Congress in 1929, and the 1930 Second Plenum of its Central
Council when it attacked any association of Russian culture
with the Church.[59] Apparently, the topic of the role of the
Church in history and culture is particularly painful to the
Soviets because of the paucity of their own history and their
unattractive record of general cultural nihilism and of wholesale destruction of cultural monuments, churches, monasteries, ancient palaces, icons and religious manuscripts;[60] and
also in view of the fact that 'probably never before has history
had such a mighty power of attraction [for the Soviet public] as
today'.[61] Publications that can safely be considered the mouthpiece of the party's general line regarding the forthcoming
Millenium, accuse the Church of capitalizing on the jubilee in
order to 'attract towards the Orthodox Church the attention of
the unbelieving citizens of the socialist state, especially those
who show interest in their nation's past, in which the Church
did play a not unimportant role'.[62]

The task, obviously set by the party for Soviet religiologists, is
to minimize and compromise this historical role of the Church.
One of the primary aims is to upset the popular Slavophile
thesis that, in contrast to most of their western neighbours, the
Slavs in general and eastern Slavs in particular had had almost
no culture and a very amorphous form of paganism prior to the
adoption of Christianity. Consequently, the new Christian
culture was grafted almost on a *tabula rasa*, and the Russian
people thus became an Orthodox Christian nation from its
foundations, a New Testament nation, a 'God-bearing' people.
As a counter-argument, Soviet authors insist that there is new
evidence of stone structures and frescoes in Kiev going back
several decades before 988, that there are written Byzantine

references to the existence of some Russian script in the late ninth century and of translation of Russo-Byzantine treaties of the early tenth century into Russian. Hence, they argue, literacy as well as arts and architecture preceded the official conversion of Russia. But this proves little. Historians, including Soviet historians (who use this argument to show the arbitrariness of the 988 date), hypothesis that the early Kiev had been largely Christianized by its pre-Riurikide princes Askold and Dir, who were treacherously killed in the early tenth century by the heathen Prince Oleg invading Kiev from Novgorod, causing the reversion to paganism. Moreover, the Byzantine reference to a Russian script relates to a Russian translation of the Scriptures and other church books in the Russian northern and eastern Black Sea areas, and both are related to and originate by Byzantium and Christian sources.

The other major attempt to minimize and neutralize the 988 date is to argue that it was merely the date of enforced mass baptism of the population of Kiev (and later Novgorod) by its authoritarian Prince Vladimir, while the conversion of the rest of the nation took several centuries, and a pagan–Christian dualism in the popular beliefs and practices of the nation survived right into the twentieth century. To further weaken the importance of the Millenium date, a 1500th anniversary of the city of Kiev was invented literally out of thin air and celebrated in 1980–82.[63]

The Soviet line regarding the importation of Christianity from Byzantium is that although it is a culture phenomenon, Christianity has had the effect of freezing cultural development. It is alleged that the first historical stage of Christianity expressed itself in the destruction of the great cultures of antiquity. They admit that during the Dark Ages the learned monks performed the role of sustaining some form of literacy and cultural development. But once culture had spread into secular society, the Church was said to have played a reactionary role, discouraging secular culture, and persecuting secular forms of drama, music and art. Eventually there was a fourth stage, which was a secular revolt against the Church and her stagnating policies, ending in the triumph of 'progressive forces' over Church culture. Jumping on the bandwagon of the currently fashionable preservationists, *Nauka i rel.*, lately the general Soviet media, has attempted to present itself and the

Soviet state as champions of the preservation of cultural and historical monuments, especially church and monastic art and architecture, and it has condemned acts of vandalism. At the same time, the 1930s attacks against the Church for an alleged lack of national patriotism have been revived. The Church hierarchy is attacked for alleged collaboration with all the invaders of Russia, from the Tatars and Poles (in the seventeenth century) to the Germans in the Second World War. It is denied that the Tatars had spared the Church from destruction out of their general respect for religion. The Soviet line is that the reason for the privileges granted by the Tatars to the Russian Church was her collaboration with and support for them because of Byzantine state interests. The clumsy evidence produced is that a Tatar khan once said the churches should not be taxed because the clergy 'prays for us'; whereas in fact such prayers 'for the caesar of this land' are a regular part of each liturgy. The fact that the Church supported Prince Dimitry Donskoy's national struggle against the Tatars is presented as an exception and a situation in which the Church could not take any other position. Similarly, the patriotic stand against the Polish invaders of Patriarch Germogen and his subsequent martyrdom at their hands is interpreted as a last-moment turn-around forced upon the Church by a surge of national patriotic sentiment, making it impossible for Germogen to take any other position. The accusation of collaboration with the Nazis is based on the simple fact that the Church and believers took advantage of greater religious tolerance of the German occupiers in the Second World War and began to open churches, establish dioceses, and reconstruct the Church out of the ruin to which it had been reduced by the Bolsheviks. These facts, of course, are overlooked and never mentioned by Soviet authors.[64]

Similarly, the impact of Byzantium and the influence of its ideas and laws in the formation of the Russian state is minimized by exaggerating beyond all proportions the pre-Christian Kievan state which 'had existed already for over a century, had politically strengthened itself and appeared before the whole world as a mighty power'.[65]

At the same time, when discussing the impact of the Church's teaching on morality and ethics of the nation, the example of the mad and psychotically cruel Ivan the Terrible is brought in;

and it is claimed that he had been brought up by the Church, was a connoisseur of theology and the Scriptures, and that he could well have been inspired by the Scriptures (particularly by the Old Testament) for his tyranny. Even the teaching of monogamy is denied to the influence of Christianity. The claim is that the pre-Christian Russians were monogamous, except for some lecherous princes, including St Vladimir who among his multiple concubines had three Christian wives (Czech, Bulgarian and Greek princesses) – that is, their Christian parents saw nothing wrong in polygamy.[66]

Much space has been dedicated to belittling and blackening the role of the monasteries in the history of Russia. The reason given by Nikolai Gordienko, one of the leading religiologists and anti-Church polemicists, for so much attention to this subject is that the Church and her authors and sermonizers have been systematically 'misinforming' the Soviet public about the true history of monasticism. Consequently, today, monasticism has become popular not only with Soviet believers, but also with 'unbelievers' (*sic*).[67]

Gordienko's polemics consist in using half-truths, presenting only one side of historical facts without their proper context, and concealing inconvenient facts. Contemporary Russian Orthodox Church historians and theologians, as well as clergy sermons, are constantly quoted and attacked. They are often accused of deliberate misinformation, which at any time can be interpreted as slander: that is, the authors can be held criminally responsible for their writings and statements on the Millenium and its impact on Russia's history, culture and morals. That the attack has been interpreted precisely in this way within the Moscow Patriarchate seems to have been confirmed by the current uncertainty within the Moscow Patriarchate of the manner and scope of Church celebrations of her Millenium that will be allowed by the Soviet state in 1988. This uncertainty has been confided by some persons within the Patriarchate to friendly visitors from abroad.[68]

However, Gordienko's policy directive, we can presume, tells him not to totally condemn the Church, which is still of great use to the Soviets in supporting their foreign policies and 'peace' propaganda at international forums. This role of the Church and its use by the Soviet state has to be somehow logically brought into focus and the duality should not appear to be too contradictory. So, regarding the contemporary Orthodox Church in the USSR, Gordienko says the Church was forced to make peace with the socialist system and accept socialism as a praiseworthy social system in order not to lose all its flock. Hence today the Russian Church is a loyal institution upholding Soviet foreign and domestic policies, having borrowed these attitudes from the Renovationists which she had fought. What is passed over in total silence, of course, is the persecutions of the 1920s–1930s and the inconsistency between the assertion that the Church was forced to the loyal positions by its laity and the (concealed) fact that the Renovationists had failed precisely because their loyalty to the Soviet system had resulted in the loss of its lay flock.

Be that as it may, Gordienko concludes that the Church is approaching the Millenium of the conversion of the city of Kiev, which she 'bastardizes' as the Millenium of Russia's Christianization, with a reduced flock, far from being in a jubilee state (again passing over in silence the Soviet state limitations and pressures imposed on her as the reason for her low profile).

After hitting the Church hard he makes the grudging admission that her role in Russian history has been quite significant:

> The baptism of the Kievites by the order of Prince Vladimir ... was a socially determined action of a far-sighted statesman pursuing concrete and quite terrestrial (political and ideological) aims: . . . to make use of religion, which had been formed in a class society, for the strengthening of the domineering role of the exploiting classes being formed at the time; for the strengthening of the princely power, for the achievement of greater firmness of the Old Russian state and of the acceptance of the growing oppression by the masses through humility and subservience [taught by the Church].

The Church, he says, was an institution 'which blessed feudal relations'. And as long as feudalism was a progressive force in history, the role of the Church was likewise historically progressive and useful. Once feudal relations began to be replaced by commerce and capitalism and thus became a reactionary force, so did the Church. Any other interpretation of the Church's role in history 'is perversion of history at it crudest', declared Gordienko menacingly,[69] while ignoring the fact that the Old Russian society, particularly the Kievan one, was not feudal by any stretch of imagination, except in the fantasies of Marxist dogmatists.

Appendix[1]

The following is a collection of the major laws and regulations governing and affecting the existence of religious organizations. Particular emphasis has been placed on the earlier bodies of laws and regulations, as these formed the basis of the relationship between the State and religion and the attitudes towards believers. Much has been omitted for the sake of brevity and to avoid repetition. In addition, some of the texts have been abbreviated in order to avoid technical details and matter not pertaining directly to believers.

ACTS OF THE SOVIET GOVERNMENT ON RELIGION AND THE CHURCH, PRECEDING THE DECREE ON THE SEPARATION OF CHURCH AND STATE

Act of the Commissar of Education, December 11, 1917

... It is declared that all control of educational matters shall be handed over to the Commissariat of Education from all religious organizations. All church/parish schools, teachers colleges, religious colleges and seminaries, ... all missionary schools, [and] all academies ... with all of their property, both movable and immovable, i.e. with all buildings ... land, with all gardens, with all libraries ... valuables, capital and vulnerable papers ... and with all that was credited to the above mentioned schools and institutions, shall likewise be handed over to the Commissariat of Education. ...

(Chairman of the Council of People's Commissars V. I. Lenin)

Decree on the dissolution of marriage, December 18, 1917

... 12 ... All records currently in the possession of any religious organization are to be handed over to the local courts without delay. ... All decisions regarding the dissolution of marriages already made or in the process of being ruled upon by any religious organization or by any of its representatives, are hereby declared destroyed and not valid, they are to be decided upon by the local courts upon their taking possession of the appropriate records. Parties not wishing to wait until this takes place have the right to issue a new petition for the dissolution of their marriage as described by this decree. ...

(Chairman of the Council of People's Commissars V. I. Lenin)

Decree on Civic marriages, on children, and on the introduction of books or records, December 18, 1917

The Russian Republic as of now recognizes only civil marriages. ...

(Chairman of the Council of People's Commissars V. I. Lenin)

132

Order of the People's Commissar of military affairs No. 39, January 16, 1918

On the prohibition of all powers of religious departments

1. All religious ministers and practisers currently employed by war departments are discharged.
2. All powers of military clergy are dissolved.
3. War committees have the right to retain religious ministers, providing this is in accordance with the desires of their members.
4. In the above case the support of such a minister will be entirely up to the concerned committees.
5. All wealth and property of military churches, without exception, is to be handed over to the war committees of the units involved for safe-keeping . . .

Order of the People's Commissar of Welfare, January 20, 1918

The distribution of subsidies for the maintenance of churches, chapels, and for the operations of religious orders are to be halted. Governmental support of clergy and teachers of religion is to be halted as of the 1st of March of this year . . . Church services and the fulfilment of the needs of believers may be continued on the condition of an expressed desire by collectives of believers who must assume the full cost of repairs and maintenance of churches, [and] of all inventory and all servers.

(People's Commissar A. Kollontai)

LAWS OF 1918

SEPARATION OF THE CHURCH FROM THE STATE AND THE SCHOOLS FROM THE CHURCH

Decree of the Soviet of People's Commissars January 21, 1918

1. The Church is separated from the state.
2. Within the territory of the Republic, it is forbidden to pass any local laws or regulations which would restrain or limit the freedom of conscience or which would grant special rights or privileges on the basis of the religious confession of citizens.
3. Every citizen may confess any religion or profess none at all. Every legal restriction connected with the profession of no faith is now revoked.
   Note: In all official documents every mention of a citizen's religious affiliation or nonaffiliation shall be removed.
4. The actions of the government or other organizations of public law may not be accompanied by any religious rites or ceremonies.
5. The free performance of religious rites is granted as long as it does not disturb public order or infringe upon the rights of citizens of the Soviet Republic. In such cases the local authorities are entitled to take the necessary measures to secure public order and safety.

6. No one may refuse to carry out his citizen's duties on the grounds of his religious views.
7. Religious vows or oaths are abolished. In necessary situations a ceremonial promise will suffice.
8. The acts of civil status are registered exclusively by the civil authorities at the departments for the registration of marriages and births.
9. The school is separated from the church. The teaching of religious doctrines in all state and public schools, or in private educational institutions where general subjects are taught, is prohibited. Citizens may receive and give religious instructions privately.
10. All ecclesiastical and religious associations are subject to the same general regulations to private associations and unions, and shall not enjoy any benefits, nor any subsidies either from the Government, nor from any of its autonomous or self-governing institutions.
11. Religious organizations are prohibited from calling obligatory gatherings for its members, from establishing membership dues, and from disciplining any of its members in any way.
12. No church or religious organizations are permitted to own property. They do not have the rights of a legal person.
13. Any and all property that any church or religious organization may have in Russia is hereby declared to be public property. Buildings and objects required specifically for religious ceremonies, are to be given only by special decrees by either local or central governmental powers, for free use for the appropriate religious organization.

(Chairman of the Council of People's Commissars, V. I. Lenin)

Constitution of the Russian Soviet Federated Socialist Republic, July 10, 1918

Chapter Five

13. For the goal of securing true freedom of conscience for workers, the church is separated from the state and the schools are separated from the church, but all citizens are free to carry out religious and antireligious propaganda.

Chapter Thirteen

65. The following categories may not vote and cannot be elected . . .:
    (b) those who do not work for their income . . .
    (d) monks and clergy . . .

Declaration of the People's Commissar of Education, February 17, 1918

All teachers of religion of all religions are relieved of all of their duties and responsibilities as of the first of January, 1918.

(People's Commissar A. V. Lunacharsky)

Declaration by the People's Commissar of Public Property, January 14, 1918

The Court Clergy is abolished.

The protection of Court churches, as artistic and national monuments, is temporarily assigned to the committees and commissars of those places and institutions to which the churches are attached. If any religious society declares a desire to celebrate in these churches, then it will have to take upon itself the full cost of supporting the clergy, other religious servers and other associated costs . . .

(Deputy People's Commissar Iu. Flakeerman)

Declaration of the People's Commissar of Justice, August 24, 1918

6. The minimum of local citizens required, in order to receive the use of religious property, shall be set by the local Soviet of Worker and Peasant Deputies, but this number may not be less than 20.

    [Thus a local Soviet could very easily prevent a Church from opening by setting the minimum number at an unrealistically high level. Ed.]

8. Those who take upon themselves the use of a church building are obligated to: . . . in the event of the revelation by the Soviet of Worker and Peasant Deputies of embezzlement or ill usage of lent property, immediately give up said property to the Soviet of Worker and Peasant Deputies upon their first demand. . . .

10. All local citizens of the corresponding faith have the right to . . . take part in the administration of the church property to the same degree as the founders of the association.

    [Thus the local administration could fill the church's administration with its agents and thus control it to such an extent as to even 'voluntarily' close the church. Ed.]

29. In government and all publicly administered buildings, it is, without exception, forbidden to:

    (a) hold religious functions or ceremonies (prayer services, funerals, etc.),

    (b) house any sort of religious items (ikons, pictures, statues of a religious nature, etc.).

31. Religious processions, and the carrying-out of any sort of religious functions outside, is allowed only with written permission from the local Soviet authority, which must be obtained for each separate occasion . . .

(People's Commissar D. Kursky)

Act #259 of the People's Commissar of Internal Affairs, July 30, 1929

4. . . . for former church/parish houses or former monastery buildings, if they are rented out to workers, they will be responsible for all repairs, and they must be charged rent equivalent to the devaluation of the property. This is to be considered as 1 per cent of the current

construction cost for stone buildings, and 2 per cent for wooden buildings.

For tenants living off non-labour income, including religious servers, the rent shall be determined as the cost of the devaluation of the property plus the interest upon the cost of the construction of the building, assumed to be up to 10 per cent per year, depending upon local conditions and the situation of the tenant.

[In other words the rent for ministers of religions was to be 5–10 times that of a worker for the same property. Ed.]

Act of the All-Russian Central Administrative Committee and Soviet of People's Commissars RSFSR, April 8, 1929

1. Persons living off non-labour income ... exceeding 3000 rubles per year, living in nationalized or municipally owned housing, cannot have their leases extended past the 1st of October 1929. ... they must be moved out without being offered alternative living space.
3. In all municipally owned or nationalized housing ... it is from now on forbidden to rent out space to those on non-labour incomes. It is also likewise forbidden to sublet, or take in as boarders those living on non-labour incomes.

    [In other words a priest cannot live with a parishioner or relative in government-owned housing. Ed.]

Decree of SNK RSFSR #23–24, 1929

1. All cemeteries ... and all funeral organizations are hereby placed in the control of local soviet deputies.

    (People's Commissar of Internal Affairs Tolmachev)

LAWS CONCERNING THE TAXATION OF RELIGIOUS CULTS AND THEIR EMPLOYEES

Circular NKF USSR, September 10, 1929 #398

1. Buildings, assigned for religious use ... and supplied free of charge for use to religious organizations, are subject to local taxes ...
4. ... nonpayment of taxes on time will result in the confiscation of the building.

    (People's Commissar of Finance Briukhanov)

Rule #21/177

1. In those municipalities where there are municipal administrators, those citizens who are deprived of civic rights [see Constitution ... 1918, chapter 13, section 65. Ed.] and thus cannot perform administrative functions are subject to a surtax.
4. ... The surtax shall not exceed 10 rubles ...

(Assistant Head of Taxation the RSFSR People's Commissariat of Finance Starobinsky)

LAWS CONCERNING CIVIL OBLIGATIONS

Law on military obligations, September 1, 1928

Section 1 . . . The armed defence of the USSR shall be carried out only by the workers. Non-worker elements are charged with the fulfilment of other tasks for the defence of the USSR.

Section 236 Citizens, freed from military service on religious ground [by local courts. Ed.] . . . are to be assigned to: in peacetime – public-benefiting work (combating natural disasters, epidemics, etc.) . . . and in wartime – special brigades for the servicing of the front and rear.

The Central Committee and the Soviet of People's Commissars of the USSR decrees:

1. Citizens assigned to home front service . . . in peacetime are subject to a special military tax for the duration of their home front service designation.
2. . . . the rate of tax shall be as follows: . . . for those with an income up to 1800 rubles – the equivalent of 50 per cent of their income tax; with an income up to 3000 rubles – 75 per cent of their income tax; over 3000 rubles – 100 per cent of their income tax . . . but the special tax shall not exceed 20 per cent of the person's taxable income.
5. The special military tax shall be collected for the first five-year period of one's home front service designation, and after this – for one year of every six years of home front service designation.

(Moscow, Kremlin, April 10, 1929)

Instruction for the fulfilment of [the above] decree, April 25, 1929

19. The maximum age for being designated for home front service is 40 . . .

(Assistant Head of Taxation)

Instruction on the elections to the Soviets, confirmed by the Presidium of the Central Committee, November 4, 1926

15. Servers of cults of all religions and beliefs, including: monks, novices, deacons, psalmers, mullas, rabbis, lamas, shamans, pastors . . . and all those who fulfil similar functions, are denied voting privileges. . . . Family members of those whose voting privileges are suspended, and if the source of their income is social benefiting labour . . .

Act of the Central Committee and the Soviet of People's Commissars, January 11, 1928

All Citizens of the USSR, who possess voting privileges . . . may organize consumer organizations to serve their consumer and household needs. . . .
[In other words, those whose voting privileges have been denied (monks, priests, etc.) could not form, participate in, or benefit from

consumer organizations. Membership in such organizations, at certain times, in some areas, was essential in order to have access to any consumer goods. Ed.]

Confirmation of the Central Committee, December 15, 1928

... Those whose voting privileges have been suspended, have the last and lowest priority in land distribution for use ... Members of land organizations [which assign all land for all use. Ed.] are considered all those who ... possess voting privileges ...

[In other words those who are not permitted to vote cannot have a voice in land allocations. This was a particularly harsh measure for village priests who often depended upon small gardens or farms for their survival. Even if the village priest did receive land, it was often the worst land available, that no one else wanted. Ed.]

Act of the Soviet of People's Commissars of the USSR, September 24, 1929

1. In all industries ... [and] in all institutions, that operate year round ... the five-day work week (four days of work and one day of rest) is to be introduced. ...

   [By this method, since only every fifth Sunday was a day of rest, regular church attendance was made impossible. The celebration of religious holidays was also made difficult by the abolition of holidays for such events as Christmas and Easter. Ed.]

The three main collections of laws and regulations governing the formal existence of religions and their relations with the state in the USSR – the 1929 Legislation on Religious Associations as amended in 1975 (LRA), the 1965 Statute of the Council for Religious Affairs (CRA), and the Instruction on the Supervision over the Fulfilment of Religious Cults (1961) – are presented below in the reverse order. The texts are abbreviated from the Russian original. The language is simplified. Some articles have simply been summarised, others were omitted in order to avoid purely technical matter or repetition from one code to the next.

THE LAWS ON RELIGIOUS ASSOCIATIONS OF 8 APRIL 1929, WITH THE JUNE 23 AMENDMENTS

Only articles directly bearing on the religious associations, their rights, etc., will be cited. The relevant Soviet authorities will appear under their current, not their 1929, designations.

3. A religious society is a local association of believers at least 18 years of age, belonging to the same religious cult, faith, orientation or sect, numbering no less than twenty persons, having come together for the joint satisfaction of their religious needs.

Laws of 1929

4. A religious society or group of believers may start its activities only after the registration of the society or group by the committee on religious matters at the proper city or district (*raion*) soviet.

5. In order to register a religious society at least 20 initiators must submit to the agencies mentioned in the previous Article an application in accordance with the form determined by the Permanent Committee for Religious Matters at the [Council of Ministers].

6. In order to register a group of believers, the representative of the group (Art. 13) must submit an application to the agencies mentioned in Article 4 of the city or district where the group is located in accordance with the form determined by the Permanent Committee for Religious Matters at the [Council of Ministers].

7. The registration agencies shall register the society or groups within one month, or inform the initiators of the denial of the registration.

Amendments of 1975

4. A religious society or a group of believers may begin to function only after the Council for Religious Affairs ... has made a decision regarding the registration of the society or group.

The decision on the registration of a religious society or a group of believers and on the establishment of a prayer house is made by the Council ... on the recommendations of the Councils of Ministers if autonomous republics or the executive committees of regional, provincial or city (Moscow and Leningrad) soviets of workers' deputies.

5. In order to register a religious society its founders, consisting of at least twenty persons, address a petition to the executive committee of the district or city soviet ... requesting the registration of the society and the opening of a prayer house ...

[The soviet] addresses the received petition of the believers with its resolution to the Council of Ministers of the autonomous republic, [or] the executive committee of the regional, provincial, city (Moscow and Leningrad) soviet ...

6. In order to effect the registration of the group, the petition signed by all the believers of the given group is submitted to the executive committee of the district or urban soviet ... which forwards this petition with its resolution attached to the Council of Ministers of an autonomous republic, to the executive committee of a regional, provincial or ([in the cases of] Moscow and Leningrad) city soviet ...

7. The Council of Ministers of an autonomous republic, or the executive committee of a regional, provincial or city (Moscow and Leningrad [only]) soviet ... having received the materials regarding the registration

8. The registration agencies shall be informed on the composition of the society, as well as on their executive and accounting bodies and on the clergy, within the period and in accordance with the forms determined by the Permanent Committee for Religious Matters at the [Council of Ministers].

10. For the satisfaction of their religious needs, the believers who have formed a religious society may receive from the district or city soviet, under a contract, free of charge, special prayer buildings and objects intended exclusively for the cult.

Besides that the believers who have formed a religious society or group of believers may use for prayer meetings other premises left to them by private persons or local soviets on lease. Such premises shall be subject to all regulations provided for in the present law relating to prayer buildings; the contracts for the use of such premises shall be concluded by individual believers on their personal responsibility. Such premises shall be subject to technical and sanitary regulations.

A religious society or group of believers may use only one prayer building or [complex of] premises.

of a society or group of believers, is to complete their scrutiny within one month and then forward them with its representation to the Council for Religious Affairs of the USSR Council of Ministers for authorization.

The Council for Religious Affairs ... studies the materials ... and makes the decision [no time limit given] whether to register or to refuse to register the ... group, and informs the latter on its decision.

8. The Council for religious Affairs keeps a register of all religious associations, houses of prayer and [other church] buildings ... [and] establishes the order of submission of data on religious societies or groups of believers, their executive and auditing organs and the clergy.

10. For the satisfaction of religious needs the believers making up a religious society may, on the decision of the Council for Religious Affairs ... receive a special building for prayer, free of charge, on the conditions ... stipulated in the agreement concluded between the religious society and a legitimate representative of the executive committee of the district or urban soviet.

In addition, believers comprising a religious society or a group of believers may use for their communal prayer other structures on leaseholding conditions placed at their disposal by individual persons or executive committees of district or urban soviets ... These structures are subject to all regulations of the legislation in force regarding house of prayer ... Moreover, these structures must correspond to the regular building and sanitary safety regulations.

A religious society or group of believers may use only one house of prayer.

11. Individual members of the executive organs of religious societies or representatives of groups of believers may make contractual agreements hiring persons to fulfil various jobs connected with guarding, repairing or procuring church property or material necessary for its preservation. [Paraphrased, D.P.]

Such contracts may not include any commercial or industrial operations, even if related to the church, e.g. leasing of candle-producing plants or printing shops for the production of religious prayer books.

Laws of 1929	Amendments of 1975
12. For each general assembly of a religious society or group of believers, permission shall be obtained: in cities from committees for religious matters of the city soviets, and in rural areas from the executive committees of the district.	12. General meetings (other than prayer meetings) of religious societies and groups of believers may take place [only] on the permission of the executive committee of the district or urban soviet . . .
18. Teaching of any kind of the religious cult in schools, boarding schools, or preschool establishments maintained by the State, public institutions or private persons is prohibited. Such teaching may be given exclusively in religious courses created by the citizens of the USSR with the special permission of the Permanent Committee for Religious Matters at the [Council of Ministers].	18. No religious doctrines whatsoever may be taught in educational institutions. The teaching of religion is permitted in theological schools only, which may be established in accordance with the existing regulations.

19. The clergy and other ministers of religion may operate only in the area of residence of members of the religious association by which they are employed and in the area of the temple where they serve.

Clergymen regularly serving two or more religious associations may minister only in the areas of residence of the members of the given religious communities.

Laws of 1929	Amendments of 1975
20. The religious societies and groups of believers may organize local, All-Russian or All-Union religious conventions or conferences by special permission issued separately for each case by: (a) the Permanent committee for Religious Matters of the [Council of Ministers] if an All-Russian or All-Union convention or congress on the territory of the RSFSR is supposed to be convoked.	20. Religious societies and groups of believers may convoke religious congresses and conferences only with the express permission of the Council for Religious Affairs in each particular case. Religious centres, spiritual administrations and other religious organizations elected at such congresses and conferences have administrative jurisdiction only over the religious (canonical) activities of religious

(b) the local Committee for Religious Matters, if a local convention is supposed to be convoked.

The permission for convocation of republican conventions and conferences shall be granted by the Committee for Religious Matters of the appropriate republic.

associations. They are supported by the contributions of religious associations collected exclusively by means of voluntary donations.

Religious centres and diocesan administrations have the right to produce church-plate and [other] objects of the religious cult, and to sell the same to societies of believers. [They also have the right] to obtain means of transportation, to rent, build and purchase buildings for their own needs in accordance with the legally established order.

25. All the property necessary for the performance of the religious rite, both that contractually leased to the believers forming the religious society, and that newly acquired or donated for the use in religious cult, is a nationalized property and is listed in the files of the local government organs.

Laws of 1929	Amendments of 1975
27. Prayer buildings and religious objects shall be leased to believers forming religious associations for use by the Committee for Religious Matters at the city or district soviet.	27. Houses of prayer and religious belongings are transferred to the believers comprising a religious society for use on conditions and in the order established in the agreement concluded between the religious society and a plenipotentiary representative of the executive committee of a district or urban soviet. . . .

28. The temples and all the cult utensils within them are handed over for the use of believers forming the religious society, on conditions stated in the agreement concluded by the religious society with a representative of the local government.

29. The agreement must state that the persons taking over the building and its contents for religious use, pledge:

(a) to preserve and protect them as state property entrusted to them;

(b) to carry out all necessary repairs and to fulfil all financial obligations connected with the rental and use of the property, e.g. for the heating, insurance, guarding, payment of taxes, special collections, etc.;

(c) to use all these properties only for the purpose of satisfying religious needs;

(d) to repay to the government the costs of any damaged or lost goods;

(e) to keep a register of all the belongings of the given temple, entering therein all additionally obtained (whether by purchase, personal donations, or receipt from other churches) objects of the religious rite . . . objects falling into disuse through wear and tear must be stricken out of the register informing the local government organ and receiving permission from the same to do so.

(f) official representatives of the local governments to be permitted by the parish executive to inspect the property and all its contents at all times except during the performance of the religious rite.

31. All local residents belonging to the same faith may add their names to those who have already signed the lease agreement, thereby obtaining equal right with the former in administering over the properties . . .

32. Every signatory may remove his/her signature at a later date, departing from the religious community. This however does not free him/her from the responsibility for the state of the property and its contents up to the moment of his/her resignation.

Laws of 1929	Amendments of 1975

33. Prayer buildings shall be subject to compulsory fire insurance for the benefit of the appropriate local government at the expense of the persons who signed the contract. In case of fire, the insurance payment may be used for the reconstruction of the prayer building destroyed by fire, or upon decision of the appropriate local government for social and cultural needs of a given locality in full accordance with the Decree of August 24, 1925 on the Utilization of Insurance Payments Acquired for Prayer Buildings Destroyed by Fire.

33. Houses of religion must be insured at the cost of the persons signing the agreement [on behalf of the religious society] [but] in favour of the executive committee of that district or urban soviet . . . on whose territory the structure is situated.

The insurance payments for prayer houses destroyed by fire and are used, in accordance with the decision of the Council of Ministers of an autonomous republic or the executive committee of a regional, provincial or city (Moscow and Leningrad [alone]) soviet . . . coordinated with the Council for Religious Affairs, for the reconstruction of the ruined buildings or for cultural needs of the district or town in which the ruined prayer house was situated.

34. If there are no persons who wish to use a prayer building for the satisfaction of religious needs under the conditions provided for in Articles 27–33, the city or district soviet puts up a notice of this fact on the doors of the prayer building.

34. If the believers do not submit a petition to lease to them for religious purposes a building and its belongings necessary for the religious cult . . . the Council of Ministers of an autonomous republic or the executive committee of a regional, provincial or city (Moscow and Leningrad [alone]) soviet . . . decides on the subsequent use of the prayer house and all its belongings in accordance with articles 40 and 41 of this enactment.

36. The transfer of a prayer building leased for the use of believers for other purposes (liquidation of the prayer building) may take place only

36. A cult building used by believers may be reassigned for other needs [i.e., a prayer house may be simply closed down] exclusively by a deci-

according to a decision of the [Council of Ministers] of the autonomous republic or oblast which must be supported by reasons, in a case where the building is needed for government or public purposes. The believers who formed the religious society shall be informed regarding such decision.

sion of the Council for Religious Affairs . . . after a request from the Council of Ministers of an autonomous republic or from the executive committee of a regional, provincial or city (Moscow and Leningrad) soviet, . . . if this building is necessary for state or public needs. Believers comprising the given religious society are to be informed of the decision.

38. Lease agreements regarding . . . houses used for religious rites can be annulled ahead of time by court action.

39. Only the CRA may close a temple by the request of the Council of Ministers of an autonomous republic, a province or a city (in the cases of Moscow and Leningrad) government.

40. Should a temple be closed, its contents are distributed thus:

(a) all goods made of precious metals and containing precious or semi-precious stones go to the local government financial organs or to the Ministry of Culture;

(b) all objects of historical and special artistic value go to the Ministry of Culture;

(c) other objects (icons, clergy vestments, etc.) having special significance for the performance of the rite are given to believers for transfer to other, active, places of worship of the same faith. . . ;

(d) . . .

(e) money, incense, candles, oil, wine, wax, firewood and coal remain with the religious society, should the latter remain in existence after the closure of the temple.

Laws of 1929

41. Prayer buildings and wayside shrines subject to liquidation, which are registered in special local agencies for State funds, may be transferred for use free of charge to proper executive committees or city soviets under the condition that they will be continuously considered as nationalized property and their use for other purposes than stipulated may not take place without the consent of the Minister of Finance.

43. When the religious association does not observe the terms of the contract or orders of the Committee for Religious Matters (on re-registration, repair, etc.), the contract may be annulled.

The contract may also be annulled

Amendments of 1975

41. Prayer houses subject to closure which are not under state protection as cultural monuments may be . . . rebuilt for other uses or demolished only be the decision of the Council for Religious Affairs . . . on the representation from the Council of Ministers of an autonomous republic [etc.]. . .

43. Religious associations may be deprived of registration if they transgress the legislation on cults.

Deregistration of religious associations is enacted by the Council for Religious Affairs . . . on the representation from the Council of Minis-

upon the presentation of lower executive committees by the [Council of Ministers] of the autonomous republic, oblast, etc.

44. When the decision of the authorities mentioned in Article 43 is appealed to the [Council of Ministers] within two weeks, the prayer buildings and property may actually be taken from the believers only after the final decision of [the Council].

45. The construction of a new prayer building may take place upon request of religious societies under the observance of the general regulations pertaining to construction and technical rules as well as the special conditions stipulated by the Permanent Committee for Religious Matters at the [Council of Ministers].

ters of an autonomous republic [etc.]. . .

44. In the case of nonobservance by the religious association of the agreement on the use of the prayer house or cult belongings the Council for religious Affairs . . . has the right to annul the agreement on a representation from the Council of Ministers of an autonomous republic [etc.]. . .

45. On the request of religious societies and with the permission of the Council for Religious Affairs . . . on the representation from the Council of Ministers of an autonomous republic [etc.] . . . believers may be permitted in individual cases to build new prayer houses out of their own resources.

46. Should the temple, owing to its age, become a hazard to the believers using it, the executive committee of the local government has the right to propose to the parish executive organ to discontinue the building's use for religious purposes until an inspection by a technical commission.

48. The technical inspection commission formed by the local government is to include a representative of the religious society in question.

49. The conclusion of the commission is final and its fulfilment is obligatory.

50. The commission's report is to state whether the building must be demolished or repaired. In the latter case the report is to detail the necessary repairs and the time needed for their conclusion.

51. In the case of the believer's refusal to carry out the required repairs, the agreement with the religious society on the lease of the property is nullified by the CRA . . .

52. The CRA also annuls the contract with the society if the commission concludes that the building must be wrecked.

Laws of 1929	**Amendments of 1975**

54. The members of the groups of believers and religious societies may pool money in the prayer building or premises and outside it by voluntary collections and donations, but only among the members of the given religious association and only for the purpose of covering the expenses for the maintenance of prayer building or premises and religious property, and for the salary of the clergy and activities of the executive bodies.

54. Religious societies and members of groups of believers may voluntarily pool their resources together and solicit voluntary collections inside the prayer house among members of the given religious association for purposes connected with the maintenance of the building, [the purchase and upkeep] of the cult belongings, the hiring of the clergy, and support of the executive organs.

57. Religious services take place in the temples without any express information to the effect of any local government organs.

Local government must be informed [advance permission has to be sought – DP] in advance, should a religious service take place in a building other than those officially assigned for such use.

58. No religious rites may be performed in any state, public or co-operative institutions and enterprises. Neither may there be any religious symbols displayed in such buildings.

This ban does not extend to special rites performed by request of a dying or gravely ill person, being in hospital or prison, if these rites are performed in special isolated rooms. Neither does the ban extend to cemeteries and crematoria.

Laws of 1929	Amendments of 1975
59. A special permission [granted] for each case separately by the Committee for Religious Matters is required for the performance of religious processions as well as the performance of religious rites in the open air. An application for such permission must be submitted at least two weeks prior to the ceremony. Such permission is not required for religious services connected with funerals.	59. Religious processions, the performance of religious ceremonies in the open air, as well as in apartments and houses of believers, may take place only by the express permission in each individual case from the executive committee of the regional or urban soviet . . . Petitions for permissions [for the above ceremonies] . . . must be submitted at least two weeks prior to the date [of the desired action] . . . Religious ceremonies in private residences requested by dying or very seriously ill believers may be performed without the [above] permission or request [of the same] . . .

60. No special permission is required for processions around the church as a part of the religious service, as long as they do not interfere with the traffic.
61. All other religious processions and all performances of religious rites outside the regular cult building require special permission of the local government in each particular case.

Laws of 1929	Amendments of 1975
63. The registration agencies of religious associations (Art. 6) submit data to the Committee for Religious Matters at the city and district soviets in accordance with the forms and within the period established by the Permanent Committee for Religious Matters at the [Council of Ministers].	63. The Council of Ministers of an autonomous republic [etc.] . . . reports all information on religious associations to the CRA . . . in accordance with the established order.

SUPERVISION OVER THE FULFILMENT OF LEGISLATION ON RELIGIOUS CULTS OF THE USSR[2]

Instruction on the application of the legislation on religious cults. Approved on 16 March 1961.

I. General

1. [Rights to believe].
2. Definition of a religious society. See LRA, Art. 3.
3. Believers forming a religious association [society or group] may:
   (a) observe religious rites, organize worship meetings as required by the given cult;
   (b) hire or elect clergymen and other personnel necessary for the observance of the cult;
   (c) use a house for prayer and other cult utensils;
   (d) collect voluntary donations within the temple for the support of the clergy, the prayer house, its property and the executive organs of religious associations.
4. On the open elections of the executive organs. The same as in the Laws on Religious Associations. See below.
5. The Council on the Russian Orthodox Affairs, the Council on Religious Cults, their local plenipotentiaries and local government organs must carry out strict supervision that the constitutional rights of believers and non-believers are observed, that no administrative methods are used in antireligious struggle, no administrative interference in the activities of a religious association, rudeness towards the clergy and insults of believers feelings.

II. The Activities of the Clergy and the Religious Associations must correspond to the following demands

6. Free performance of religious rites is warranted as long as it does not disturb public order and is not accompanied by acts infringing on the rights of Soviet citizens. Otherwise, organs of national government may take any measures deemed necessary to restore public order and security.
7. Religious associations and clergy may not:
   (a) use religious services for political pronouncements, contradicting the interests of Soviet society;
   (b) urge the believers to abstain from fulfilling their citizens' duties;
   (c) carry on propaganda aimed at tearing the believers away from active participation in the state, and the cultural and socio-political life of the country;
   (d) perform religious rites and ceremonies in the state, public and co-operative institutions and enterprises. [Exception for the sick and the dying. . .]
8. Religious associations and the clergy may not engage in any activities, except those aimed at satisfying believer's needs.
9. Meetings and processions. Same as in LRA below.

10. Religious centres, religious associations and the clergy may not:
    (a) organize special groups, etc. – as in LRA below;
    (b) organize pilgrimages to the so-called 'holy places', perform fraudulent actions aimed at raising superstitions in the masses of population in order to derive some kind of benefits (declaration of all sorts of miracles, e.g. curing of illness, prophecies, etc.);
    (c) make any compulsory collections or imposing dues on believers for the support of religious associations or other purposes;
    (d) apply any forms of compulsion or punishment to believers.
11. Religious centres, diocesan administrations and other religious organs are forbidden to:
    (a) use their resources and funds for charity or for the support of churches and monasteries, not supported by the population as it drifts away from religion, or for any other needs except for the covering of expenses required for the sustenance of the organs themselves;
    (b) convoke religious congresses and councils, establish theological schools, publish religious literature, without the express permission each time of the Council on Religious Cults or the Council for the Russian Orthodox Church Affairs.
12. & 13. Technicalities, repeated in LRA (CRA's inspections, etc.).

III. Supervision over the fulfilment of the Legislation on Cults
14. Technical.
15. On the discovery of breaches of the Legislation on Cults in the activities of a religious association or a clergyman, state of organs and officials of the CROCA/CRC must ask the said clergyman or religious association's executive organ to remove the breaches by a certain date.
    Should the said bodies continue to disregard the rules and refuse to do otherwise, the said government organs must raise the question of depriving the clergyman or the religious association of registration . . . and, in special circumstances, bring the guilty ones to justice.
16. Technical: on keeping registers, listing and reporting . . .
17. [On the duty of local CROC/CRC officials to inform the central offices on all details of local religious life, breaches of legislation by the church organs, etc.]

IV. Order and Procedures regarding Registration of Religious Associations, Opening and Closing of Prayer Houses
18. No religious association may begin its functioning without first registering with the organs of the state government.
19. Technicalities of the procedure. Basically the same as in LRA.
20. The executive committee of the local government addresses the believers' petition with its resolution attached to the provincial government or to the Council of Ministers of the given autonomous republic, adding to it all the necessary information as established by the CROCA/CRC.
21. On the instruction of the provincial government . . . the local official of the CROCA/CRC reviews the believers' petition and checks its soundness.

22. The Provincial Government or Council of Ministers of an autonomous republic makes the decision to register or not to register the petitioners as a religious association.
23. Religious societies and groups of believers belonging to the sects the teachings and character of activities whereof is of an anti-state and fanatical nature, may not be registered. To these belong: The Jehovah Witnesses, Pentecostals, the True Orthodox Christians, The True Orthodox Church, the Adventist-Reformists, Murashkovites, etc.
24. Religious associations may be deprived of registration in cases of breaking the Soviet legislation on religious cults.

    The Procedure is the same as in the LRA below, except that the registration is revoked by local government rather than by the CRA or its predecessors.
25. Prayer houses may be closed in the following cases:

    (a) if the religious association using it has been deprived of registration;

    (b) if the building has to be demolished owing to the reconstruction of the area or owing to the dilapidated state of the building as confirmed by a technical inspection document and co-ordinated with the local official of the CROCA/CRC.
26. No Orthodox, Old Believer, Armenian-Gregorian, Roman-Catholic, Lutheran churches, Moslem mosques, Judaic synagogues, sectarian places of worship, Buddhist temples, actively in use by their religious societies may be closed without the express permission of the provincial government or Council of Ministers of an autonomous republic, co-ordinated with the central CROCA/CRC.
27. Registration and de-registration of clergy. The same as in LRA.
28. Provincial governments and their equivalents may order a limitation on tolling church bells, should this become necessary and be supported by the local population.

V. Rules on the Use of Objects (Utensils) of the Cult
Basically the same as in LRA. A lesser role is given to the CROCA/CRC; a greater to local governments.

The texts of these rules and of the CRA Statute are taken from a closed Soviet publication (not for general sale), *Zakonodatel'stvo o religionznykh kul'takh* (Moscow: Iuridicheskaia literatura, 1971), marked 'For Official use'. In other words, at least until the publication of the revised Soviet Laws on Religious Associations, the average Soviet citizen could only guess that there were some new regulations, increasing administrative control over the Church and giving new powers to the CROCA/CRC, which in 1965 were amalgamated into a single body: Council for Religious Affairs (CRA).

The above booklet was somehow leaked out of the USSR and reprinted in 1981 in New York by the Chalidze Publishers.

If we compare the stipulations of this Instruction with both the CRA Statute and the 1975 version of the Legislation on Religious Associations (LRA), we see even there a considerably changed role of the CRA compared with its predecessors. The latter were rather consulting and professional information bodies on religion (its needs and requirements) for the Soviet Government. In some instances (Art. 26, for instance) CROCA/CRC's function appears to be almost a protector for the believers and the churches against undue encroachments by the state.

In contrast, in the CRA Statute and the 1975 LRA, CRA is a watchdog over the Church with very wide arbitrary and dictatorial powers over her.

Articles 24–26 spell out quite clearly for which offences and/or in which circumstances alone a house of prayer may be liquidated. Although, in view of the arbitrariness of Soviet power and its monopoly over the interpretation of law, these regulations leave much room for abuse, the 1975 LRA does not provide even this flimsy protection to the church (see Art. 36, LRA). That the protection was flimsy enough was testified by the mass arbitary closures of thousands of churches in 1959–64, eleven years before the adoption of the 1975 amendments.

Articles 6, 7, 10 and 11 in the above Instruction render themselves to much abuse. What religious rites disturb public order? Choral singing, processions (of which the Orthodox Church has traditionally had much), not to mention church bells, may be interpreted as disturbing public order and be banned.

Art. 7/a–c can be applied to any sermon the regime does not like. Furov, for instance, complained that Bishop Khrizostom of Kursk in his sermons criticized the basic premises of 'scientific atheism' and maintained that science likewise depended on faith as a motive power for research and investment. For such sermons he was taken to task by the CRA. Refusing to budge, he soon lost his post as deputy head of the Department of External Ecclesiastical Relations, and by the end of 1984 was moved to a distant Ural diocese.

Similarly, monastic sermons calling on people to concentrate on their spiritual life and belittling the material temptations of the secular world can be interpreted as 'propaganda aimed at tearing believers away from active participation in the life of the state'. This apparently was the reason for the harassment and expulsion in 1976 of Fr. Amvrossi – a highly revered monastic priest (born 1937) – from the Zagorsk Holy Trinity Lavra and seven years later from the Pochaev Lavra. In both places his sermons attracted many thousands of pilgrims from all corners of the USSR.

Art. 10/b forbids priests to organize pilgrimages, and attributes belief in miracles and other manifestations of God's power to 'fraudulent actions'. But belief in these manifestations is an essential part of belief in God of all religious faiths. Priests have been struck from the register and even imprisoned for witnessing such manifestations to their parishioners. One of them the late Fr. Sergii Zheludkov who lost registration by the CRA in the 1960s for taking some of his parishioners to a site of icon renewal. This is an inexplicable phenomenon when suddenly an icon (sometimes all icons in a church), dark and almost invisible from centuries of soot from candles and oil lamps, suddenly begins to shine anew as if recently painted. What sort of freedom of religion can there be if a believer may not testify to his faith in, what he believes to be, manifestations and signs of God!?

Finally, Art. 11 deprives the Christian of his or her basic 'good Samaritan's' duty and calling. And then: it is not the Church who decides how many theological colleges she needs or when to have a council, but the CRA!

Such is, Dr Billy Graham, your religious freedom in the USSR. But perhaps the 1975 legislation has improved the situation? Let us look.

PROVISIONS ON THE COUNCIL FOR RELIGIOUS AFFAIRS OF THE COUNCIL OF MINISTERS OF THE USSR

1. The CRA . . . has been formed for the implementation of the policies of the Soviet Government regarding religions.
2. The main functions of the CRA are:
   (a) [to make sure that the constitutional and all other legal provisions regarding Church–State relations are observed];
   (b) to study and draw conclusions regarding the practice of the laws on religious cults, to draft new laws and decrees in this sphere . . .;
   (c) to inform the Soviet Government on the activities of religious organizations;
   (d) to help religious organizations in making international contacts, in participating in the struggle for peace and strengthening friendship between nations.
3. The CRA's duties include:
   (a) assuring the realization of the constitutional right of Soviet citizens to profess a religion or not to profess any;
   (b) supervision over the correct fulfilment of the laws on religion by religious organization and the clergy;
   (c) liaison functions between the religious organization and the Soviet Government on questions needing a governmental decision;
   (d) keeping a register of all religious associations prayer houses and buildings;
   (e) study and decision-making regarding questions arising out of activities of religious organizations in the USSR;
   (f) checking the application of the laws on religion by central and local organizations;
   (g) issuing resolutions on the union republican draft laws relating to religion;
   (h) receipt of information and materials on religion from the central and local government organs.
4. The CRA has the right to:
   (a) make decisions on the registration or de-registration of religious associations, on the opening and closing of temples and prayer houses;
   (b) check the activities of religious organizations in regard to their observance of Soviet laws on religion; its orders to discontinue any abuses of the laws must be met without fail;
   (c) raise the question of initiating penal administrative or criminal procedure against those in breach of the laws on religion;
   (d) clarify questions relating to the laws on religion to central and local government organs and other Soviet organizations;
   (e) suggest to local and higher administrative organs abolition of instructions that contradict Soviet laws on religion.

6. (Structure and staffing of the CRA)
7. The CRA of the Soviet Council of Ministers at its meetings studies questions related to the practical application of the Soviet religious policies . . . makes decisions on the registration and de-registration of religious temples and prayer houses . . . [and regarding all the other issues enumerated in article 1–5].
8. The CRA has its plenipotentiary officials in each union and autonomous republic and in every province, subordinate to the central CRA.
9. [The local CRA official is responsible for all the actions on the local level, stipulated in the above articles. Has the same controlling powers over local church organizations and bishops as, in principle, the central CRA Office has over the whole Church. He also informs the CRA central office on all details of life and activities of local churches and clergy.]
10. More details of the kind enumerated under No. 9.
11. & 12. Additional details on the relationship between the local CRA and local governments, and on the CRA stamp.

Adopted on 8 December 1965
Confirmed on 10 May 1966.

Criminal Code of the USSR, January 1, 1979
Article 142
The breaking of the laws on the separation of Church and State, and Schools and Church – is punishable by correctional labour for up to one year, or by a fine of up to fifty rubles. . . . Repeat offenders are to be imprisoned for up to three years.
Article 143
The hindrance or prevention of the fulfilment of religious functions, so far as they do not harm the social order or infringe upon individual rights – is punishable by correctional labour for up to six months or by a public reprimand.
[Here it is made clear that article 142 applies only to believers who break the laws on the separation of Church and State, while article 143 applies only to those opposing believers. Thus, even in the very unlikely eventuality of a group of believers suing a Soviet official, and an even less likely eventuality of their winning the suit, all that the guilty administrator would likely face would be a public reprimand. No matter how many times an official or a citizen is found guilty of preventing believers from exercising their religious rights, the maximum sentence to which he could be subjected is six months or correctional labour, while believers who repeatedly are found guilty under article 142 face up to three years of imprisonment. Ed.].
Article 190
The systematic distribution of false information, harmful to the Soviet government, or to the social order, whether in oral, written, or any other form – is punishable by imprisonment for up to three years, or by correctional work for up to one year, or by a fine up to 100 rubles.
[This would include sermons condemning religious persecutions. Ed.]

Article 199

...The unlicensed construction of a dwelling or an addition – is punishable by correctional work for a period of 6 months to one year with a confiscation of the construction or addition.

[This punishes the expansion of a church without government authorization. Ed.]

Article 277

Organizations or the leadership of a group, which function under the guise of fulfilling religious duties, that are harmful, or that enlist other citizens into harmful activities by threat of expulsion from the religious group, or attempt to enlist or force others to enlist minors into the group – is punishable by imprisonment for up to five years, or banishment for up to five years with or without confiscation of property....

[This article gives licence to brand as harmful to society any missionary work and threaten with imprisonment any clergyman or layperson who attracts converts or who strengthens religious convictions. The article also allows for the punishment of those clergymen who try to achieve proper spiritual discipline by subjecting parishioners to ecclesiastical punishments for immoral or spiritually demoralizing behaviour. Ed.]

Notes and References

INTRODUCTION

1. Bociurkiw in *Lenin: the Man, the Theorist, the Leader*, Leonard Schapiro and Peter Reddaway, eds (London: Pall Mall Press, 1967) pp. 107–8; Thrower, *Marxist-Leninist 'Scientific Atheism' and the Study of Religion and Atheism in the USSR* (Berlin-Amsterdam: Mouton Publishers, 1983) pp. 110–11 *et passim*. Among Western scholars who have under-estimated the role of atheism and antireligious campaigns in Soviet policy-making should be named John Curtiss, the leading American scholar in this field of the elder generation who adversely influenced the whole American scholarship on the subject. Billy Graham's declarations after his 1982 trip to the USSR that there is religious freedom there and that the party and the government ought to be separated in our perceptions on the status of religions, have ever since been skilfully used by Soviet propaganda: for example, Vladimir Kuroedov (the late chairman of the Council for Religious Affairs [CRA]) in *Nauka i religiia*, no. 10 (October 1982) p. 5.
2. Many believers and the Church herself at first thought that the term 'social organization' (*obshchestvennaia organizatsiia*) applied to the Church, after the publication of the 1936 Constitution, believing that she could now put forward candidates for the elections to the soviets. A Krasnov-Levitin, *Likhie gody, 1925–1941* (Paris: YMCA Press, 1977) pp. 299–300. Leading Soviet atheist authors attacked believers and the Church for the 'misconception', stating that the Church was an ideologically alien organization and therefore could not be a social or public organization in a socialist state. See: F. Oleshchuk, *O zadachakh antireligioznoi propagandy* (Moscow, 1937) pp. 12–17; Iu. Kogan and F. Megruzhan, *O svobode sovesti* (M.: OGIZ, 1938) pp. 64–5; F. Putintsev, *Vybory v sovety i razoblachenie popovshchiny* M., 1937) p. 20 *et passim*; 'Predvyborvye manevry tserkovnikov' and 'Luchshikh liudei – v Verkhovnyi Sovet SSR!', *Bezbozhnik*, respectively no. 6 (June 1938) and no. 11 (November 1937) pp. 3–4 and 2–3.
3. *Constitution of the Union of Soviet Socialist Republics*, supplement to *New Times*, no. 41 (1977). In the Constitution of 1936 (English edn, e.g., M.: Foreign Languages Publishing House, 1962) the relevant Articles are 124 and 126, which read respectively: 'Freedom of religious worship and freedom of anti-religious propaganda is recognized for all citizens; and 'the Communist Party of the Soviet Union ... is the vanguard of the working people ... and is the leading core of all organizations of the working people, both public and state.'
4. See Marx and Engels: *The Holy Family, The Communist Manifesto, German Ideology, Ludwig Feurebach and the End of the Classical Philosophy, The Origins of the Family, Private Property and the State, The Dialectics of Nature, Anti-Duering*.

5. *Voprosy nauchnogo ateizma v kurse istorii KPSS* (M.: Vysshaia shkola, 1975) pp. 14 and 34; Karl Marx, *On Religion*, Saul Padover (ed. and transl.) (N.Y.: McGraw-Hill, 1974) p. 356.
6. *Voprosy...*, pp. 22–3; *KPSS v rezolutsiiakh i resheniiakh s'ezdov, konferentsii i plenumov Tsk* (M.: Izd. polit. literatury, 1969–72) vol. 1, p. 60.
7. Pospielovsky, *The Russian Church Under the Soviet Regime, 1917–1982* (Crestwood, N.Y.: St. Vladimir's Seminary Press, 1984) ch. 2.
8. 'Ob otnoshenii rabochei partii k religii', as cited in: F. Putintsev, 'Lenin i bor'ba s religiei', *Pod znamenem marxizma*, no. 3–(1932) p. 65.
9. Ibid, and: a. Lenin, 'O znachenii voinstvuiushchego materializma' *Polnoe sobraine sochinenii*, 5th edn (M., 1964) vol. 45, pp. 22–33 (first published in *Pod znamenem marxizma*, no. 3, March 1972); b. 'Novyi etap' and 'Rezolutsii II Vsesoiuznoi konferentsii marxistsko-leninskikh nauchno-issledovatel'skikh uchrezhdenii', *P. znam. marx.*, no. 5 (1929) pp. 1–6 and 7–11, resp.; c. 'O zhurnale P. znam. marx. (Postanovlenie TsK VKP(b) ot 25 ianvaria 1931 g.)' and editorial, 'Vazheishii istoricheskii dokument', *P. znam. marx.*, no. 10–12 (1930) pp. 1–2 and 3–13 resp. Also: editorial in *P. nam. marx.*, no. 9–10 (1931) pp. 3–5.
10. Vlad. Oll-sky, 'Stoimost' Kul'tov', *Prosveshchenie*, no. 3 (St Pbg., March 1913) pp. 40–9; S, no. 6 (June 1913) pp. 1–19.
11. Iu.k., 'A. Lunacharsky, *Religiia i sotsializm*, v. II, Spbg. 1911'. A book-review, *Prosv.*, no. 1 (1912) p. 86; Lenin, *Collected Works*, vol. 35 (M.: Progress Publishers, 1966) p. 122.
12. A. Lunacharsky, *Vvedenie v istoriiu religii* (M-Pgd.: Gos. izdat., 1923) p. 3.
13. Ibid, chs 1–4.

CHAPTER 1: THE PHILOSOPHICAL FOUNDATIONS OF SOVIET ATHEISM

1. L. Feuerbach, *Essence of Christianity* (New York: Harper Torch Books, 1957) pp. 13–14.
2. Ibid, p. 152.
3. Karl Marx and Friedrich Engels, *Historich-Kritische Gesamtausgabe* (Frankfurt, 1927–35) II (1), p. 175.
4. D. Aikman, *The Role of Atheism in the Marxist Tradition*, PhD dissertation (Seattle: University of Washington, 1979) pp. 7 and 183–4.
5. Ibid, p. 9. He accepts this formula from the Soviet Russian mathematician and religious thinker, Igor' Shafarevich, *Sotsializm kak iavlenie mirovoi istorii* (Paris: YMCA Press, 1977) p. 260.
6. Ibid, p. 164.
7. Marx and Engels, *Collected Works* (London: Lawrence & Wishart, 1975) vol. 3, p. 176.
8. Ibid, vol. 5, p. 7.
9. Engels, *Anti-Düring* (Moscow: Foreign Language Publishing House, 1954) p. 440.
10. Ibid, pp. 65–6.
11. Ibid, p. 192.

12. V. I. Lenin, *Collected Works*, 5th edn (M.: Foreign Languages Publishing House, 1962) vol. 4, p. 2.
13. Ibid, vol. 4, pp. 83–4.
14. Marx and Engels, *Collected Works*, vol. 3, p. 296.
15. Ibid, vol. 5, p. 45.
16. Aikman, *Role of Atheism*, pp. 190–2.
17. Marx and Engels, *Collected Works*, vol. 5, p. 8.

CHAPTER 2: ANTIRELIGIOUS POLICIES, 1917–41

1. Vorontsov, *Leninskaia programma ateisticheskovo vospitaniia v deistivii (1917–1937gg.)* (Leningrad: izd. LGU, 1973) *passim.*
2. The exact dating of this decree is most frustrating. Originally it appeared in *Izvestia*, no. 16 of 21 January (Old Calendar, henceforth o.s. for Old Style) 1918 under the title of 'Decree on the Freedom of Conscience, Ecclesiastical and Religious Associations' over the signatures of Lenin and eight other people's commissars, as well as Vladimir Bonch-Bruevich, Director of the Office of People's Commissars, and N. Gorbunov, its secretary. So presumably the decree should have come down into history as that of 20 January (o.s.) or 2 February (n.s.), and this is the date of the document given in 'K istorii otdeleniia tserkvi ot gosudarstva i shkoly ot teserkvi v SSSR', *Voprosy istorii religii i ateizma* (henceforth *VIRA*) vol. 5 (M:. Academy of Sciences, 1958) pp. 7–8; but a footnote on p. 7 adds that in a codification of Soviet decrees issued on 26 January it appeared under its current name of 'Decree on the Separation of Church From the State and the School From the Church'. Thus so far the decree could be dated by 20, 21, 26 January (o.s.); yet all subsequent official Soviet collections of laws date it 23 January, 1918: for example, *Sistematicheskoe sobranie zakonov RSFSR...*, vol. 2 (Moscow: Iuridicheskaia literatura, 1968) pp. 537–8.
3. Lev Regel'son, *Tragediia russkoi Tserkvi, 1917–1945* (Paris: YMCA Press, 1977) p. 90 – he erroneously calls it the V Department. In fact it was the VIII Department of the Commissariat of Justice. For example, 'Otchet VIII (likvidatsionnogo) Otdela Narkoma Iustitsii Vserossiiskomu s'ezdu Sovetov', *Revolutsiia i tserkov'*, no. 9–12 (1920) p. 70.
4. Pospielovsky, *Russ. Church*, chs 1 and 3.
5. 'Ob antireligioznoi propagande', *Rev. i ts.*, no. 1 (1919) pp. 13–16; Vorontsov citing B.-B.'s memoirs, *Leninskocia programma*, p. 30.
6. *KPSS v rezolutsiiakh...*, vol. 2, p. 49. According to Vorontsov (p. 28), the author of Article 13 was Krasikov. One of the most aggressive leaders of Soviet atheism and the chief prosecutor at the trial of Metropolitan Veniamin of Petrograd in 1922, Krasikov requested the death penalty for him along with the death of numerous other leading church personalities in Petrograd. The metropolitan was absolutely innocent, but since he was much too popular among the masses of the population to be tolerated, he was executed.
7. This is the opinion of Joan Delaney Grossman, 'The Origins of Soviet Antireligious Organizations', in Richard H. Marshall, Jr (ed.), *Aspects of*

Religion in the Soviet Union, 1917–1967, (Chicago: University of Chicago Press, 1971) pp. 103–30.

8. *Bezbozhnik*, no. 1, 4 January, Year 8 (1925) p. 1.

9. David E. Powell, *Antireligious Propaganda in the Soviet Union: A Study of Mass Persuasion* (Cambridge, Mass.: MIT Press, 1975) p. 34; and *KPSS v rezolutsiiakh*, vol. 2, p. 242.

10. Trotsky, 'Vodka, tserkov' i kinematograf', *Pravda* (12 July 1923) p. 2. The very title of the article shows Trotsky's carelessly contemptuous attitude to religion, not unlike Alfred Rosenberg who brushed aside the Orthodox Church as nothing but a meaningless folk ritual, while his subordinates in occupied Russia soon became convinced that it was the single most important consolidating power of the Russian people. Underestimation of the importance of the Church in the Russian tradition stems from a confusion of popular anticlericalism with non-belief (see my *Russ. Church*, Introduction and ch. 2).

11. Lunacharsky's position, beginning with his 1919 article 'Ob antireligioznoi propagande', see *Pochemu nel'zia verit' v boga?*, F. Oleshchuk (ed.) (M.: Nauka, 1965) pp. 229–33 and 308. Skvortsov-Stepanov, *Mysli o religii* (M.: Gosizdat.antirel.lit., 1936) *passim*. On the matter of attack on all religions, not just the Orthodox, he agreed with Lunacharsky at least as early as 1922 (see *The Russ. Ch.*, vol. 1, 91 nn.). On Trotsky, contrast his article in *Pravda* 12 July 1923 (above) with his 'Antireligioznaia propaganda', *Pravda*, 24 July 1924.

12. 'Dekret ob uchrezhdenii Komissariata po delam musul'man', *Izvestiia*, 21 January 1918 (o.s.).

13. The Moslems had enjoyed direct Soviet support until 1920; both the Moslems and the Protestant sects enjoyed relative toleration until 1928–9 and were allowed a wide range of activities, including publications, seminaries, youth work, etc., which were banned to the Orthodox. See, for example, Bernhard Wilhelm, 'Moslems in the Soviet Union, 1948–54', and Andrew Q. Blane, 'Protestant Sectarians in the First Years of Soviet Rule' in *Aspects of Religion. . .*, pp. 257 and 301, respectively.

14. D. Grossman, 'Antireligious Organizations', p. 114.

15. Ibid, p. 127.

16. 'Vodka, tserkov'. . . ' (n. 21); on Rosenberg: *The Russian Church*, vol. 1, ch. 7, p. 225.

17. See Lenin's objection to the arrest of the Patriarch in his 'secret letter' on Shuia, below. Note that Trotsky's article (n. 18) was published in *Pravda* in July 1923, when, after the Renovationist Schism had begun to decline, the Patriarch was released from prison and made his declaration of civic loyalty to secular authorities of the Soviet Union. Hence, Trotsky must have lost hope of destroying the Church by means of the split, but at the same time he was calmed by Tikhon's declaration. A year earlier he was much more militant. Fr. Mikhail Polsky claims that also in response to Tikhon's excommunication of the Bolshevik leaders (19 January, 1918 o.s.) Lenin refused to permit his arrest and execution suggested by Trotsky, saying: 'We shall not allow him to be turned into a second Germogen'. (The latter was the patriotic Russian patriarch martyred by the Polish occupying forces at the Moscow Kremlin in 1612.) *Novye*

mucheniki rossiiskie, vol. 1. (Jordanville: H. Trinity Monastery Press, 1949) p. 150.

18. For example, Emelian Yaroslavsky, *Na religioznom fronte* (M.-L., 1925) *passim*. He uses such primitive antireligious arguments as, for instance, that the Easter cake blessed by a priest with holy water still dries like any other. He repeats similar 'challenges' in his *Bible for Believers and Unbelievers*, a collection of his articles published earlier in *Bezbozhnik*. Each article deals with a paradoxical episode or story from the Old Testament which Yaroslavsky interprets in its primitive literal sense, and 'proves' its inaccuracy in the context of the scientific theories of his time or of naturalistic realism. There is much mockery and blasphemy in the book. *Bibliia dlia veruiuschchikh i neveruiushchikh* (M.: OGIZ, 1936) 417 pp., circulation 20 200 copies.

19. 'O znachenii. . .', pp. 23−9; 'K itogam vsesoiuznogo soveshchaniia OVMD' (editorial), *P. znam. marx.*, no. 3 (1931) p. 8; 'Vazhneishii. . .', p. 5.

20. For the complete original text and the date on the Shuia events, see *VRSKhD*, no. 98 (Paris, 1970) p. 54.

21. In fact, Lenin and the Soviet propaganda misrepresented the position of the Church on the famine. It was the Patriarch who had originated the charity campaign by appealing to Church leaders in the West and forming a special Church Committee for aid to the victims of famine. The government ordered this committee to be dissolved and all collected funds handed over to it. The Church complied. When the government ordered the confiscation of Church valuables, the Patriarch issued a pastoral letter permitting the submission of all of them except those used directly for Eucharistic purposes, offering instead to collect their money value by a special plate collection. Pospielovsky, *Russian Church*, ch. 3.

22. *Izvestia*, 19 December, 1922; E. Belov, 'Sud'ba tserkovnykh tsennostei, iz'iatykh sovetskoi vlast'iu v 1922 g.', *VRSKhD*, no. 104−5 (1972) pp. 325−7 (in. edit. note).

23. Vorontsov, pp. 90 and 132; Grossman, 'Antireligious Organizations', pp. 120−8.

24. Vorontsov, p. 72.

25. *KPSS v rezolutsiiakh*, vol. 2 p. 468; vol. 3, p. 84.

26. 'Rezolutsiia Obshchestva voinstvuiushchikh materialistov o tekushchikh zadachakh obshchestva', *P. znam. marx.*, no. 12 (1926) p. 236; 'Ot pravleniia Obshchestva voinstvuiushchikh materialistov-dialektikov' and 'Ustav O-va VMD', ibid, No. 12 (1928) pp. 216−22.

27. N. Krupskaia, 'Obstanovka, v kotoroi pisalas' stat'ia Lenina 'O znachenii voinstvuiushchego materializma', no. 1 (1933) pp. 147−9; Gr. Bammel', 'Ob idealisticheskoi filosofii posle Oktiabria', ibid., no. 5 (1930) pp. 36−61; V.V. (Vaganian?), 'S krestom i bogom protiv materializma', ibid, no. 4 (1922) p. 82−94.

28. *The Russ. Church*, vol. 1, p. 51.

29. P. K. Lobazov, I. A. Serebriankin, *Voprosy nauchnogo ateizma v kurse istorii KPSS* (Moscow: Vysshaia shkola, 1975) pp. 196−7.

30. On Vvedensky: A. Levitin and V. Sharvrov, *Ocherki po istorii russkoi tserkovnoi smuty* (Kuesnacht, Switzerland: Institut 'Glaube in der 2 Welt',

1978), vol. 1, p. 53 *et passim*; on Martsinkovsky and in general on the debates: V. Martsinkovsky, *Zapiski veruiushchego* (Prague, 1929) *passim*; on the surgeon-bishop Voino-Iasenetsky generally, see: Mark Popovsky, *Zhizn' i zhitie Voino-Iasentskogo, arkiepiskopa i khirurga* (Paris: YMCA Press, 1979) *passim*.

31. Martsinkovsky, p. 278.

32. The very first Soviet film, produced in November 1918, was anti-religious propaganda based on the Demian Bedny poem, 'on the Priest Pankrat, Aunt Domna and an Icon in Kolomna', *Voprosy...*, p. 100. Note that 'Cinematography' is the third word in the title of the cited Trotsky 1923 *Pravda* article. There he attaches great importance to the cinema in the struggle against religion on a mass scale.

33. N. A. Krylov, 'Iz istorii propagandy ateizma v SSSR (1923–25)', *Voprosy istorii religii i ateizma* (V. VIII, M., 1960) pp. 183–7. Also: Zatko, pp. 103, 117.

34. The 8 April 1929 'Law on Religious Associations' restricted believers to services within the church walls; the 14th Congress of the Soviets a month later made religious propaganda illegal, restricting the right of propaganda to atheism alone.

35. Thrower, *Marxist-Leninist 'Scientific Atheism' and the Study of Religion and Atheism in the USSR* (Berlin and Amsterdam: Mouton Publisher, 1983) pp. 70–100.

36. 'Novyi etap', *P. znam. marx.*, no. 5 (1929) pp. 1–5; I. Skvortsov-Stepanov, 'Obshchestvo voinstvuiushchikh materialistov', ibid, no. 2–3 (1927) pp. 256–60; responses to Skvortsov-Stepanov, by Nik, Karev, Vas. Slepkov, and the Presidium of the Society of Militant Dialectical Materialists, ibid, no. 4 (1927) pp. 252–80; editorial, ibid, no. 10–11 (1929) p. 1; 'O zhurnale 'Pod znamenem marxizma' (Postanovlenie TsK VKP(b) ot 25 ianvaria 1931 g.), followed by the editorial 'Vazhneishii istoricheskii dokument', and unsigned 'Itogi filosofskoi diskussi', ibid, 10–12 (1930) pp. 1–2, 3–14, and 15–24, respectively.

37. *KPSS v rezolutsiiakh...*, pp. 164–5. It is interesting how this document betrays that 'voluntary' in Soviet semantics means *compulsory*: 'Confirming the CC resolution on the voluntary character of political education, the CC at the same time considers it an error to interpret the principle of voluntariness as permission to refuse political education.'

38. *KPSS...*, vol. 4, pp. 415 and 469.

39. Pospielovsky, *Russ. Church*, ch. 5; also: N. Struve, M. Spinka, etc. The decree is no. 301, *Sobranie zakonov i rasporiazhenii Rabochekrestianskogo pravitel'stva SSSR* (M., 1929) p. 641.

40. F. N. Oleshchuk, introductory article to Lunacharsky's, *Pochemu nel'zia....*, pp. 5–28.

41. Ibid, p. 304; Oleshchuk contradicts the author of the book he edited when in his introduction he says that only 40 per cent of the teachers were religious believers.

42. Pokrovsky, 'K uchitel'skomu s'ezdu', *Na putiakh k novoi shkole, No. 1* (M.: Rabotnik prosveshcheniia, January 1925) pp. 4; Lunacharsky, *Pochemu nel'zia...*, pp. 239 and 303.

43. Vorontsov, p. 117. On the Academy of Sciences purge, see: N.

Voznesensky, 'Imena i sud'by' and 'Materialy k istorii Akademii nauk', *Pamiat'*, a historical miscellany of *samizdat* (respectively: no. 1, Moscow, 1976 – New York: Khronika Press, 1978; and no. 4, M., 1979 – Paris: YMCA Press, 1981) pp. 353 and 459.

44. Lunacharsky as long ago as 1925 showed his implicit disagreement with the general party line which at that time tolerated sectarians. He argued in his speech at the first congress of the LG that they were more dangerous than the traditionalists, because they (Tolstoyans and other radical sects) by their dress and behaviour appeared to be modern, revolutionary and even communistic. In a March 1929 article in *Izvestia* he strongly reiterated *Pravda's* new line: '*It would be a crime to pervert the struggle in such a way as to turn it entirely against the Orthodox Church ... leaving in the shade the struggle against sectarianism, Islam, Judaism or any other religion*', *Pochemu nel'zia.* . ., pp. 241, 308.

45. 'Antireligioznaia propaganda i klassovaia bor'ba', *Pravda*, 25 Dec. (1928); for example, M. Galaktionov, 'Shire front antireligioznoi bor'by', *Koms, pr.*, 30 Aug. (1929), etc.

46. Vorontsov, respectively pp. 153, 113. The evidence that this circular instruction' was never published lies in its reference to an unpublished documents' section of the Institute of Marxism–Leninism Archives. The same is true of vitally important decisions concerning a total attack on religion adopted by special party conferences in 1928–9, the only reference to it in Vorontsov is again to the above archival section (106–7). Hence, the most important policy decisions, guidelines and regulations are not those which were published and known to the citizens, but those that remained secret and unknown.

47. See Edgar C. Bundy, *How the Communists Use Religion* (N.Y.: The Devin–Adair Co., 1966) *passim*; William Fletcher, *Religion and Soviet Foreign Policy* (London: Oxford University Press, 1973) *passim*.

48. Vorontsov, p. 112.

49. Ibid, pp. 91–3; Yaroslavsky, 'Marxizm i anarkhizm v antireligionoi propagande', *Bol'shevik*, no. 7–8 (15 July 1924) pp. 61–71, and 'Marx i religiia', no. 5 (14 March 1933) p. 89.

50. It is interesting that while the Soviet Government was pursuing the policy of divide and rule towards religion in 1918–27, Skvortsov-Stepanov declared publicly that this was only a temporary manoeuvre. In reality, the party was equally hostile to all religions and aimed at the liquidation of all of them. Pospielovsky, *Russ. Church*, vol. 1, 91 n. M. Enisherlov's article in *Voinstvuiushchee bezbozhie v SSSR za 15 let*, M. Enisherlov, A. Lukachevsky, M. Mitin (eds), (M.: Gos. antirel. izd., 1932) p. 342, etc. Yaroslavsky himself, apparently, narrowly escaped these purges: his name had disappeared from the list of *Bol'shevik*'s editors after its 6th issue in 1934, but he remained one of its regular authors until his death in 1943(?).

51. 'Izuchenie sotsial'nykh kornei religii v SSSR' (M.: 1930) pp. 5–14; *Mybezbozhniki*, a book of antireligious readings for grade schools compiled by I. A. Flerov, lists its whole first section under the subtitle 'Religion, a brake on the construction of socialism' (M.: Gos. antirel. izd., 1932) pp. 19–90.

52. *Pochemu nel'zia verit'* . . ., p. 229.
53. Ibid, pp. 248, 334, 339. In June 1929 he writes in *Izvestia*: 'Religion is like a nail: if you hit it on the head, you'll drive it only deeper.' Hence he rules out persecutions, but then says: 'You need pliers. Religion must be grabbed, squeezed from below . . . and removed with roots.' This, he alleges, can be achieved '*only by a scientific propaganda, moral and artistic re-education of the masses*' (*Pochemu nel'zia verit'* p. 222). And what if this is ineffective? What if persecution appears to be more effective in physical terms, which alone should count for a consistent Marxist, for matter determines the state of mind? After all, Lunacharsky offers no moral objections against the use of compulsion. On the 1929 legislation and its effect see *Russ. Church*, vol. 1, chs 4 and 5, and vol. 2, appendix 6.
54. I. Bobryshev, 'K perevooruzheniiu na odnom iz boevykh uchastkov', and Yaroslavsky, 'Nauchites' pravil'no vladet' oruzhiem marxizma' – both in *Antireligioznik*, no. 9 (Sept. 1929) pp. 57 and 65 resp.
55. Levitin–Krasnov, *Likhie gody* (Paris: YMCA Press, 1977) p. 256.
56. See the shorthand report of the LMG Second Plenum for its attacks on the Peoples' Commissariat of Enlightenment for allegedly upholding their 1924–5 line of 'a religious education' rather than antireligious. *Antirel. cit.*, p. 118 *et passim*.
57. *Rezolutsii II vsesoiuznogo s'ezda soiuza voinst. bezb.*, 2nd edn (M.: Akts. obshch. 'Bezb.', 1930) pp. 3, 77.
58. 'Rabochie 25 i 26 dekabria budut rabotat'', *Kom.pr.*, (11 Dec. 1929). On the antireligious function of the six-day week, see: Bullo, 'Za shestidnevnuiu nedeliu', *Bezbozh.*, no. 8 (17 Feb. 1929); N. Fominov 'Protiv Blagodushiia i Bespechnosti v antireligioznoi rabote', *Bol'shevik*, no. 20 (15 Oct. 1937) pp. 36–8. According to soviet emigrants of the pre-war generation, throughout the 1930s there existed three parallel systems: most schools and enterprises worked five days having the sixth day off; medical doctors and many other professions worked four days having the fifth day for rest; but in the more distant provinces, at least in industry, the old seven-day week was retained (to get more production out of the worker) – six days of work, one day off. In 1940 the seven-day week with Sunday as the only off-day was universally restored.
59. *XVI s'ezd Vserossiiskoi kommunisticheskoi partii (bol'shevikov). Stenograficheskii otchet* (M.: Gosizdat, 1930) p. 740.
60. *Antireligioznik*, no. 3 (1932) p. 61. Also, N. Amosov, 'Antireligioznoe vospitanie v deistvii', *Voinstvuiushchee bezbozhie* . . ., p. 299. Amosov admits, however, that the natural trend is that as soon as a lull occurs in the antireligious offensive of direct and brutal persecutions (for this is what the euphemism 'administrative measures' stands for), the antireligious character of the school withers away and antireligious activities come almost to a standstill.
61. G. Struchkov, 'Antireligioznaia rabota v Krasnoi armii', *Voinstvuiushchee bezbozhie v SSSR za 15 let*, M. Enisherlov, A. Lukachevsky, M. Mitin (eds), (M.: Gos. antirel., izd., 1932) p. 418.
62. *Derevnia kak ona est'* (M.: Krasnaia nov', 1923) p. 68.
63. Contrast V. Cherniavsky, 'Sektanty i voina', *Kom. pr.*, 1 Aug. 1929; and I.

Kryvelev, *Pochemu my boremsia protiv religii* (M.: Gos. antirel. izd., 1940) p. 7.

64. Contrast: G.Z., '5,000 rabochikh "Trekhgorki" trebuiut: . . . tserkov' pod detskii klub', *Kom. pr.*, 16 Oct. 1929; and K. Berkova, an antireligious lecturer–propagandist who complained that even the best antireligious lectures cannot break the resistance and power of the religious workers who cast 3000 votes in favour of the church at the above factory. In other words, the 5000 atheists claimed by the *Kom. pr.* article must have been a gross exaggeration or else they abstained from voting. Berkova asks Lukachevsky, why, despite all the propaganda and lectures, 'there is a growth of religiosity among some working class strata'. At the Trekhgornaia, workers replied to her lectures: 'tell us better why we have had no bread for three days. . . . Stop muddling our heads, and no one asked you to lecture to us.' Lukachevsky, *Izuchenie sotsial'nykh kornei religii v SSSR* (M.: 1930) p. 24.

65. Lukachevsky, *Izuchenie*, pp. 5–14.

66. The claim that 'komsomol cells become a tool of anti-Soviet politics' may have been nothing more than 'left–right deviation' purge hysterics in which the LMG was scrupulously imitating Stalin's party policies. See *Rezolutsii II Vsesoiuznogo s'ezda SVB*, pp. 33–6.

67. Ibid, p. 14.

68. Amosov, p. 30.

69. *Desiatyi s'ezd VLKSM, 11–12. IV. 1936 g.* (M.: Partizd., 1936) pp. 426 and 432.

70. John Curtiss, *The Russian Church and the Soviet State, 1917–1950* (Boston: Little, Brown, 1953) p. 205; F. Oleschuk, *O zadachakh antireligioznoi propagandy* (M.: 1937) p. 16. The Smolensk LMG section reported the 'dissolution of some of its cells' as early as 1926 (one year after LMG's national establishment). While 850 churches of all denominations functioned in the province with 836 priests and ministers 'and there has been marked increase in church attendance, especially by young people', the documents complained about the difficulty of recruiting young people to the LMG cells. In the whole city of Smolensk of some 70 000 inhabitants at the time, with four Orthodox, one Roman Catholic and one Evangelical church and a functioning synagogue, the League could not secure even twenty attendants for a regular seminar on 'scientific atheism', although the nominal Smolensk provincial LMG membership was 1395. 'Protocol No. 1', 9.1.1926, LMG; 'Secret Circular on the Activities of the Churches and on the State of the LMG in the Western Oblast''; A. Gagarin, 'Results . . . of Antireligious Work', an internal report. *Smolensk Archives* XT 47 (documents resp.: 458/56, 499, pt, II of 2, and 458/35).

71. Curtiss, *The Russian Church*, p. 205. N. Amosov, *Antireligioznaia rabota na poroge vtoroi piatiletki* (M.: Gos. antir. izd., 1932) p. 11; Yaroslavsky, 'Zadachi antireligioznoi propagandy', *Antireligioznik*, no. 5 (May 1941) p. 2; *Bol'shaia sovetskaia entsiklopediia*, 3rd edn, vol. 3 (Moscow 1970) p. 225; A. Lukachevsky, '10 let zhurnala "Antireligioznik"', *Bezbozh.*, no. 2 (Feb. 1936) p. 8; and my scrutiny of Soviet antireligious periodicals at the Hoover Institution and at the libraries of Harvard and Columbia

universities. According to a Soviet–Ukrainian source, there were 25 LMG periodicals in 1932. Ák. nauk Uht. RSR, Inst. Suspil'nykh nauk, *Stanovlenniavî rozvytok masovoho ateizmu v zakhidnikh oblastiahh URSR* (Kyiv, 1981) pp. 139–40.

72. Vorontsov, pp. 130–34; Second LMG Central Council Plenum, report by Stal'. Similar reports could also be seen in the daily press, e.g. 'Vylazka tverskikh sektantov: ubili aktivnuiu antireligioznitsu', *Kom. pr.* (16. Oct. 1929).

73. Curtiss, *The Russian Church*, p. 205.

74. Vorontsov, pp. 130–34 and 101.

75. Murray Feshbach, 'The Soviet Union: Population Trends and Dilemmas', *Population Bulletin*, vol. 37 no. 3 (Aug. 1982) p. 30. One of such claims for failure of the religious debaters is made by Struchkov, p. 416.

76. A. Lukachevsky, *Izuchenie sots. kor. rel.*, p. 19.

77. Vorontsov, p. 151. Incidentally, Yaroslavsky, who was hailed as a great Marxist scholar, used this fraudulent statistic as late as 1937 in his 'Antibol'shevitskaia propaganda v sovremennykh usloviakh', *Bol'shevik*, no. 4 (15 Feb. 1937) p. 32.

78. Compare: *Antirel. krestianskii uchebnik* (M.: Moskovskii rabochii) p. 14; with his *Religion in the USSR* (N.Y.: International Publishers, 1934) p. 48. In this duplicity he also followed his mentor, Lunacharsky, who, while participating in public debates with the Renovationist bishop Vvedensky (1925), calls him: 'a respectable opponent . . . who is dedicated supporter of justice in the world'. But addressing the first LG congress in the same year he calls the same Vvedensky 'a talented cheater'. *Pochemu nel'zia verit'. . .*, respectively pp. 83 and 241.

79. Nikita Struve, *Christians in Contemporary Russia* (London: Harvill Press, 1967) p. 54. Vorontsov denied such a plan, p. 115, although he admits there that a Five-Year Plan was adopted in 1930 to co-ordinate and rationalize the League's activities, including 'enactment of mass anti-religious work'. See also, V. Dulov, 'O podgotovke kadrov voinstvuiushchikh bezbozhnikov', *Antirel.*, no. 5 (1930) p. 52. On role in Five-Year Plans see, 'Bezbozhniki prodvigaiut zaem 3-go reshaiushchego goda Piatiletki', no. 10 (1931) pp. 102–4.

80. 'Stenogrammy Vtorogo plenuma TsS SVB', *Antirel., cit.*, p. 116. Oleshchuk hints that Lunacharsky's retirement may have been caused by his opposition to the destruction of cultural treasures (churches) and by the attacks 'on the part of the atheistic public opinion' on his Commissariat of Public Enlightenment for its slowness in introducing militant atheism into school programmes. He adds that L. was lucky to die in 1933, thus 'avoiding the sad fate of many of his comrades . . . who would fall victim to Stalin's . . . arbitrary rule'. Introd. to *Pochemu nel'zia. . .*, p. 23.

81. Vorontsov, p. 148, citing Yaroslavsky. It is also general knowledge that the 1937 population census, that last one which contained a question on religious convictions, was suppressed owing to embarrassingly high figures of religious believers. Another census was taken in 1939. It and all subsequent ones do not contain any question on religious belief, under the official pretext that owing to the separation of church and state, religion is a private affair of no interest to the state. The other reason for

the SVB decline may have been the imminence of war requiring a greater national unity for defence, rather than an atmosphere of internal civil strife fomented by constant attacks on the religious masses.

82. 'K voprosu o kreshchenii Kievskoi Rusi', *Istorik—marxist*, no. 2 (1937) pp. 40–77. Even *Bezbozhnik* had to follow suit with an article by Grekulov, 'Kreshchenie Rusi', in no. 5 (1938). Characteristically, at the above 1930 LMG CC plenum schoolteachers were attacked for teaching that the Church had disseminated culture in the past. *Antirel. cit.*, p. 118.

83. Yaroslavsky, 'Antireligioznaia propaganda v sovremennykh usloviiakh', *Bol'shevik*, no. 4 (15 Feb. 1937) p. 31. Also compare: Oleshchuk, 'Boevye voprosy antireligioznoi propagandy', *Bol'shevik*, no. 16 (15 August 1938) pp. 35–8 (he also says that 'priests have gone into the underground, formed illegal church organizations, secret worship, underground monasteries', p. 38); and Oleshchuk, 'Kommunisticheskoe vospitanie mass i preodolenie religioznykh perezhitkov', *Bol'shevik*, no. 9 (1 May 1939) pp. 46–8; and 'Kommunizm i religiia', *Bol'shevik*, no. 8 (1 April 1940) pp. 39–40.

84. 'Zadachi antireligioznoi . . ., pp. 1–8. He also cites interesting statistics on the dynamics of Soviet atheism: LMG ran 484 antireligious courses in 1939, 622 in 1940, but the total number of course attendants in the same two years *declined* from 12 662 to 10 968, less than 17 per course; similarly, the number of LMG study circles increased from 5089 to 9698, but the number of participants declined from 82 536 to 71 982 – just over 7 members per circle; similarly, the number of LMG seminars grew from 4824 to 5068, but the number of participants declined slightly from 77 231 to 77 011 despite the addition of the western territories.

85. Theofanes Stavrou and Vasili Alexeew, *The Great Revival* (Minneapolis: Burgess Publishing Co., 1976) *passim*.

86. Its activities petered out by the end of 1941. Its formal abolition date remains questionable. The *Soviet Historical Encyclopedia* gives no date. The third edition of the *Great Soviet Encyclopedia* (Russian edn, 24, M., 1976, p. 266) gives 1947, the year of the establishment of *Znanie* Society, as the year of dissolution of LMG. Antireligious articles likewise disappeared from the flagship of Soviet atheism, *Under the Banner of Marxism*, immediately after the German attack of June 1941; and were soon replaced by nationalistic articles praising Russian (and to a lesser extent those of other Soviet nationalities) historical personalities, the Russian people, the heroism of Soviet soldiers, etc. Having been launched as the leading organ of *militant* atheism, the journal lost its *raison d'être* and ceased publication in 1944.

87. N. 88. Also: Fominov, 'Protiv blagodushiia . . .', p. 36; n. 62; and Oleshchuk, 'Boevye voprosy . . .', pp. 34–5. The figures on believers must have come from the suppressed 1937 population census. The 1941 figure in Pospielovsky, *Russ. Church*, vol. 1, p. 174.

88. 'Fedor Mikhailovich Dostoevsky protiv nemtsev', *Bol'shevik*, no. 16 (August 1942) p. 38.

CHAPTER 3: THE POST-WAR ATHEISTIC SCENE

1. Characteristically, the 27 Sept. resolution uses very cautious language. There is no direct reference to atheism or religion; the term 'scientific-enlightenment propaganda' is used instead. 'Postanovlenie Tse-Ka VKP(b) ob organizatisii nauchnoprosvetitel'noi propagandy', *KPSS v rezolutsiiakh* . . ., vol. 6, pp. 121–3. See also: Powell, *Anti-religious Propaganda*, p. 38.

2. Pospielovsky, *Russian Church*, ch. 9; and (on the text of the 1961 Instruction) *Zakonodatel'stvo o religioznykh kul'takh*, a reprint from a secret internal publication (M.: Iuridicheskaia literatura, 2nd edn, 1971) by Chalidze Publications (New York, 1981) p. 80.

3. One would have thought this issue had already been resolved in 1928–9 (see Chapter 2). But apparently the quiet resistance of the secretly believing or of simply civilized and tolerant teachers minimized the implementation of the official policy of aggressive atheism in school wherever possible.

4. S. Kovalev, 'Kommunisticheskoe vospitanie trudiashchikhsia i preodolenie perezhitkov kapitalizma v soznanii mass', *Bol'shevik*, no. 5 (March 1947) pp. 20–21; and N. Yakovlev, 'Sovetskaia shkola – vazhneishee orudie vospitaniia molodiozhy', *Bol'shevik*, no. 11 (June 1947) pp. 6–22. The fact that Yakovlev was a regular contributor of highly patriotic articles to the journal throughout the war, but had never mentioned religion in any one of them prior to this one, indicates a policy decision at the level of the CPSU Central Committee.

5. S. Kaftanov, 'Vsemerno uluchshat' prepodavanie osnov marxizma–leninizma v vysshei shkole', *Bol'sh.*, no. 12 (30 June 1949) pp. 22–3; but also in *Bol'sh.*: S. Kovalev, 'O preodolenii perezhitkov kapitalizma v soznanii liudei', no. 19 (Oct. 1950) pp. 19–31; unsigned editorial 'Stroitel'stvo kommunizma i propaganda marxizma–leninizma', no. 18 (Sept. 1951) pp. 3–12; V. Kuroedov, Secretary of the Sverdlovsk Prov. Party Committee (the future chairman of the Council for Religious Affairs), 'Obkom partii i voprosy prepodavaniia osnov marxizma–leninizma v vuzakh', no. 14 (June 1950) pp. 57–62.

6. A. Sobolev, 'Lektsionnaia propaganda sredi naseleniia', *Bol'shevik*, no. 24 (Dec. 1950) pp. 67–70.

7. I have no direct evidence of the late Kapitsa's *Znanie* membership, but most probably, in view of the above resolution and its size, he was a member. The text of the resolution in *KPSS v rezolutsiiakh* . . ., vol. 6, pp. 281–6. Additional information on *Znanie* received from Dimitry and Taisia Lenkov, young former Soviet scholars who had institutional *Znanie* membership during their conversion to Christianity. Oral testimony given to this author, San Francisco, June 1984. See also, 'Primechaniia' to Lunacharsky's *Pochemu nel'zia verit'*. . ., 423.

8. *Russian Church*, vol. 2 pp. 316–17.

9. Akademiia nauk SSSR. Institut istorii, *Voprosy istorii religii i ateizma. Sbornik statei* (M.: Akad. nauk., 1950) circ. 10 000 copies.

10. Grossman, 'Khrushchev's Anti-Religious Policy and the Campaign of 1954', *Soviet Studies*, vol. XXIV no. 3 (1973) pp. 377–9. B.-B., 'Svoboda

sovesti v SSSR', *Vop. ist. rel. i at.*, no. 2 (1954) pp. 11–28; 'Lenin o religii' in
his posthumous *Izbrannye ateisticheskie proizvedeniia* (M.: Mysl', 1973)
pp. 40–1; F. N. Oleshchuk, 'Voprosy ateisticheskoi propagandy v rabote
V. I. Lenina' O znachenii voinstvuiushchego materializma', *Vop. ist.
rel. . . .*, pp. 29–44.

11. *KPSS v rezolutsiiakh*, vol. 6, pp. 502–20.
12. The preparatory steps for the future onslaught were most likely made at
a strictly in-camera conference of 350 theorists of atheism and atheistic
militants in Moscow in August 1957. *Vop. fil.*, no. 5 (1958), cited by N.
Struve, p. 293. On the secret atheistic Seven Year Plan this author was
informed in Moscow in 1964 by the now deceased highly respected
Moscow priest, Fr. Vsevolod Shpiller. The *NiR* editorial was entitled
'Kommunisticheskoe stroitel'stvo i preodolenie religioznykh perezhitkov', pp. 4–8. See also: Powell, *Anti-Religious*, pp. 39–40; Popovsky,
Zhizn'. . ., p. 467; William Stroyen, *Communist Russia and the Russian
Orthodox Church, 1943–1962* (Washington, D.C., 1967) pp. 89–93.
13. The *Zhurnal Moskovskoi patriarkhii* (Journal of the Moscow Patriarchate,
henceforth *ZhMP*) circulation is cited in the secret report of V. Furov, the
deputy chairman of the Council for Religious Affairs (CRA), to the
CPSU Central Committee (undated, but apparently 1975): 'Tserkovnye
kadry i mery po ogranicheniiu ikh deiatel'nosti ramkami zakona', *Vestnik
RKhD* (Paris, 1979, no. 130) p. 328. Circulation of the other important
publication, *Theological Endeavours*, organ of the theological schools in
the USSR, appearing once or twice a year, is given by the same source as
3000 copies.
14. *KPSS v rezolutsiiakh . . .*, vol. 6, p. 507; Stroyen, *Church*, pp. 89–94, etc.
15. Donald A. Lowrie and William C. Fletcher, 'Khrushchev's Religious
Policy, 1959–1964', *Aspects of Religion*, p. 132.
16. *KPSS v rezolutsiiakh . . .*, vol. 7, p. 378; Grossman, 'Khrushchev's . . .',
p. 381.
17. G. V. Vorontsov and N. P. Krasnikov, 'XXII s'ezd KPSS i zadachi
ateisticheskogo vospitaniia trudiashchikhsia', *Ezhegodnik muzeia . . .*,
no. 6 (1962) p. 6.
18. The implication of this statement is that the natural state of man is
conservative, i.e. a materialistic *Weltanschauung* is *unnatural* and contradicts human nature if it has to be brought about by force. There is no
evidence to show communist society is the inevitable result of human
history or that it represents man's return to his natural state.
19. Kryvelev, 'Sovremennyi fideizm i nauka', no. 13 (Sept. 1959) pp. 96–
108; and almost every issue of *Kommunist* for 1959.
20. 'Kazhdyi intelligent–propagandist ateizma', *NiR*, no. 2 (Feb. 1962)
p. 15.
21. 'O zadachakh partiinoi propagandy v sovremennykh usloviiakh', *Kom.*,
no. 1 (Jan. 1960) pp. 10–24.
22. 'Iz otchetnogo doklada Pravleniia Vsesoiuznogo ob-va po rasprostrane-
niiu politicheskikh i nauchnykh znanii III s'ezdu Ob-va', *NiR*, no. 2 (Feb.
1960) p. 6; I. P. Tsamerian *et al.* (eds), *Osnovy nauchnogo ateizma. Uchebnoe
posobie. Tret'e, pererabotannoe izdanie* (M.: izd. polit. literatury, 1964).
23. 'K novomu pod'emu ideologicheskoi raboty', *Kom.*, no. 14 (Sept. 1960)
pp. 22–40; also, F. Lukinsky, 'Zametki o nauchno-ateisticheskoi prop-

agande' (*Kom.*, no. 9, June 1960), who argues that 'individual work' is necessary because believers do not attend atheistic lectures and do not subscribe to atheistic literature – i.e. such atheistic efforts simply miss their target (pp. 112–14). Il'ichev later quotes an Orthodox priest as saying that atheistic propaganda does not bother the believers: atheists do not attend churches, believers do not attend atheistic lectures. See his 1963 CC Plenum report, n. 39 below.

24. Pospielovsky, *Russian Church*, ch. 10 and sources there cited; also Lowrie and Fletcher, p. 141.
25. Lowrie and Fletcher, ch. 10, pp. 141–3.
26. Ibid, ch. 10.
27. Ibid, particularly nn. 11 and 74 in ch. 10.
28. 'Pochemu shkola otstupaet bez boia?' and 'Otvet ministra prosveshcheniia RSFSR, t. E. I. Afanasenko', *NiR.*, no. 9 (Sept. 1960) pp. 3–7.
29. A. A. Vershinskaia, V. I. Nosovich and R. F. Filippova, 'Massovaia rabota muzeia po preodoleniiu religioznykh perezhitkov', *Ezhegodnik*, no. 5 (1961) pp. 350–7.
30. Economic and Philosophic Manuscripts of 1844, *Marx-Padover*, 42.
31. Vorontsov and Krasnikov, pp. 10–11; N. S. Khrushchev, *O kommunisticheskom vospitanii* (M.: Izd. polit. literat., 1964) p. 149.
32. *XIV s'ezd Vsesoiuznogo Leniniskogo kommunisticheskogo soiuza molodezhi. 16–20 aprelia 1962 g. . Stenograficheskii otchet* (M.: Molodaia gvardiia, 1962) pp. 536 and 553. Trade unions were also brought into line. The resolution of the 12th Congress of Trade Unions, meeting some months after the 21st Party Congress, states that 'it is the duty of trade unions to improve the scientific–atheistic upbringing of workers'. In contrast, the new statute adopted at the 13th Congress in 1963 states that the unions include workers irrespective of their religious convictions, contradicting the job discrimination of religious workers, widely practised from late 1950s again. See: V. Podzerko, *XII s'ezd sovetskikh profsoiuzov* (M.: Profizdat, 1969) p. 36; *Materially XIII s'ezda professional'nykh soiuzov SSSR* (M.: Profizdat, 1964) *passim*.
33. They all refer to the 22nd Party Congress and the new CP Programme as starting-points for the new consolidated offensive against religion as part and parcel of progression towards communism. For example: Oleshchuk, 'Torzhestvo kommunizma i zakat religii', and V. F. Zybkovets, 'Programmnye polozheniia KPSS v bor'be protiv religii' – both in *Vop. istor. rel. i at.*, no. XI (1963) pp. 3–25, 26–42 respectively; editorial 'Novaia programma KPSS o preodolenii religioznykh predrassudkov', ibid, no. X (1962) pp. 3–19; V. Stepakov, 'Leninskie printsipy kommunisticheskogo vospitaniia', *Kom.*, no. 5 (March 1963) pp. 11–21. *Vop. ist. rel. i at.* roughly from 1960 became less academic and more militant in tone and content, but apparently not sufficiently so for Khrushchev, for its circulation continued to decline. The last, 12th, issue (1964) dropped to 2100 copies.
34. *KPSS v rezolutsiiakh*, vol. 8, pp. 367–73.
35. *Filosofkie problemy ateizma* (M.: Ak. nauk, 1963) pp. 30–1.
36. For example, N. Sviridov, 'Glavnoe – znat' liudei!', *NiR*, no. 12 (Dec. 1962) pp. 70–3.
37. 'Kazhdyi intelligent – propagandist ateizma', n. 20 above.

168   *Notes and References*

38. See, for example, 'Programma partii – rukovodstvo k deistviiu', *NiR*, no. 2 (1962) pp. 3–18, and no. 3 (1962) pp. 9–20; 'Vsesoiuznoe soveshchanie ateistov', *NiR*, no. 5 (1962) pp. 7–14, etc.
39. 'Doklad tov. L. F. Il'icheva na Plenume TsK KPSS. 18 iiunia 1963 g.', *Pravda* (19 June 1963), followed by an aggressively militant antireligious editorial on the plenum: 'Ideologicheskii front', *Kom.*, no. 10 (July 1963) pp. 6–14; on Leninist 'legality': 'Formirovanie nauchnogo mirovozzreniia i ateisticheskoe vospitanie', *Kom.*, no. 1 (Jan. 1964) pp. 29–30. Ideological-atheistic conferences, praising Il'ichev's aggressive stand and drawing policy conclusions; e.g. and expanded session of the CPSU CC Ideological Commission, *NiR*, no. 1 (1964) pp. 31–60; a conference of Central Asian atheists, *NiR*, no. 5 (1964) pp. 12–19.
40. See Resolutions (*Postanovleniia*) nos. 1160 (16 October 1958), 1251 (6 November 1958), 1159 (16 October 1958) respectively, in: *Zakonodatel'stvo o religioznykh kul'takh* (M.: Iuridicheskaia literatura, 1971). 'Only for internal use.' (Reprint N.Y.: Chalidze, 1981) pp. 35–6.
41. Fr. Gleb Yakunin, 'O sovremennom polozhenii Russkoi Pravoslavnoi Tserkvi . . .', *Vol'noe slovo* (*Samizdat* reprint), no. 35–6 (1979) pp. 46–7.
42. Prot. Dimitri Konstantinov, *Gonimaia Tserkov'* (New York: Vseslavianskoe izdatel'stvo, 1967) pp. 286–7, and (London: Macmillan, 1969) chs 4 and 5.
43. For the decline of functioning seminaries, see *ZhMP*, nos. 5 (1961) p. 38 and 3 (1964) p. 22. On the Volhyinian Seminary, see Feodosii, Archb. of Poltava, letter to L. I. Brezhnev, *Vestnik RKhD*, no. 135 (1981) pp. 236–7. On the Belorussian Seminary this author was informed by a former professor of that seminary. There it was a case of overzealous communists of the Belorussian republican government, while the central government in Moscow opposed the closure for several years. Consequently, for over two years the seminary officially continued to be open, while the local Soviet authorities prevented any registration of new students, using the above described methods.
44. For example, editorial 'Molodezh' i religiia', *NiR*, no. 8 (1962) pp. 3–7.
45. Vorontsov and Krasnikov, p. 16.
46. Lowrie and Fletcher, *Aspects of Religion*, p. 133.
47. Ibid, pp. 133–5; N. Struve, pp. 295–6.
48. On the comparison of closing of Orthodox churches and synagogues see: David Powell, *Anti-religious Propaganda*, pp. 40–1; on Baptists: Michael Bordeaux, *Religious Ferment in Russia* (London: Macmillan, 1968) *passim*. Powell's maximum total of Orthodox churches in the USSR in 1959 is 17 500 and his figure for 1966, 7500. The late Metropolitan Boris of Odessa at a press conference in Montreal in 1955 gave a figure of 'about 25 000'. A high-ranking priest of the Moscow Patriarchate told this author in 1979 that the 1975 internal figure of the Patriarchate was 6800 functioning Orthodox churches in the whole Soviet Union, not counting Georgia.
49. The purpose of this law originally was to make employers responsible for providing living quarters for their employees, an excellent example of misuse for oppressive purposes of an originally beneficial law.
50. Pospielovsky, *Russian Church*, ch. 10 (Boris Talantov's documents).

51. Pospielovsky, *Russian Church*, ch. 10 (Talantov's testimonies); the above Archb. Feodosii letter, pp. 222–34, and many *samizdat* documents.
52. Lowrie and Fletcher, *Aspects of Religion*, pp. 143.
53. Ibid, p. 145.
54. See articles 66 and 6, and the 'Preamble' to the Constitution, as cited below.
55. This refers to the 'wandering priests'. After the closing of churches and deprivation of their priests of 'registration', the more dedicated ones among them began to wander from village to village secretly performing pastoral duties and religious services in private homes of the faithful in the areas left without open churches. This has been confirmed to this author by several Russian clerics, including V. Rev. Konstantin Tivetsky, a Moscow priest who emigrated to the USA in 1980 (San Francisco, June 1980).
56. This author saw this instruction originally in the BBC Central Research Unit in 1967 (see *Russian Church*, ch. 10, n. 20); published in full in *Vestnik RKhD* no. 136 (1982) pp. 273–6. The earlier versions, see in *Zakonodatel'stvo o kul'takh*, pp. 187–96 and 88–103.
57. See, 'Archpriest Shpiller and His Parish', *Patriarch and Prophets: Persecution of the Russian Orthodox Church Today*, Michael Bourdeaux, ed. (London: Macmillan, 1969) pp. 304–29; V. Rev. Vsevolod Shpiller's letter in *Vestnik Russkogo Zapadnoevropeiskogo ekzarkhata*, Paris, avril–juin 1967, no. 58 pp. 107–9; and other documents.
58. *Russian Church*, ch. 10.
59. *Zakonodatel'stvo o kul'takh*, pp. 35 6.
60. For example: E. Maiat and I. Uzkov, 'Rushatsia monastyrskie steny', *NiR*, no. 9 (1961) pp. 22–31; A. Andreev and G. Gerodnik, 'Krest na sluzhbe u svastiki', *NiR*, no. 11 (1963) pp. 43–8; Iu. M. Vesela, 'Dvi doli. Rozpovid' kolyshnioi chernytsi', *Voiovnychyi ateist*, no. 7 (July 1964) pp. 4–7.
61. A. Shamaro, 'Mezhdu sinikh vetvei', *NiR*, no. 11 (1963) pp. 23–8; L. Khvolovsky, 'Byvshie liudi', *NiR* no. 7 (1964) pp. 24–32.
62. Pospielovsky, *Russian Church*, ch. 10.
63. D. Ushinin (this author's earlier pseudonym), 'Novye veianiia v ateisticheskoi propagande SSSR', *Grani* no. 60 (1966) p. 206. An article in *Nauka i religiia* compares the liveliness, human warmth and popularity of the churches in Tambov with the emptiness and coldness of the atheist section of the local 'House of Political Education'. In the latter there could have been no visitors whatsoever for a long time because it was locked and the correspondent had considerable difficulty obtaining the keys to visit it. The church was packed with services, baptisms, funerals, confessions and communions almost round the clock.
64. Powell, *Anti-religious*, p. 69 *et passim*; 'Novye sovetskie obriady i ritualy', *Radio Liberty Research Bulletin* (Russian edn) (Munich, 16 August 1974, no. 258/74); G. Chebotar', 'Novye obriady v drevnem Polotske', *Nauka i religiia*, no. 7 (1970) pp. 33–4; N. P. Lobacheva, 'O protsesse formirovaniia novoi semeinoi obriadnosti', *Sovetskaia etnografiia*, no. 1 (1972) pp. 3–13.
65. Veresaev, 'Ob obriadakh', *Krasnaia nov'*, no. 11 (Nov. 1926) pp. 174–85;

and his other publications mentioned in the article, e.g. 'Khudozhestven-nomu oformleniiu byta', ibid, no. 1 (Jan. 1926), and *Ob briadakh starykh i novykh*.

66. Compare the idea of the mission of 'the new revolutionary theatre' with N. Gogol's idea of a Christian (Orthodox) theatre's role in a religious transfiguration of man. *Ocherki po filosofii marxizma* (S. Pbg., 1980); esp. V. Bazarov's 'Mistitsizm i realizm nashego vremeni', pp. 3–71; Lunacharsky's 'Ateizm', pp. 107–61; P. Yushkevich's 'Sovremennaia energetika s t. zr. empiriosimovolizma', pp. 162–214; and Bogdanov's 'Strana idolov i filosofiia marxizma', pp. 215–42. Also: M. Laskovaia, *Bogoiskatel'stvo i bogostroitel'stvo prezhde i teper'* (M.: Moskovskii rabochii, 1976) pp. 11–78; M. P. Gapochka, 'Uroki bogostroitel'stva', *Vop. nauch. at.*, no. 25 (M.: 1980) pp. 186–204.

67. For example: 'idealism is clericalism . . . But a philosophical idealism is the road to clericalism.'; 'God-seeking differs from god-building . . . just as much as a yellow devil differs from a blue devil.'; 'Any idea of any God, any attempt to flirt with God is a loathsome abomination . . . the most dangerous abomination, the most infamous infection.' These and similar statements the Soviet author calls Lenin's destruction of the god-builders' theories. Laskovaia, *Bogoiskatel'stvo* pp. 21, 22, etc.

68. N. Valentinov in *Vstrechi s Leninym* (N.Y.: Chekhov Publishing House, 1953) pp. 283–305, gives a vivid description of Lenin's philosophic illiteracy and primitiveness of argumentation.

69. See Chapter 1 of this work, and Lunacharsky's *Pochemu nel'zia.* . . .

70. The German 'theological' school originating from the pastor–martyr Bonnhoefer; or the fact that Dr Robinson, the Anglican Bishop of Woolwich, safely retained his episcopal seat even after publishing his *Honest to God*, which rejected the concept of a personal God.

    In Russia, on the other hand, even under the Soviet regime, an outstanding theology professor at the Leningrad Theological Academy, Alexandr Osipov, when he ceased to believe in God, left the Academy and, after publishing his attack on religion, was excommunicated by the Orthodox Church. See the Patriarchal *Ukaze* to this effect in *ZhMP*, no. 1 (1960); 'Vypiska iz postanovleniia . . .', no. 23 (30 Dec. 1959). Similarly when a bishop even of the Renovationist Church, Nikolai Platonov, had developed similar doubts, he retired from all church positions and went into civilian life. That these were hardly more than doubts seems to be attested to by the fact that just before his death in 1942 he returned to the Church and received the last rites. See Levitin, *Orcherki* . . ., vol. 3, pp. 349–69.

71. This rubric appeared in 1965. See also, Ushinin in *Grani*, no. 60 (1966) pp. 198–222.

72. P. P. Kampars, *Sovetskaia grazhdanskaia obriadnost'* (M.: Mysl', 1967) *passim*.

73. Chebotar' in *Nauka i Religiia*, no. 7 (1970), Lobacheva in *Sovetskaia etnografiia*, no. 1 (1972); also, Janis Sapiets, 'Soviet Atheists Adopt Pagan Folklore Rites', *BBC Central Research Unit Talk* (no. 80/69, 22 April 1969), citing Galina Terekhova in *Sovetskaia kul'tura* (4 January 1969) and Efim Dorosh, 'Raionnye budni', *Novy mir* (M.: no. 1, Jan. 1969). About the

concern of the Soviets with Siberia this author was informed by several Moscow Patriarchate sources. The other possible reason given by them for permission to reopen a few Orthodox churches was the proximity of China and the need for building Russian national identity.

74. Pospielovsky, *Russian Church*, ch. 10; Bohdan R. Bociurkiw, 'Religion and Atheism in Soviet Society', *Aspects of Religion*, pp. 49–53.

CHAPTER 4: ANTIRELIGIOUS POLICIES AFTER KHRUSHCHEV

1. The specialized atheistic journals which appeared in these years were: *Science and Religion (Nauka i religiia)*, a mass *Znanie* Society monthly (from 1959); its Ukrainian counterpart, *The Militant Atheist (Voiovnychyi ateist*, 1960), later renamed *Man and World (Liudyna i svit)*; the *Yearbook of the Museum of the History of Religion and Atheism*, vols I – VII (1957–64), and *Problems of History of Religion and Atheism* (1950–64, an irregular miscellany) – both published by the Academy of Sciences; both were superseded in 1966 by the similarly irregular *Problems of Scientific Atheism (Voprosy nauchnovo ateizma)*, published by the Institute of Scientific Atheism attached to the Academy of Social Sciences of the CPSU Central Committee, but, in contrast to the meagre circulation figures of its predecessors, *Vop. nauch. at.* reached over 24 000 per issue by the late 1970s, falling to 22 500 by 1985. See, L. Andreev, B. Evdokimov, etc., 'Naychnyi ateizm za 50 let', *Voprosy filosofii*, no. 12 (1967).

2. There are plenty of documents to show that thousands of believers signed petitions begging for the reopening of a church and their requests were never granted. The most famous case is that of the city of Gorky which has only three small churches on the outskirts serving a population of 1.5 million. Nearly 2000 people have been fighting since 1969 for the reopening of five churches in five inner districts of the city without success. See this and other cases in, *Documents of the Christian Committee for the Defence of Believers' rights in the USSR* (San Francisco: Washington Research *Samizdat* Reprints, vv. 1–12, 1979–80); also: *Religion in Communist Lands* (Keston College, Keston, England) vol. 6, no. 1 (1978) p. 45; vol. 7, no. 4 (1979) pp. 258–61; vol. 8, no. 2 (1980) p. 13.

The *Journal of the Moscow Patriarchate* has been reporting the reopening and even building of at least 19 Orthodox churches in the period between 1977 and 1982; while the Baptist Church had managed to open over 50 new churches in 1976 alone, although each Baptist community is considerably smaller than the Orthodox parishes. See: *ZhMP*, Partriarch Pimen's Report (no. 8, 1978) p. 11, and church chronicle in other issues during the above years; for Baptists: 'New Baptist Churches Opened', *Religion in Communist Lands* (henceforth RCL) vol. 5, no. 3 (1977) p. 200.

3. Dr William Fletcher wrongly views the removal of atheistic research from the auspices of the Academy of Science to the Academy of Social Sciences as a positive factor, on the basis that their work henceforth

became 'more practical, immediately usable'. He ignores the fact that having been placed under the direct control of the CPSU Central Committee *Agitprop* it became even more mobilized to serve immediate party needs than before. See Fletcher's *Soviet Believers. The Religious Sector of the Population* (Lawrence: Regents Press of Kansas, 1981) p. 11. Angered by the fact that neither he nor a number of his protégés were elected to the Academy, Khrushchev wanted to disband it altogether in the last years of his reign. Hence, the creation of the Institute of Scientific Atheism at the CPSU CC Academy of Social Sciences and the attachment of *Vop. nauch. at.* to it must have been a carry-over from Khrushchev's time.

4. Pospielovsky, *Orthodox Church*, ch. 6, n. 18. Also, Fathers Gleb Yakunin and Nikolai Eshliman, 'An Open Letter to Patriarch Alexii', *Grani*, no. 61 (1966) p. 126.

5. 'From the Report of the Council for Religious Affairs to Members of the CPSU Central Committee', *Vestnik RKhD*, no. 130 (1979) p. 277.

6. In fact, the correspondence (extramural) sector was reopened immediately after Khrushchev's fall in the 1965–6 academic year, having been closed in the last years of Khrushchev's reign: Ushinin, 'Novye veiania', p. 199. Patriarch Pimen, in his report on the occasion of the sixtieth anniversary of the restoration of patriarchate in Russia, cites the following figures for 1977: 788 day students and 814 extramural ones: *ZhMP* (8 August 1978) p. 14. by 1981 this grew to 900 day students and 1000 extramural, according to another leading cleric of the Moscow Patriarchate, Archbishop Khrizostom of Tambov. See Pospielovsky, *Russian Church*, ch. 12, n. 31.

7. Powell, *Anti-religious*, p. 81; and 'Za deistvennost' ateisticheskoi propagandy', *Pravda*, 27 July 1968. also, 'Nauka, tekhnika, progress', *NiR*, no. 6 (1977) p. 2.

8. The graphs are based on Powell up to 1969 and 1973 (*Anti-religious*, pp. 88–90). The continuation to 1981–2 and 1984 and the circulation figures on books published have been found, compiled and formed into graphs by my research assistant and son, Andrew Pospielovsky.

9. *Inter alia* see Pospielovsky, 'Intelligentsia and Religion: Aspects of Religious Revival in the Contemporary Soviet Union. The Orthodox Church', *Religion and Communist Society*, Dennis J. Dunn, ed. (Berkeley: Berkeley Slavic Specialties, 1983) pp. 11–44; Pospielovsky, *The Russian Church*, vol. 2, pp. 454–60.

10. *KPSS v rezolutsiiakh* . . ., vol. 9, pp. 30–4, 222–3, 346–53; vol. 10, pp 361–3 and 434–6.

11. *Tovarishch Komsomol* Documents of the Komsomol congresses, conferences and CC resolutions (M.: Molodaia gvardiia, 1969) vol. 2, pp. 358–9, 375, 407, 476 and 488–90.

12. 'V Tsentral'nom komitete KPSS', *Pravda* 6 May 1979, pp. 1–2. Why did it take so long to publish a document adopted on 26 April? There must have been some behind-the-scenes disagreements. Both the 25th and 26th Party congresses avoided direct attacks on religion, preferring the usual euphemisms.

13. Feodossii, *Letter to Brezhnev*, pp. 222–3. He describes the destruction in

1971, by a group of 20 Komsomol members led by the village soviet chairman and protected by a policeman, of brick walls just built by the villagers in order to enlarge and improve the tiny village prayer house.

14. *Tov. Komsomol*, pp. 275 and 163. It is more than a question of euphemisms; the emphasis in all Komsomol documents of the post-Khrushchev era is on mobilizing youth for work on the industrial and rural objects of the Five Year Plans.

15. See Soviet sources in Pospielovsky, *The Russian Church*, vol. 2, p. 454.

16. Oral testimony to this author by Irina Evsikova, Washington, D.C., June 1985.

17. See text related to note 39 below. Perhaps some of this classified material from unpublished surveys found its way into Veniamin Arsenkin's *Krizis religioznosti i molodezh'* (M.: Nauka, 1984) whose average for the non-atheistic sector of the population is 48 per cent, and that of convinced believers 26 per cent – both far greater figures than those usually given in Soviet publications. See, Oxana Antich, 'Kak byt' s religioznost'iu?', *Rus. m.*, 12 July 1985, p. 6.

18. M. Mchedlov, 'Religioznoe "obnovlenchestvo" pod natiskom zhizni', *Kom.*, no. 15 (Oct. 1964) pp. 88–9; N. Baranova, 'Chto takoe ekumenizm?', *NiR*, no. 5 (1968) pp. 82–4.

19. 'Vospitanie molodezhi – delo partiinoe', *Kom*, no. 3 (Feb. 1965) pp. 15–28.

20. See note 5 above; and 'U ateistov Moskvy', *Nauka i rel.*, no. 4 (1968) p. 41.

21. See the whole resolution in *KPSS v rezolutsiiakh*, vol. 9, pp. 342–57.

22. *Vop. fil.*, no. 1 (January 1972) pp. 25–39, cited in Pospielovsky, 'The Philosophic Society of the Union of Soviet Socialist Republics', *Radio Liberty Research* (Munich, 15 March 1972) CRD 64/72. Its president, F. Konstantinov, repeats the same instruction to Soviet philosophers once again eleven years later in, 'Marxistko–Leninskaia filosofiia . . ., *Vop. fil.*, no. 7 (1982) pp. 37–45.

23. In the 1940s (and probably in the 1950s) bishops still dared to appoint to parishes priests who were residing illegally, without any papers (fugitives from concentration camps or those sought by KGB prosecutors). For example 'Starets Sampson', *Nadezhda*, no. 8 (Samizdat, 1981; Possev Repr., 1983) p. 126. Nowadays a bishop can make no such appointments without the approval of and a registering licence from a local CRA plenipotentiary. See the Bishop Feodosi letter to Brezhnev, cited below; or Fr. Gleb Yakunin, *Vol'noe slovo*.

24. R. P. Platonov, 'Organizatsiia propagandy nauchnogo ateizma i povyshenie eio effektivnosti na asnove komplexnogo podkhoda', *Vop. nauch. at.*, no. 26 (1980) pp. 5–20.

25. 'XXV s'ezd KPSS i voprosy ideino-vospitatel'noi raboty', *Vop. nauch. at.* no. 21 (1977) pp. 14–15.

26. See, in particular, the vicious publications written jointly by A. V. Belov and A. D. Shilkin: *Ideologicheskie diversii imperializma i religiia* (M.: Znanie, 1980) 45 pp., circulation 44 300; *Religiia v sovremennoi ideologicheskoi por'be* (M.: Znanie, 1971) 62 pp., circulation 90 000; *Diversiia bez dinamita* (M.: Izd. politicheskoi literatury, 1972) 175 pp.

27. See the article on the occasion of the seventieth birthday of M. M.

Sheinman, an SVB veteran from its foundation: *N. i rel.*, no. 3 (March 1972) p. 96 etc.; a similar article on another SVB veteran, Guliaev: no. 7, pp. 22–4; colour reproductions of the title pages of *N. i rel.'s* 1922 namesake, in no. 8 (August 1972).

28. For example, a joint conference of the Institute of Scientific Atheism with the Soviet trade-union leaders, the Ministry of Culture and the *Znanie* Society at the end of 1967. Some of its proceedings were published in *N. i rel.*, no. 4 (1968). See 'Eschche odin prizyv k novym metodam i formam ateisticheskoi propagandy', *Biulleten' radio Svobody*, no. 255/68 (27 June 1968).

29. 'Budut li studenty-vypuskniki slushat' kurs "Osnovy nauchnovo ateizma"?', *Biulleten' radio Svobody* 199/68 (27 June 1968); M. Danilov, 'Vazhnyi razgovor', *NiR*, no. 10 (1975) pp. 12–13.

30. Contrast: Kurochkin, 'Ubezhdennost'', *NiR*, no. 1 (1980) pp. 2–4, and L. A. Filippov, 'O voinstvuiushchem materializme i ateizme', *Vop. fil.*, no. 3 (March 1972).

31. V. Furov, deputy CRA chairman; particularly pp. 277–86. The bishop in question is Nikolai, moved from Rostov-on-Don to Vladimir, then to Kaluga, thence to Gorky. The report has to be read in the knowledge that its intention was to impress the Central Committee with CRA's real or fictitious achievements in suppressing the Church.

32. See note 2 above and 'The Forty-First All-Union Congress of the Evangelical Baptists of the Soviet Union', *St Vladimir's Theological Quarterly*, vol. 19, no. 4 (1975) pp. 246–53; *Religiia i tserkov' v sovetskom obshchestre* (M.: Polit. literatura, 1984) pp. 144 and 108.

33. Fr. Gleb Yakunin, 'O sovremennom polozhenii Russkoi pravoslavnoi Tserkvi i perspektivakh religioznovo vozrozhedeniia v Rossii (a report to the Christian Committee for the Defence of Believers' Rights in the USSR) (M.: *samizdat*) repr.: *Vol'noe slovo* (no. 35–36, Frankfurt/M., 1979) p. 32 *et passim*. A concrete case cited in *Khronika tek. sob.*, no. 54 (M., 1979–N.Y., 1980) p. 102.

34. See almost every issue of the *Chronicle of Current Events* for arrests and prison sentences. In particular, the prison terms meted out to A. Ogorodnikov, T. Shchipkova, V. Poresh and other members of the unofficial Moscow religio-philosophic seminar: *Khronika . . .*, nos 54, 55, 58, resp. pp. 28–30, 17–18, 33–4; *Russian Church*, ch. 12; the 1982 arrest of Zoia Krakhmal'nikova for putting out a miscellany of religious and theological readings *Nadezhda* (*Posev*, no. 10, October 1982) title page and inside; on a church youth choir, see *Khronika . . .*, no. 60; (M., 1980–N.Y., 1981) p. 73. In January 1985, Vladimir Frenkel, a young Orthodox Christian thinker who had apparently led a religio-philosophic circle in Riga, was likewise arrested and sentenced to 18 months hard labour. *Russkaia mysl'*, 5 July 1985, p. 7.

35. Peter Reddaway and Sidney Bloch, *Russia's Psycho-prisons*; V. Nekipelov, *Institute of Fools* and multiple reports in the *Chronicle of Current Events*.

36. For example, Fr. Alexandr Pivovarov, see: 'Sud nad o Alexandrom Pivovarovym', *V.R.Kh.D.*, no. 141 (1984) pp. 227–30.

37. *Vop. nauch. at.*, no. 28 (1981), particularly section 3, 'Aktual'nye problemy ateisticheskogo vospitaniia v regionakh rasprostraneniia

katolitsizma', pp. 202–58. Also P. K. Kurochkin (ed.), 'Problemy nauchnogo ateizma v svete reshenii XXVII s'ezda KPSS', *Vop. nauch. at., no. 28*, pp. 3–20.

38. See the texts of two such pro-pagan nationalistic writings in M. Meerson-Aksenov and B. Shragin (eds), *The Political, Social and Religious Thought of Russian Samizdat* (Belmont, Mass.: Nordland, 1977) pp. 420–48. Ideas placing the national above God, and the pagan tribalization of God, also occur in the writings of the extremist Ukrainian nationalist Valentyn Moroz. See 'Nationalism as a Factor of Dissent', *Canadian Review of Studies in Nationalism*, vol. 2, no. 1 (1974) p. 103; Powell, 'Rearing the New Soviet Man', *Religion and Atheism in the USSR and Eastern Europe*, B. Bociurkiw and J. Strong (eds) (Toronto: University of Toronto Press, 1975).

39. I. A. Kryvelev, 'Preodolenie religiozno-bytovykh perezhitkov u narodov SSR', *Sovetskaia etnografiia*, no. 4 (1961) pp. 37–43. Igor' Golomshtok of Oxford University and formerly of Moscow, an art critic, has observed a similar phenomenon among the remnants of the north Russia peasants in the area north and north-west of Vologda. there, deprived of priests and officially functioning churches, the peasants observed a mixture of Christian and Pagan traditions in their churches. Oral testimony made to this author in 1974.

40. 'Novye sovremennye obriady . . .' and 'Novye obriady v drevnem gorode', *Nauka i religiia*, no. 7 (July 1970) pp. 33–4; N. P. Lobacheva, 'O protsesse formirovaniia novoi semeinoi obriadnosti', *Sovetskaia etnografiia*, no. 1 (January 1972) pp. 3–13.

41. Fr. Dimitrii Dudko, 'Kreshchenie na Rusi' (a diary of adult conversions from 1962 to 1973), *Vestnik RKhD*, no. 117 (1976) pp. 188–208; Feodosii, *Letter to Brezhnev*, p. 235; Larisa Volokhonskaia's oral testimony to the author (Crestwood, N.Y., 16 April 1980). She is a recent émigrée who described her own secret baptism in Leningrad in 1972.

   On Soviet concerns: 'Ateisticheskoe vospitanie', *Pravda*, 15 September 1972, p. 1; Kurochkin, 'Problemy nauchnogo ateizma v svete reshenii XXVI s'ezda KPSS', *Vop. nauch. at.*, no. 28 (1981) p. 15, where he cites the rate of young Komsomol members within different attitudes to religion as being 44 per cent in central Russia. The rate for young people (generally members and non-members of Komsomol) is as high as 50 per cent in some regions.

42. See respectively: Pospielovsky, 'Soviet Family Policy', *The Soviet Union and Eastern Europe*, a handbook ed. by George Schopflin (London: Anthony Blond, 1970) p. 427; and V. A. Kapitanchuk, F. V. Karelin, G. P. Yakunin, 'K priniatiiu "osnov zakonodatel'stva Soiuza SSR i soiuznykh respublik o narodnom obrazovanii"', *Vol'noe slovo* (no. 17–18: selections from *Veche*, nos 7, 8, 9, 10 (1975)) p. 79. See confirmation of this in Kuroedov, *Religiia* (1984) pp. 129–30.

43. See Kuroedov: (1) 'Svoboda sovesti i zakon', *Nedelia/Izvestiia*'s weekend magazine, no. 44 (31 Oct. 1971) p. 16; (2) 'Torzhestvo leninskikh printsipov svobody sovesti', *Nauka i rel.*, no. 1 (1978) pp. 3–4; (3) *Religiia i tserkov' v sovetskom gosudarstve* (M.: polit. literatura, 1981) pp. 130–212. Furov, 'Stanovlenie zakonodatel'stva o kul'takh', *NiR*, no. 8 (1979) pp. 16–18; his secret report: *VRKhD*, no. 130 (1979) pp. 283–8;

summary in Pospielovsky, *The Russian Church*, vol. 2, pp. 409–15.

44. *Vedomosti Verkhovnovo soveta RSFSR*, no. 12 (March 1966) p. 219.
45. Fr. Gleb Yakunin and Lev Regel'son, 'Pis'mo General'nomu sekretariu VSTs Filippu Potteru', *Vol'noe slovo*, no. 24 (1976) pp. 27–33 *et passim*.
46. See the Furov report and Archbishop Feodosii, letter to Brezhnev, *passim*. Fr. Yakunin claims that the unwritten condition for the episcopal consecration of a candidate since the 1960s has been a prior written pledge of the candidate given to the KGB to co-operate with it upon consecration. This was not necessary under Stalin because the KGB could arrest anyone without any regard for due process of law. But with the so-called 'return to Leninist legality' the need for internal police informers in the Church has increased, hence the above KGB–CRA ruling. Yakunin, 'O sovremennom . . .', pp. 17–18.
47. Oral testimony to this author by clergy of the Moscow Patriarchate. Also 1985 statements by Yuvenali, Metropolitan of Krutitsy, and Vladimir, Metropolitan of Rostov. *Keston News Service* (Keston College, Centre for the Study of Religion and Communism, Keston, Kent, England), 21 February 1985, p. 22, and 4 April 1985, p. 7. *Vedomosti*, no. 27 (June 1975) pp. 487–91.
48. *Sbornik po finansovomu zakonodatel'stvu* (M.: Iuridicheskaia literatura, 1980) pp. 239–40; USSR Supreme Soviet Presidium *Ukaz*, no. 1061 (1 January 1981); also, L. Sergeeva, 'V tiskakh sistemy', *Posev*, no. 7 (1981) p. 32.
49. Yakunin, 'O sovremennom', *passim*.
50. 'Nashi iuridicheskie konsul'tatsii', *ZhMP*, no. 6 (1985) p. 80, and no. 10, (1985) p. 80. The journal regularly publishes items on clergy who had in the past gallantly served in the Soviet armed forces, with photos of them in their uniforms and with medals, to counter the antireligious propaganda depicting the Church and the clergy as unpatriotic.
51. 'Nashi. . .konsul'tatsii', *ZhMP*, no. 1 (Jan. 1986) p. 80. Indeed, in the last few years many issues of *ZhMP* have reported construction of new diocesan and other secular buildings for administrative and other needs of the Church. The most grandiose of them was the solemn opening of a large plant at Sofrino near Moscow, on 15 September 1980, for the production of church plate and other articles used in the Orthodox Church services and for the private use of religious believers (*ZhMP*, no. 11, 1980, pp. 12–15). The change of taxation rate, of course, does not apply to articles produced and sold by the Church. The Sofrino income remains taxable according to Article 19.
52. B. N. Konovalov, E. G. Filimonov, 'Kompleksny podkhod v ateisticheskom vospitanii – reshaiushchii faktor povysheniia ego effektivnosti', *Vop. nauch. at.*, no. 22 (1978) pp. 168–70; 'Povyshat' ideino-teoreticheskii uroven' i effektivnost' nauchno-ateisticheskogo vospitaniia', ibid, no. 19 (1976) pp. 11–13; *XXV s'ezd Kommunisticheskoi partii Sovetskogo Soiuza*, vol. 1 (M.: Izd. polit. lit., 1976) pp. 26–115; 'Otchet Tsentral'nogo komiteta KPSS XXVI s'ezdu . . . Doklad . . . Brezhneva', *Pravda*, 24 February 1981, pp. 2–9.
53. 'Novaia konstitutsiia SSSR i svoboda sovesti', *Vop. nauch. at.*, no. 23 (1978) pp. 6–24; also: A. Olulov, P. Kurochkin, 'S uvazheniem k cheloveku',

Pravda, 1 Sept. 1977, p. 3; Kurochkin, 'Ubezhdennost', p. 2.

54. Contrast *XVIII S'ezd Vsesoiuznogo Leninskogo Kommunisticheskogo soiuza molodezhi, 25–28 aprelia 1978 g. . Stenogr. otchet*, vol. 2 (M: Molod. gvard., 1978) pp. 196–221, with *XIX S'ezd . . ., 18–21 maia, 1982 g.*, vol. 2, pp. 205–25.

55. 'Voinstvuiushchii materializm – filosofskoe znamia kommunizma', *Kom.*, no. 4 (March 1982) pp. 56–68.

56. 'Boevaia programma tvorcheskogo marxizma', *Vop. fil.*, no. 3 (March 1982) pp. 3–16.

57. Andropov's and Chernenko's speeches followed by an editorial and by the 14–15 June 1983 CPSU CC Plenum Resolution, *Kom.*, no. 9 (June 1983) pp. 4–46; editorial, 'Aktual'nye voprosy ateisticheskogo vospitaniia v svete reshenii iiun'skogo (1983) Plenuma TsK KPSS'; and L. K. Shepetis, 'Ateisticheskomu vospitaniiu–deistvennost' i nastupatel'nost'' – both in *Voprosy nauchnogo ateizma* (henceforth *Vopnat*) vol. 32 (1985) pp. 5 and 35 respectively; *Pravda* editorial, 14 December 1983, gives also a militantly atheistic policy interpretation to the June CC Plenum Resolution.

58. Oral testimony to this author by a very well-informed source who had visited both the Patriarchate and the monastery in question in 1985. For obvious reasons the source prefers to remain unnamed.

59. Pospielovsky, *The Russian Church*, vol. 2, chs 10 and 12, and Chapter 3 of present volume.

60. Pospielovsky, 'More on Historic Preservation Policy in the USSR', *Canadian Slavonic Papers*, vol. XVIII, no. 4 (1975) pp. 641–9; and, *inter alia*, such writings of Vladimir Soloukhin as: *Chernye doski, Pis'ma iz Russkovo muzeia*, 'Prodolzhenie vremeni', *Nash sovremennik* (no. 1, 1982), and *Vremia sobirat' kamni* (M.: Sovremennik, 1980).

61. Apollon Kuz'min, 'Pisatel'' i istoriia', *Nash sovremennik*, no. 4 (M.: 'Literaturnaia gazeta', April 1982) p. 148.

62. N. S. Gordienko, *'Kreshchenie Rusi': fakty protiv legend i mifov* (Leningrad: Lenizdat, 1984) p. 274. For a similar platform but presented less polemically and in a more scholarly fashion, with many interesting historical details not directly related or totally unrelated to the task of 'killing' religion, see M. S. Korzun, *Russkaia pravoslavnaia tserkov' na sluzhbe ekspluatatorskikh klassov. X vek – 1917 god.* (Minsk: Belarus', 1984). Predictably, Gordienko's book was published in 75 000 copies, the much more scholarly Korzun's, in 5000. Many anti-Millenium articles have appeared in *Vopnat.*, including one which was surprisingly scholarly and 'unorthodox' from the Marxist-Soviet policy viewpoint: L. V. Poliakov, 'Khristianizatsiia i stanovlenie filosofii v Kievskoi Rusi', vol. 32 (1985) pp. 268–92.

63. Gordienko, *Kreshchenie, passim*; A. F. Zamaleev, V. A. Zots, *Mysliteli Kievskoi Rusi* (Kiev: Vyshcha shkola, 1981), is one of the official publications dedicated to the alleged 1500th anniversary. Ironically, the subject of the book is a very confused and confusing analysis of the writings of the first Russian bishops and monastics, and of the very pious Prince Vladimir Monomakh (12th c.). The authors invent a division between the Byzantine denial of the world expressed in the ascetic and

pessimistic Christianity of the monks, and the joyous *Weltanschauung* of Metropolitan Ilarion, which was a legacy of Bogumil and some other heresies mixed in with the Pagan background of the Russians. Much of Polaikov's article argues that such an artificial duality is the product of the authors' fantasy and incomprehension of Christian theology.

64. *Vopnat.*, no. 30 (1982) *passim*; A. Gusev, 'Pis'mo veruiushchemu rodstvenniku', *NiR*, no. 8 (1975) pp. 27–8; F. Gorbacheva, 'Dormidont i voina', *NiR*, nos 2, 3, 4 and 5 (1975); Alexandr Shamaro, 'Kak ustoiala Rus'', *NiR*, no. 7 (1980) pp. 18–28; Gordienko, *Kreshchenie, passim*; Korzun, *passim*.

65. Gordienko, *Kreshchenie*, pp. 30–4.

66. Korzun, pp. 69–70, 95 and 17. In contrast to the 'cruelty' of the Scriptures, he stresses that the common Russian people never came to terms with Ivan's tyranny: 'In Russian folk songs Ivan the Terrible appears as a wild beast.' Korzun is wrong about the Greek princess: he received her as his wife only after his conversion and abandonment of polygamy and of all his former wives and concubines.

67. Gordienko, *Kreshchenie*, pp. 190–205.

68. Oral testimony to this author by a source that may not be named, June 1985. The threat of the Church must be very real if so much energy and attention is given to polemics with its publications, which amount to a monthly journal with a circulation of less than 50 000 copies, and with priests' oral sermons; whereas millions of copies of antireligious publications, printing houses, the whole educational, TV and broadcasting systems are a monopoly of the Communist Party.

69. Gordienko, *Kreshchenie*, pp. 205–80.

APPENDIX

1. This Appendix includes some earlier translations of this author in his *Orthodox Church under the Soviet Regime* (St Vladimir's Seminary Press, 1984), as well as from a brochure by this author on the legal situation of the Church in the USSR to be published by the Orthodox Church in America as a hand-out. Other parts have been newly translated and edited by Andrew Pospielovsky, the compiler and editor of this section.
2. To the best of our knowledge, these regulations remain unpublished for the general public to the present day.

Bibliography

The following bibliography consists of materials directly used and cited in the current volume, books and other materials scrutinized in the course of research directly relevant to this book, as well as those materials encountered by this author and pertaining to the subject of Soviet atheism which would be of use for further reading on the subject. The list does not include materials, known to the author, which in his view add nothing to an inquisitive reader's knowledge. This was the rationale for the selection of some books by, for instance, a Western author for inclusion in the list, and exclusion of other writings by the same author. Of course, the writer does not pretend to have a total encyclopaedic knowledge of all sources, and may have missed some useful ones as well.

ARCHIVES, DOCUMENTS, AND OTHER PRIMARY SOURCES

Constitution of 1936. English edn. Moscow: Foreign Languages Publishing House, 1962.

Constitution of the Union of Soviet Socialist Republics, supplement to *New Times*, no. 41. Moscow: 1977.

Documents of the Christian Committee for the Defense of Believers Rights in the USSR. San Francisco: Washington Research *Samizdat* Reprints, vols 1–12, 1979–80.

Feodosii, Archb. of Poltava, 'Letter to L. I. Brezhnev', *Vestnik RKhD.*, no. 135. Paris, 1981.

Furov, V., 'Tsekovnye kadry i mery po ogranicheniiu ikh deiatel'nosti ramkami zakona', *Vestnik RKhD.*, no. 130, Paris, 1979.

KPSS – Communist Party of the Soviet Union, Congresses: XVI S'ezd Vsesoiuznoi Kommunisticheskoi partii (bol'shevikov). Stenograficheskii otchet. Moscow: Gosizdat, 1930. *XXV S'ezd Kommunisticheskoi partii Sovetskogo Soiuza*. Moscow: Izdatel'stvo politicheskoi literatury, 1976.

KPSS v rezoliutsiiakh i resheniiakh S'ezdov, Konferentsii i Plenumov TsK., 10 vols. Moscow: Izdatel'stvo politicheskoi literatury, 1970–72.

Lenin, V. I., 'Neizdannoe pis'mo V. I. Lenina chlenam politburo', 'Top Secret', *Vestnik RSKhD.*, no. 98. Paris, 1970.

Materially XIII S'ezda professional'nykh soiuzov SSSR. Moscow: Profizdat, 1964.

Rezoluitsii II vsesoiuznogo s'ezda soiuza voinstvuiushchikh bezbozhnikov, 2nd edn. Moscow: Akts. obshch. Bezbozhnik, 1930.

Samizdat Archives. Radio Liberty, Munich.

Samizdat Religious Archives. Keston College, Keston, Kent, England.

Sbornik po finansovomu zakonadetel'stvu. Moscow: Iuridicheskaia literatura, 1980.

Sistematicheskoe sobranie zakonov RSFSR. . . . Moscow: Iuridicheskaia literatura, 1968.

179

Smolensk Archives. Widener Library. Harvard University, Cambridge, Mass.
Sobranie zakonov i rasporiazhenii Raboche-krestianskogo pravitel'stva SSSR. Moscow, 1929.
Tovarishch Komsomol, 2 vols. Moscow: Molodaia gvardiia, 1969.
Ugolovnyi kodex RSFSR. Moscow: Iuridicheskaia literatura, 1979.
VLKSM – All Union Leninist Communist Union of Youth, Congresses: X S'ezd VLKSM, 11–12 IV, 1936g. Moscow: Partizdat, 1936. *XIV S'ezd VLKSM, 16–20 aprilia, 1962g. Stenograficheskii otchet*. Moscow: Molodaia gvardiia, 1962. *XVII S'ezd VLKSM, 25–28 aprilia, 1978g. Stenograficheskii otchet*. Moscow: Molodaia gvardiia, 1978.
XIX S'ezd VLKSM, 18–21 maia, 1982g. Moscow: Molodaia gvardiia, 1982.
Zakonodatel'stvo o religionznykh kul'takh, 2nd edn. Moscow: Iuridicheskaia literatura, 1971. 'Only for Internal Use'. Reprinted: New York: Chalidze Publications, 1981.

SERIAL PUBLICATIONS

Antireligioznik, monthly. Moscow: 1926–41.
Ateist, irregular/monthly. (Superseded by *Voinstvuiushchii ateizm*.) Moscow: 1925–31.
Bezbozhnik illustrated, monthly until 1926, bimonthly from 1926 to 1933 and monthly after 1933. Moscow: 1925–41.
Bezbozhnik newspaper, irregularly, thrice monthly, and weekly. Not published from January 1935 until March 1938. Moscow: December 1922–July 1941.
Bezbozhnik u stanka, monthly. Moscow: 1923–32.
Biulleten' radio svobody, weekly. Munich: since mid-1950s.
Bogoslovskie trudy, once to twice annually. Moscow: Patriarkhiia, since early 1960s.
Bol'shevik, monthly. (Superseded by *Kommunist*.) Moscow: 1923–52.
Derevenskii bezbozhnik. Moscow: 1928–32.
Ezhegodnik muzeia istorii religii i ateizma. Moscow: Akademia nauk SSSR, 1957–62.
Grani, quarterly. Frankfurt am Main: since 1946.
Istorik-marxist, monthly. Moscow: 1926–41.
Izvestiia, daily. Moscow.
Khronika tekushchikh sobytii, irregularly. Moscow: Samizdat, since 1968. Reprinted: Frankfurt am Main: Possev, 1968–72; New York: Chalidze publications, since 1973.
Kommunist, 18 issues annually. (Superseded *Bol'shevik*.) Moscow: since 1952.
Komsomol'skaia pravda, daily. Moscow.
Krasnaia nov', monthly. Moscow: 1921–41.
Liudyna i svit, monthly. Kiev: Znanie, since 1967(?).
Na putiakh k novoi shkole. Moscow: 1922–33.
Nadezhda: khristianskoe chtenie, irregularly. Moscow: Samizdat, since 1977. Reprinted: Frankfurt am Main: Possev, since 1977.
Nash sovremennik, monthly. Moscow: since 1933.

Nauka i religiia, monthly. (1) Moscow: 1921; (2) Moscow: Znanie, since 1959.
Nedelia, weekly supplement to *Izvestiia*. Moscow.
Novy mir, monthly. Moscow: since January 1925.
Pamiat', 5 vols. Moscow: Samizdat, 1976–81. Reprinted: V. I – New York: Khronika Press, 1978; vols. II–V – Paris: YMCA Press, 1979–82.
Pod znamenem Marxizma, monthly. Moscow: 1922–44.
Posev, weekly 1945–67; monthly since January 1968. Frankfurt am Main.
Pravda, daily. Moscow.
Prosveshcheniie, irregular/monthly. St Petersburg, 1912–14.
Religion in Communist Lands, quarterly. Keston, Kent, England: Keston College, since 1973.
Revoliutsiia i tserkov', irregular/monthly. Moscow: 1919–24.
Ruskaia mysl', weekly. Paris: since 1947.
Saint Vladimir's Theological Quarterly. Crestwood, New York: St Vladmir's Orthodox Theological Seminary, since 1957.
Sovetskaia etnografiia, bimonthly. Moscow: since 1931.
Sovetskaia kul'tura, twice weekly. Moscow: since 1973.
Veche, 9 issues. Rozhdestvo, Vladimir, USSR: Samizdat, 1971–4.
Vedomosti verkhovnogo soveta RSFSR., weekly. Moscow: since 1936.
Vestnik russkogo studencheskogo khristianskogo dvizheniya (Vestnik RSKhD, or VRSKhD), and since issue no. 112–113, 1974 – *Vestnik russkogo Khristianskogo dvizheniya (Vestnik RKhD, or VRKhD)*, presently a quarterly. Paris: since 1926.
Voinstvuiushchii ateizm, irregular/monthly. Moscow: 1931–2.
Voiovnychyi ateist, monthly. Kiev: Znanie, since 1960, superseded by *Liudyna i svit* (approx. since 1967).
Vol'noe slovo, formerly *Possev, spetsial'nyi vypusk*, 4 to 6 times annually. Frankfurt am Main: Narodno-trudovoi soiuz, 1972–81.
Voprosy filosofii, monthly. Moscow: Pravda, since 1947.
Voprosy istorii religii i ateizma. Moscow: Akadmeiia nauk SSSR, until 1964.
Voprosy nauchnogo ateizma, irregularly. Akademiia obshchestvenikh nauk, since 1964.
Zhurnal Moskovskoi Patriarkhii, monthly. Moscow: Patriarkhiia, 1931–5 irregularly, regularly since September 1943.

BOOKS AND ARTICLES

Amosov, N., *Antireligioznaia rabota na poroge vtoroi piatiletki*. Moscow: Gosudarskoe antireligioznoe izdatel'stvo, 1932.
Antireligioznyi krestianskii uchebnik. Moscow: Moskovskii rabochii, sixth revised edn, 1931.
Arsenkin, Veniamin, *Krizis religioznosti i molodezh'*. Moscow: Nauka, 1984.
Bakhrushin, S., 'K voprosu o kreshchenii Kievskoi Rusi', *Istorik–marxist*, no. 2, 40–77. Moscow: 1937.
Bammel', Fr., 'Ob idealisticheskoi filosofii posle Oktiabria', *Pod znamenem marxizma*, no. 5, 36–61. Moscow: 1930.
Belov, A. V. and A. D. Shilkin, *Diversiia bez dinamita*. Moscow: Izdatel'stvo

politicheskoi literatury, 1972.
——, *Ideologicheskie diversii imperializma i religiia*. Moscow: Znanie, 1980.
——, *Religiia v sovremennoi ideologicheskoi bor'be*. Moscow: Znanie, 1971.
Belov, E., 'Sud'ba tserkovnykh tsennostei, iz'iatykh sovetskoi vlast'iu v 1922g.', *Vestnik RSKhD.*, no. 104–105, Paris, 1972.
Bociurkiw, Bohdan, 'The Catacomb Church: Ukrainian Greek Catholics in the USSR', *Religion in Communist Lands*, v. V, no. 1, Keston, Kent, England: Keston College, 1977.
——, 'Lenin and religion', *Lenin: The Man, the Theorist, the Leader*. Leonard Schapiro and Peter Reddaway, eds. London: Pall Mall Press, 1967.
——,'Religious situation in Soviet Ukraine', *Ukraine in Changing World*. New York: Ukrainian Congress Committee of America, 1977.
——, and J. Strong (eds), *Religion and Atheism in the USSR and Eastern Europe*. Toronto: University of Toronto Press, 1975.
Bogolepov, Alexander A., *Tserkov' pod vlast'iu kommunizma*. Munich: 1958.
Bol'shaia sovetskaia entsiklopediia, 30 vols, 3rd edn. Moscow: 1970–78.
Bonch-Bruevich, V. D., *Izbrannye ateisticheskie proizvedeniia*. Moscow: Mysl', 1973.
——, 'Svoboda sovesti v SSSR', *Voprosy istorii religii i ateizma*, no. 2, pp. 11–28. Moscow: 1954.
Bourdeaux, Michael, *Faith on Trial in Russia*. London: Hodder & Stoughton, 1971.
——, (ed.), *Patriarch and Prophets: Persecution of the Russian Orthodox Church Today*. London: Macmillan, 1969.
——, (ed.), *Religious Ferment in Russia*. London, 1968.
Bundy, Edgar C., *How the Communists Use Religion*. New York: The Devin-Adair Co., 1966.
Casey, Robert Pierce, *Religion in Russia*. New York: Harper & Brothers, 1946.
Chrysostomus, J., *Kirchengeschichte Russlands der neusten Zeit*, 3 vols. Munich-Salzburg: 1965–8.
Conquest, Robert, *Religion in the USSR*. New York: Praeger, 1968.
Curtiss, John, *The Russian Church and the Soviet State, 1917–1950*. Boston: Little, Brown, 1953.
Drujski, A., *Religious Life in Belorussia: The Orthodox Church*. Chicago: 1976.
Dudko, Fr. Dimitrii, 'Kreshchenie na Rusi', *Vestnik RKhD.*, no. 117, pp. 188–208. Paris: 1976.
Dunn, Denis J. (ed.), *Religion and Communist Society*. Berkeley: Berkeley Slavic Specialties, 1983.
Enisherlov, M., A. Lukachevsky and M. Mitin (eds), *Voinstvuiushchee bezbozhie v SSSR. za 15 let*. Moscow: Gosudarstvennoe antireligioznoe izdatel'stvo, 1932.
Feshbach, Murray, 'The Soviet Union: Population Trends and Dilemmas', *Population Bulletin*, vol. 37, no. 3, pp. 1–44. Washington, D.C.: August 1982.
Feuerbach, Ludwig, *The Essence of Christianity*. George Eliot, trans. New York: Harper & Brothers, 1957.
Filosofskie problemy ateizma. Moscow: Akademiia Nauk, 1963.
Flerov, I. A. (ed.), *My – bezbozhniki*. Moscow: Gosudarstvennoe antireligioznoe izdatel'stvo, 1932.

Fletcher, William, *Religion and Soviet Policy*. London: Oxford University Press, 1973.
——, *The Russian Orthodox Church Underground, 1917–1970*. Oxford: University Press, 1971.
——, *A Study in Survival*. New York: Macmillan, 1965.
Gapochka, M. P., 'Uroki bogostroitel'stva', *Voprosy nauchnogo ateizma*, no. 25, pp. 186–204. Moscow, 1980.
Gordienko, N. S., *Kreshchenie Rusi': fakty protiv legend i mifov*. Leningrad: Lenizdat, 1984.
Grekulov, E. F., *Pravoslavnaia tserkov' – vrag prosveshcheniia*. Moscow: Akademiia nauk, 1962.
——, *Tserkov', samoderzhavie, narod (2ia polovina XIX – nachalo XX v.)*. Moscow: Nauka, 1969.
Grossman, V., 'Khrushchev's antireligious policy and the campaign of 1954', *Soviet Studies*, V, XXIV, no. 3. Glasgow, 1973.
Hutten, Kurt, *Iron Curtain Christians*. Minneapolis: Augsburg Publishing House, 1967.
Kampers, P. P., *Sovetskaia grazhdanskaia obriadnost'*. Moscow: Mysl', 1967.
Khrushchev, N. S., *O kommunisticheskom vospitanii*. Moscow: Izdatel'stvo politicheskoi literatury, 1964.
Khudyakov, S. N., *O preodolenii religioznykh perezhitkov v SSSR*. Moscow 1958.
Kischkowsky, S., *Die sowjetische Religionspolitik und die Russiche Orthodoxe Kirche*. Munich, 1960.
Kline, George, *Religious and Anti-Religious Thought in Russia*. Chicago: University Press, 1968.
Kogan, Iu. and F. Megruzhan, *O svobode sovesti*. Moscow: OGIZ, 1938.
Konstantinov, Prot. Dimitri, *Gonimaia tserkov'*. New York: Vseslavianskoe izdatel'stvo, 1967.
Korzun, M. S., *Russkaia pravoslavnaia tserkov' na sluzbe ekspluatatorskikh klassov. X vek – 1917 god*. Minsk: Belarus', 1984.
Krasnov-Levitin, A., *Likhie gody, 1925–1941*. Paris: YMCA Press, 1977.
——, and V. Shavrov, *Ocherki po istorii russkoi tsekovnoi smuty*. Kuesnacht, Switzerland: Institut 'Glaube in der 2 Welt', 1978.
Kryvelev, I. A., *Pochemu my boremsia protive religii*. Moscow: Gosudarstvennoe antireligioznoe izdatel'stvo, 1940.
——, *Protiv Paskhi*. Moscow: Gosudarstvennoe antireligioznoe izdatel'stvo, 1936.
Kuroedov, V. A., *Religiia i tserkov' v sovetskom gosudarstve*. Moscow: Politicheskaia literatura, 1981.
——, *Reilgiia i tserkov' v sovetskom obshchestve*. Moscow: Politicheskaia literatura, 1984.
Laskovaia, M., *Bogoiskatel'stvo i bogostroitel'stvo prezhde i teper'*. Moscow: Moskovskii rabochii, 1976.
Lenin, V. I., *Collected Works*, 4th edn. Moscow: Foreign Languages Publishing House, 1962.
——, *Izbrannye ateisticheskie proizvedeniia*. Moscow: Mysl', 1973.
——, *Polnoe sobranie sochinenii*, 5th edn. Moscow, 1964.
Lisavtsev, E. I., *Kritika burzhuaznoi fal'sifikatsii polozheniya religii v SSSR*. Moscow, 1971.

Lobazov, P. K. and I. A. Serebriankin, *Voprosy nauchnogo ateizma v kurse istorii KPSS*. Leningrad: Vysshaia shkola, 1975.
Lukachevsky, A., *Izuchenie sotsial'nykh kornei religii v SSSR*. Moscow, 1930.
Lunarcharsky, A. V., *Ob ateizme i religii*. Moscow: Mysl', 1972.
——, *Khristianstvo ili kommunizm: Disput s mitr. A. Vvedenskim*. Leningrad, 1926.
—— (ed.), *Ocherki po filosofii marxizma*. St Petersburg, 1908.
——, *Religiia i sotsializm*, 2 vols. St Petersburg, 1911.
——, *Vvedenie v istoriiu religii*. Moscow-St Petersburg: Gosudarstvennoe antireligioznoe izdatel'stvo, 1923.
Marshall, Richard H. Jr. (ed.), *Aspects of Religion in the Soviet Union, 1917–1967*. Chicago Press, 1971.
Martsinkovsky, V., *Zapiski veruiushchego*. Prague, 1929.
Marx, Karl, *On Religion*. Saul Padover, trans. and ed. New York: McGraw-Hill, 1974.
Marx, Karl, and Fredrick Engels, *Anti-Düring*. Moscow: Foreign Languages Publishing House, 1954.
——, *Collected Works*. London: Lawrence & Wishart, 1975.
——, *Historisch-Kritische Gesamtausgabe*. Frankfurt, 1927–35. Meerson-Aksenov, M. and B. Shragin (eds), *The Political, Social and Religious Thought of Russian Samizdat*. Belmont, Mass.: Nordland, 1977.
Nekipelov, V., *Institute of Fools: Notes From Serbsky*. New York: Farrar, Straus, Giroux, 1980.
Oleshchuk, F. O. (ed.), *Pochemu nel'zia verit' v boga?* Moscow: Nauka, 1965.
——, *Vybory v Sovet Deputatov Trudiashchikhsia i antireligioznaia propaganda*. Moscow: Molodaia gvardiia, 1938.
——, *O zadachakh antireligioznoi propagandy*. Moscow, 1937.
Orleansky, H., *Zakon o religioznykh ob'edineniiakh RSFSR. i deistvuiushchie zakony . . . po voprosam sviazannym s otdeleniem tserkvi ot gosudarstva i shkoly ot tserkvi*. Moscow: Bezbozhnik, 1930.
Pantskhava, I. P., *Konkretno-sotsiologicheskoe izuchenie sostoianiia religioznosti i opyta ateisticheskogo vospitaniia*. Moscow, 1969.
Pavliuk, V. V., *Psikhologiia sovremennykh veruiushchikh i ateisticheskoe vospitanie*. L'vov, 1976.
Podzerko, V., *XII s'ezd sovetskikh profsoiuzov*. Moscow: Profizdat, 1969.
Pol'skii, M. (ed.), *Novye mucheniki rossiiskie*. Jordanville: Holy Trinity Monastery Press, vol. I – 1949, vol. II – 1957.
Popovsky, Mark, *Zhizn' i zhitie Voino-Iasentskogo, arkiepiskopa i khirurga*. Paris: YMCA Press, 1979.
Pospielovsky, D., 'Nationalism as a factor of dissent', *Canadian Review of Studies in Nationalism*, vol. II. no. 1, 1974.
——, 'More on historic preservation policy in the USSR', *Canadian Slavonic Papers*, vol. XVIII, no. 4, pp. 641–9. Ottawa, 1975.
——, 'The Philosophic Society of the Union of Soviet Socialist Republics', *Radio Liberty Research Bulletin*, CRD 64/72. Munich, 15 March 1972.
——, *The Russian Church Under the Soviet Regime, 1917–1982*, 2 vols. Crestwood, New York: St Vladimir's Seminary Press, 1984.
Powell, David E., *Antireligious Propaganda in the Soviet Union: a Study of Mass Persuasion*. Cambridge, Mass.: MIT Press, 1975.
Putintsev, F., *Vybory v sovety i razoblachenie popovshchiny*. Moscow, 1937.

Rakusheva, L., *Komsomol protiv religii*. Leningrad: Lenizdat, 1939.
Reddaway, Peter, and Sidney Bloch, *Russia's Political Hospitals: The Abuse of Psychiatry in the Soviet Union*. London: Gollancz, 1977.
Regel'son, Lev, *Tragediia Russkoi tserkvi, 1917–1945*. Paris: YMCA Press, 1977.
Russkaya pravoslavnaya tserkov' v SSSR: sbornik. Munich, 1962.
Sapiets, Janis, 'Soviet atheists adopt pagan folklore rites', *BBC Central Research Unit Talk*, no. 80/69. London, 22 April 1969.
Scheffbusch, Winrich, *Christians Under the Hammer and Sickle*. Grand Rapids, Mich.: Zondervan Publishing House, 1974.
Schöpflin, George (ed.), *The Soviet Union and Eastern Europe*. London: Anthony Blond, 1970.
Shpiller, V. Rev. Vsevolod, 'Letter', *Vestnik russkogo zapadnoevropeiskogo ekzarkhata*, no. 58, pp. 107–9. Paris, April–June 1967.
Simon, Gerhard, *Church, State and Opposition in the USSR*. London, 1974.
Skvortsov–Stepanov, I., *Mysli o religii*. Moscow: Gosudarstvennoe izdatel'stvo antireligioznoi literatury, 1936.
Soloukhin, Vladimir, *Pis'ma iz russkogo muzeia*. Leningrad, 1968.
——, *Vremia sobirat' kamni*. Moscow: Sovremennik, 1980.
Sovetskaia istoricheskaia entsiklopediia, 16 vols. Moscow, 1961–76.
Spinka, Matthew, *The Church in Soviet Russia*. New York: Oxford University Press, 1956.
Stavrou, Theofanes, and Vasili Alexeev, *The Great Revival*. Minneapolis: Burgess Publishing Co., 1976.
Stanovlennia i rozvytok masovogo ateizma v zahidnyh oblastiah Ukrainskoi RSR. Kiev: Naukova dumka, 1981.
Stroyen, William B, *Communist Russia and the Russian Orthodox Church, 1943–1962*. Washington D.C.: Catholic University Press, 1967.
Struve, Nikita, *Christians in Contemporary Russia*. London: Harvill Press, 1967.
Thrower, James, *Marxist-Leninist 'Scientific Atheism' and the Study of Religion and Atheism in the USSR*. Berlin-Amsterdam: Mouton Publishers, 1983.
Tsamerian, I. P. *et al*. (eds), *Osnovy nauchnogo ateizma. Uchebnoe posobie. Tret'e, pererabotannoe izdanie*. Moscow: Izdatel'stvo politicheskoi literatury, 1964.
Ushinin, D. (pseudonym of D. Pospielovsky), 'Novye veianiia v ateisticheskoi propagande SSSR.', *Grani*, no. 60. Frankfurt am Main, 1966.
Valentinov, A., *Religiia i tserkov' v SSSR*. Moscow, 1960.
Valentinov, N., *Vstrechi s Leninym*. New York: Chekhov Publishing House, 1953.
Voprosy istorii religii i ateizma. Sbornik statei. Moscow: Akademiia nauk, 1950.
Voronitsyn, I., *Istoriia ateizma*, 2nd edn, vyp. IV. Moscow: Ateist, 1929.
Vorontsov, I., *Leninskaia programma ateisticheskogo vospitaniia v deistvii (1917–1937gg.)*. Leningrad: Izdatel'stvo LGU, 1973.
Yakovlev, Ya, *Derevnia kak ona est'*. Moscow: Krasnaia nov', 1923.
Yakunin, Fr. Gleb, 'O sovremennom polozhenii Russkoi pravoslavnoi tserkvi i perspektivakh religioznogo vozrozhdeniia v Rosii', Moscow: Samizdat/ reprint: *Vol'noe Slovo*, no. 35–36. Frankfurt/Main: 1979.
Yaroslavsky, Emelian, *Bibliia dlia veruiushchikh i neveruiushchikh*. Moscow: OGIZ, 1936.
——, *Kak rodiatsia, zhivut i umiraiut bogi*. Moscow: GAIz, 1938.

——, 'Marx i religiia', *Bol'shevik*, no. 5. Moscow, 14 March 1933.

Yaroslavsky, Emelian, 'Marxizm i anarchizm v antireligioznoi propagande', *Bol'shevik*, no. 7–8. Moscow, 15 July 1924.

——, *Protiv religii i tserkvi: Sobranie sochinenii v 5 tomakh.* Moscow, 1935.

——, *Razvernutym frontom. O zadachakh i metodakh antireligioznoi propagandy (Doklad na 2m vsesoiuznom S'ezde Soiuza bezbozhnikov).* Moscow: Akts. ob. Bezbozhnik, 1929.

——, *Religion in the USSR.* New York: International Publishers, 1934.

——, *Na religioznom fronte.* Moscow-Leningrad, 1925.

Zamaleev, A. F. and V. A. Zots, *Mysliteli Kievskoi Rusi.* Kiev: Vyshcha shkola, 1981.

Zatko, James, *Descent into Hell: The Destruction of the Roman Catholic Church in Russia, 1917–1923.* Notre Dame, Indiana: University Press, 1965.

Zybkovets, Vladimir, *Natsionalizatsiia monastyrskikh imushchestv v Sovetskoi Rossii (1917–1921gg).* Moscow, 1975.

Index

187